AIM Higher!

New York ELA Review

Level F

Robert D. Shepherd

Victoria S. Fortune

aim higher!®
Great Source Education Group
Wilmington, MA

Editorial Staff

Dan Carsen
Victoria S. Fortune
Robert D. Shepherd
Barbara R. Stratton

Design & Production

Paige Larkin

Cover Design

Seann Dwyer, Studio Montage, St. Louis

Cover Photo

© Rommel

Consultant

Victor Jaccarino
　English Department Chairperson, Herricks High School
　Hyde Park, NY

aim higher! More than just teaching to the test™

First Edition

Printed in the United States of America

1 2 3 4 5 6 7 8 9 10　DBH　08 07 06 05 04

International Standard Book Number: 1-58171-629-X

Contents

Part 4: Writing Skills Review

Pretest

English Language Arts

Session 1

This session contains two parts. In Part 1, you will read passages and answer multiple-choice questions about them. You may look back at passages as often as you like. In Part 2, you will listen to a passage and then write about it. You will hear the listening passage twice.

Session 1
Part 1: Reading

Directions *Read the following article about a contest between a man and a machine. Then answer questions 1 through 5.*

Machine Beats Man
by Karim Howard, from *Computer Games Universe*

You might wonder who would pay $25 to watch a human play chess against a computer. Well, I would—and I did. Why? To begin with, this was not your normal computer. IBM had spent years developing their machine, which they called Deep Blue. It could consider more than 200 million possible chess moves in one second. The human brain can consider no more than a few moves in that time.

Deep Blue would not be playing an ordinary human being, however. Garry Kasparov was by far the best chess player in the world. Some even said he was the best in history.

The match was set to last for six games. Each player would receive one point for each win and half a point for each draw, or tie. If a competitor reached three and a half points, he or it would be declared the winner. I was sure that Kasparov would win. No computer had ever beaten him in a match. I did not think any computer ever would.

On Saturday, May 3, 1997, I made my way to the Equitable Building in Manhattan for the first game. The actual chess match was being played on the thirty-fifth floor. My ticket gave me access only to an auditorium at ground level where three huge monitors had been set up to show spectators what was happening in the match. As it turned out, Deep Blue was not even in the same room as Kasparov.

GO ON

The computer was in a remote location. A person in the room with Kasparov received Deep Blue's instructions and then moved chess pieces for the computer. I sat among a crowd of 450 people and watched the first game unfold. Millions more watched the game over the Internet.

Early in the match, Kasparov took off his gold watch and set it down on the table next to him. The woman sitting next to me leaned over and said, "He's thinking. He always does that when he's thinking." Only forty-five moves into the game, Kasparov grabbed the watch and put it back on his wrist. He knew the game was his! The crowd in the auditorium went wild. Deep Blue conceded Kasparov's victory. Game 1 went to the human. I was right—Kasparov would beat the machine.

The next day, however, Deep Blue won. The loss was especially disappointing because Kasparov missed a move that might have forced a draw. After two games, the series was even: The score was one to one.

Kasparov was never the same after the second game. The next three games ended in draws. As I watched from my seat in the auditorium, I grew uneasy. Anything that Kasparov tried, the computer was able to match. What really worried me was what Kasparov was saying. He called Deep Blue "an outstanding scientific achievement" and said that the machine "showed signs of intelligence."

The last chance to reclaim human superiority came crashing down in the sixth game, only eight days after Kasparov's first victory. In just one hour, Deep Blue whipped Kasparov. At the end of the game, Kasparov bolted from the table angrily. The woman who had been sitting next to me got up quietly and left. I sat in my seat, unable to believe my eyes. In front of me, the monitors displayed a gigantic image of the chess board, confirming Deep Blue's triumph. No move could be taken back; the match was over. The best chess player in the world was a computer! ○

1. This article is MOSTLY about
   Ⓐ the factors that make chess such an interesting game.
   Ⓑ the origins and history of the game of chess.
   Ⓒ a chess match between a human and a computer.
   Ⓓ how scientists at IBM designed Deep Blue.

2. Which of these events happened FIRST?
   Ⓐ Kasparov put his watch back on his wrist.
   Ⓑ Kasparov said that Deep Blue "showed signs of intelligence."
   Ⓒ Deep Blue won its first chess game.
   Ⓓ Kasparov bolted from the table angrily.

3. Read this sentence from the article:

   The computer sat in a remote location.

   What does *remote* mean?
   Ⓐ in the same room
   Ⓑ unknown, undetectable
   Ⓒ not in the same place; distant
   Ⓓ face to face

4. The narrator watched the match
   Ⓐ over the Internet.
   Ⓑ in a theater, with the game on stage.
   Ⓒ from outside the Equitable Building.
   Ⓓ on a TV monitor in an auditorium.

5. How does the narrator seem to feel about Deep Blue's victory?
   Ⓐ He is pleased to know that people can make such powerful computers.
   Ⓑ He is stunned that a computer could beat the best human chess player.
   Ⓒ He is angry that Kasparov did not show better manners after losing the match.
   Ⓓ He is satisfied that his prediction about the match had come true.

GO ON

Directions *Read the following poem. Then answer questions 6 through 9.*

No Spring Fling
by Denise Gunderson

When I slide up the sash,
The screen is all that remains
Between inside and out.
The first freshness of spring
Blows the mustiness of winter
From under the sofa
And other hidden places of the room.
I shed my winter coat.
Timothy still has most of his.
I stand hunched over him.
He sits, alert, his striped fur against my
   striped shirt.
Our noses press with equal eagerness
Against the rusty woven wire.
Three furry forms scamper,
Heedless, through the yard.
"Rowl?" he implores,
As though I might just slide the screen up
And indulge him in
A bit of March madness.

I scratch his head and make no reply.
I'm not quite able to look him in the eye.
Which of us is right?
Later, dozing, we both start awake
As yowling cries pierce the night.
We look at each other, and I feel vindicated[1]
By what he is missing. ○

———————————

[1]**vindicated.** Proved right

6. What is this poem MOSTLY about?

   Ⓐ a cat that wants to get outside to chase a bird

   Ⓑ a bird that is being terrorized by a cat

   Ⓒ a cat that wants to be let out at springtime

   Ⓓ a pet owner who is looking for his cat

7. The chart below lists some similarities between Timothy (the cat) and the speaker of the poem. From the answers below, choose the one that belongs in the blank box.

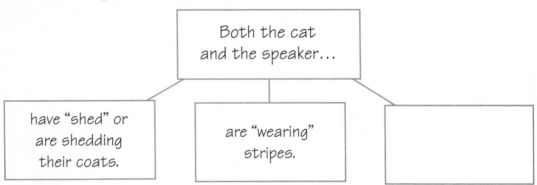

Both the cat and the speaker...

have "shed" or are shedding their coats.

are "wearing" stripes.

   Ⓐ are anxious to clean the house.

   Ⓑ are eager to be outdoors.

   Ⓒ are looking forward to climbing trees.

   Ⓓ enjoy the sounds of a summer night.

8. What is the speaker referring to when he or she mentions "rusty woven wire"?

   Ⓐ a chain-link fence

   Ⓑ the way the cat's fur looks

   Ⓒ the way a sweater feels

   Ⓓ a window screen

9. What does the speaker of the poem mean when he or she says, "I feel vindicated"?

   Ⓐ The speaker feels confident that he or she did the right thing.

   Ⓑ The speaker wants to get back at someone for hurting him or her.

   Ⓒ The speaker feels unsure about whether he or she did the right thing.

   Ⓓ The speaker is frightened by what he or she is hearing outside.

GO ON

Directions *Read the following article. Then answer questions 10 through 15.*

The Sea Monster That Wasn't
by Bernie Taubman

In 1977, Japanese fishermen off the coast of New Zealand hauled up something amazing in their nets. Fisherman aboard the boat called the *Zuiyo-maru* got something enormous caught in their nets. Using the powerful winches on board, the fishermen raised the thing out of the water, even though it weighed almost four thousand pounds. When they got the huge creature to the surface, it looked like a gigantic plesiosaur!

The **plesiosaurs** were large reptiles that lived in the sea at the same time that the dinosaurs lived on land. There were two kinds of plesiosaur, the plesiosauroids and the pliosauroids. **Plesiosauroids** had a long neck, a short head, a turtlelike back, and powerful flippers. **Pliosauroids** had a short neck, a long head, and powerful jaws. Plesiosaurs grew to lengths of up to fifty feet and were superb predators who swam after other creatures and captured them using sharp teeth. These creatures lived from about 200 million to 65 million years ago, during the **Mesozoic Era.**

The Mesozoic Era, 248 to 65 million years ago		
Triassic Period 248 to 206 million years ago	**Jurassic Period** 206 to 144 million years ago	**Cretaceous Period** 144 to 65 million years ago
Time of the first dinosaurs and the first mammals, reptiles, and amphibians.	Time of many dinosaurs and the first birds.	Time of the first flowering plants. Though this was in many ways the heyday of the dinosaurs, the period ended with their extinction.

The creature hauled up in the nets of the Japanese fisherman looked like the long-necked kind of plesiosaur. However, it was extremely rotten. The fishermen were afraid that the foul-smelling carcass would contaminate their catch. Therefore, they made a decision to throw their "find" back overboard. As they were trying to do so, they accidentally dropped the slimy creature on deck. It was revolting because of its horrible smell. After some struggle, the fishermen finally managed to push the creature overboard, but not before one person on board was able to take some pictures of its body and make some sketches. This person, whose name was Michihiko Yano, also managed to get some tissue samples from the creature.

When the fishing boat got back to port, the fishing company told the press about the discovery and shared the pictures with them. The news caused an immediate sensation. Throughout Japan and, indeed, throughout the rest of the world, people were amazed by this discovery. What if it turned out to be a creature that people believed had died out more than 65 million years earlier? The idea of finding a "sea monster" that might be a living relic of another era was very exciting.

Could it be that fishermen had found some kind of creature that had gone undetected for all that time? Absolutely. In 1938, fishermen off the coast of South Africa caught a fish that turned out to be a **coelacanth,** a type of fish that supposedly had died out 400 million years ago! So, it is possible that other life forms from the distant past might still exist out there somewhere, perhaps in a remote jungle or the deepest part of an ocean.

Unfortunately, the "sea monster" caught by Japanese fishermen turned out not to be a plesiosaur at all. In fact, it was a basking shark. Basking sharks are the second largest of all fish. (Only the whale shark is larger.) The beast caught in the fishermen's nets did not look much like a shark because some of its flesh had rotted away and its lower jaw had dropped off, making it look as if it had the long neck and small head of a plesiosauroid. Scientists who tested the samples taken by Michihiko Yano found out that the tissue came from a basking shark, not from a lost giant of the seas. ○

10. How were plesiosauroids DIFFERENT from pliosauroids?

    Ⓐ Plesiosauroids had long necks and short heads, whereas pliosauroids had short necks and long heads.

    Ⓑ Plesiosauroids had flippers and lungs, whereas pliosauroids had fins and gills.

    Ⓒ Plesiosauroids were carnivorous, whereas pliosauroids were vegetarians.

    Ⓓ Plesiosauroids breathed by means of gills, whereas pliosauroids had to come to the surface in order to breathe.

11. Read these sentences from the article:

    The news caused an immediate sensation. Throughout Japan and, indeed, throughout the rest of the world, people were amazed by this discovery.

    What does the word *sensation* mean, as it is used in the first sentence?

    Ⓐ a feeling on the skin

    Ⓑ feelings of excitement

    Ⓒ something that is smelled, touched, tasted, heard, or felt

    Ⓓ the tingling that happens as numbness starts to wear off

12. Why did many people think that the creature the Japanese fishermen found was a plesiosaur?

    Ⓐ The fishermen had altered the pictures as a joke, to make the creature look like an ancient sea monster.

    Ⓑ The coelacanth had recently been discovered, so people were ready to believe that another ancient creature had been found.

    Ⓒ Some of the creature's flesh had rotted away, so its head and neck looked a lot like that of a plesiosaur.

    Ⓓ Other plesiosaurs had been found in the same area where the fishermen had pulled up this creature.

13. According to the article, plesiosaurs lived from about 200 million to 65 million years ago. Therefore, they were around for what part of the Mesozoic Era?

    Ⓐ a tiny part of it

    Ⓑ about a quarter of it

    Ⓒ half of it

    Ⓓ most of it

14. The word web below lists some facts about plesiosaurs. From the answer choices below, choose the fact from the article that belongs in the blank circle.

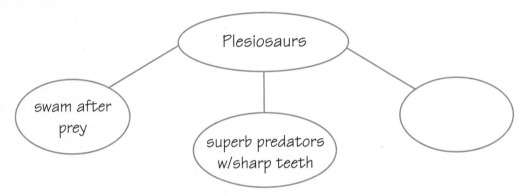

    Ⓐ lived during time of dinosaurs

    Ⓑ first of the sea mammals

    Ⓒ small & didn't weigh much

    Ⓓ ancestors of basking sharks

15. The author would probably agree with which of these statements?

    Ⓐ The creature caught by the Japanese fishermen was actually a plesiosaur.

    Ⓑ The coelacanth was a fake; it wasn't really an ancient type of fish.

    Ⓒ There may be some "living fossils" somewhere on Earth that haven't been discovered yet.

    Ⓓ Pictures are more reliable than laboratory tests when scientists need to identify the remains of a creature.

Directions *Read the following story. Then answer questions 16 through 20.*

What Matters Most
by Jun Ming Lok

"OK, you guys! Listen up. Everybody got his helmet and life jacket on? Good. We've got a radio onboard if we need help, and we've got kayakers and other rafts along-side us, so we're going to be safe. But just in case, let's go over a few rules: First, keep your hands inside the raft. Second, everyone needs to wear a life jacket, no matter how good a swimmer you are."

I glanced quickly at Enrique. He already had on his life jacket. I was surprised that he had even signed up for this trip, knowing how he feels about the water, but I was glad he was here.

"Third," the guide called, "pick a buddy and keep an eye on that person. If your buddy gets into any trouble, you should be aware of it and let me know immediately."

"All right," he said. "LET'S GO RAFTING!"

The guide shoved his oars against the rocks, and the raft was caught by the current and started its way down Tennessee's Upper Pigeon River. During our brief training session before the trip, we had been taught what to do. I leaned forward, planted my paddle in the water, and kept my feet firmly jammed between the wall and floor of the inflatable raft.

As the raft plunged forward, a hard, cold wall of water slapped us in the face. In a second, we were all drenched. Then we were out again, breathless and laughing. We had run our first rapid! The kayakers, who were gliding alongside us, darted around the rocks and whirlpools like large, yellow fish.

When the river grew peaceful for a stretch, I gazed around to take in the sights. Towering trees lined the banks. I glimpsed a bald eagle perched high in the branches of a tall pine.

The echoing roar of crashing water brought me back from my sightseeing. In seconds, the river was transformed from a smooth, green surface to a seething mass of white. The water bubbled and churned, diving over rocks and crashing down on itself. Suddenly, a large boulder appeared directly in our path. The guide tried to turn the raft, but it was too late. We all lurched forward as the raft slammed into the boulder. I looked around to see Enrique, watching in horror as his bright orange backpack fell overboard. Before I knew it, Enrique had leaped into the water after it.

"Man overboard!" I yelled, just as the guide had taught us to do. It was clear from Enrique's expression that he was stunned from the force of the cold current pushing him along. He had abandoned any notions of swimming for his backpack. Now he was desperately trying to keep his head above water and his feet out in front of him, so his head wouldn't hit the rocks first.

The guide was already on the radio, calling for help. The kayakers were working their way toward Enrique, but the river's unpredictable currents kept them away. At that moment, the wildlife, the sky, the towering trees all melted away. All I saw was Enrique, the rocks ahead of him, and the kayakers behind him. I found myself wondering what could have been so important about that backpack.

Suddenly, the river flattened out and grew quiet again. The kayakers closed in on Enrique. In a matter of moments, he was on shore, and two of the kayakers, who were also lifeguards, were checking him thoroughly. The raft came to a halt on the riverbank. I leaped out and ran to Enrique.

He wasn't hurt, but he seemed very upset. "My backpack…" he choked, coughing up water.

"Kid, forget your backpack," said the guide. "You're lucky to be alive."

Enrique blinked hard, as if he were fighting back tears. Just as the lifeguards finished inspecting him, one of the kayakers who had been trailing behind us paddled up to shore. He hopped out of his kayak and pulled out the orange backpack.

"Someone looking for this?" he called out.

Enrique's face lit up. He jumped to his feet and lunged toward the backpack. He took it from the kayaker with a quick but sincere "Thanks." Then he plopped down on the ground and dumped out its contents. Everyone swarmed around him, eager to get a glimpse of the precious loot that the backpack held: a flashlight, a soggy paperback, spare socks, a candy bar, bug spray, a wet baseball cap, and a small, black

plastic bag. It was this final item that Enrique grabbed and clutched tightly in his fist.

"What is it?" I asked. Everyone had the same question in mind.

Enrique reached inside the bag, drew out a small, hard case, and carefully opened the lid. Inside was a brass star attached to a red, white, and blue ribbon. "It's a Silver Star," Enrique said, holding the medal up so everyone could see it.

"Did you win it?" David Nickels asked.

"Or buy it online?" Reese Stephens snickered.

Enrique's eyes narrowed as he glared at Reese. "If you want to know," Enrique replied, "my grandfather was awarded this medal in World War II. Even though he was wounded in the leg, he saved his commanding officer from a burning building. When my grandfather died, my dad inherited it. He gave it to me for my birthday, just before I left for camp." Enrique stared thoughtfully at the medal. "He said I was responsible enough to be trusted with it now."

"Looks like you inherited your grandfather's courage along with his medal," the guide said as he took the Silver Star and pinned it to Enrique's shirt. "Why don't you keep that there, where it'll be safe for the rest of the trip down river. OK gang, ALL ABOARD," the guide hollered.

Enrique beamed with pride as we climbed back into the raft. ○

16. What does the narrator mean when he says he is "surprised that [Enrique] had even signed up for this trip"?

    Ⓐ that he and Enrique are not getting along

    Ⓑ that Enrique does not like the water

    Ⓒ that Enrique usually does not like outdoor activities

    Ⓓ that Enrique does not enjoy anything that involves danger

17. Read these sentences from the story:

    > He had abandoned any notions of swimming for his backpack.
    > Now he was desperately trying to keep his head above water and
    > his feet out in front of him, so his head wouldn't hit the rocks first.

    What is a *notion?*

    Ⓐ a thought or an idea

    Ⓑ an accessory

    Ⓒ a daydream or fantasy

    Ⓓ a friend

18. According to the narrator, in what way are the kayakers like fish?

    Ⓐ They do not smell good unless they are fresh.

    Ⓑ They are flashy but do not talk at all.

    Ⓒ They move very easily through the water.

    Ⓓ They are there one minute and gone the next.

19. Why was Enrique so determined to retrieve his backpack after it fell overboard?

    Ⓐ He was afraid that he would be punished if he lost his brand new backpack.

    Ⓑ He wanted to prove to the other kids that he was not afraid of the water.

    Ⓒ The medal that was in his backpack was made of silver and was worth a lot of money.

    Ⓓ His father had trusted him with his grandfather's medal, which was in the backpack.

20. Based on the information in the story, what conclusion can you draw about river rafting?

    Ⓐ Rafting is a dangerous activity, and only properly trained professionals should attempt it.

    Ⓑ Rafting does not require any particular skill, and it is a fun activity for adults and children of all ages.

    Ⓒ Rafting is an activity that requires some training and the use of proper safety equipment.

    Ⓓ Rafting is a very dangerous activity, and no one should ever attempt to do it.

GO ON

Directions *Read the following article about viruses. Then answer questions 21 through 25.*

The Smallest Microbes
by Soo Jin Kim

Did you know that the world is crawling with tiny, invisible creatures? These creatures are microbes. They can be seen only under a microscope. Viruses and bacteria are two kinds of microbe. Viruses are, by far, the smallest of all the microbes. Despite their small size, however, viruses have a huge impact on the world around them. They are best known for the illnesses that they can cause. Some illnesses caused by viruses include colds, Ebola, influenza (the flu), polio, rabies, and yellow fever.

Viruses are very tiny, very simple microbes. They are basically just packs of DNA or RNA. **DNA** and **RNA** are two types of genetic material. (Genetic material carries the instructions that tell a body how to operate, grow, and reproduce.) How small are viruses? Well, your body is made up of millions of cells. If one of the cells in your body were the size of an

Virus Sizes

Viruses are measured in **nanometers** (nm), the smallest unit of measurement in the metric system. There are ten million nanometers in a centimeter. Here are the maximum sizes of some viruses:

Virus	Size
Ebola virus	20 nm
Influenza (flu) virus	100 nm
Polio virus	27 nm
Rhino virus (cold virus)	2 nm
Yellow Fever virus	30 nm

average high-school baseball field, then a virus would be about the size of a softball. Pretty small, right?

Viruses have only one goal: to make replicas of themselves. They try to create as many copies as possible. In fact, the only time that viruses appear to be alive is when they are reproducing. And they can only reproduce within another living body, or **host.** If left alone outside a suitable host, most viruses just lie there, as lifeless as a doormat. When a virus comes in contact with the right kind of creature, however, it usually springs into action.

First, the virus attaches itself to a cell in the host—the living thing it has invaded. Then, the virus may pump its DNA straight into the cell, or it may trick the cell into accepting the DNA along with its food. Then the virus makes as many copies of itself as possible inside the cell of its new

Ebola Virus

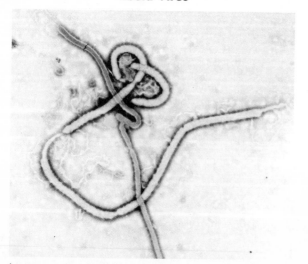

Image courtesy of the Center for Disease Control/C. Goldsmith.

Polio Virus **Flu Virus** **Yellow Fever Virus**

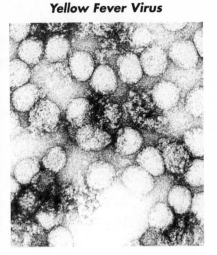
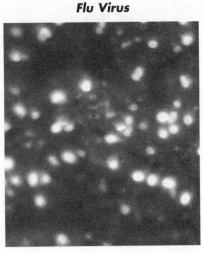

Images courtesy of the Center for Disease Control.

host. Either the host cell releases the new viruses, or the host cell becomes overstuffed with copies of the virus and eventually explodes. The host cell is often badly damaged by the virus. Sometimes, the host cell dies, which prevents the virus from making more copies of itself. Then the virus has to find a way to get to a new host cell.

Viruses cannot travel on their own. To get from one host to another, viruses have to travel through fluids or through the air. Airborne viruses can travel from one person to another in saliva or mucus from a sneeze or a cough. Sometimes viruses are carried by insects, which bite an infected animal or person and then spread the virus to others. Sometimes, a virus gets into a host when a hypodermic needle is used for more than one person.

The effect of the virus depends on the type of host invaded. A virus may enter a cell in one creature and cause no damage. If that same virus gets into another type of host, however, it can cause illness or death. That's why some viruses live quietly in

some creatures, with no ill effects, but become deadly if they get into another type of host.

If the virus gets into the right host and reproduces enough copies of itself, it makes that host sick. When that happens, the host's body tries to fight the illness. The body fights back against the virus, trying to kill it or to protect itself against the virus. The body might, for example, raise its temperature to a fever to slow the spread of the virus. Some illnesses caused by viruses, such as colds and flu, are over quickly. Other viral illnesses can cause permanent damage, however, and affect the body for life. Still other viral illnesses can cause death. The best defense against viruses is to avoid coming into contact with them in the first place. To avoid catching or spreading viruses, wash your hands often and always cover your mouth when you sneeze or cough. Vaccines[1] have also been developed that can be given to humans or animals to prevent certain viruses from invading. ○

---

[1]**vaccine.** A special medicine that helps protect people or animals from getting a certain type of illness

21. What is the article MOSTLY about?
    Ⓐ vaccines that protect humans against viruses
    Ⓑ the differences between viruses and bacteria
    Ⓒ what viruses are and how they work
    Ⓓ the Ebola virus and ways to avoid getting it

22. Why does the author compare a cell in the body to a baseball field and a virus to a softball?
    Ⓐ to explain the difference between viruses and bacteria
    Ⓑ to help readers understand how a virus moves to a new host
    Ⓒ to help readers understand how a virus works
    Ⓓ to help readers understand how tiny viruses are

23. According to the chart, which of the following viruses is the largest?
    Ⓐ influenza
    Ⓑ polio
    Ⓒ yellow fever
    Ⓓ Ebola

24. The chart below lists some of the ways mentioned in the article that viruses can travel from one host to another. From the answer choices below, choose the answer that belongs in the blank box.

Some Ways That Viruses Travel
in saliva or mucus from a sneeze or cough
in hypodermic needles used for more than one person

    Ⓐ in pollen that floats through the air
    Ⓑ in insects that have bitten an infected person
    Ⓒ in bacteria that grow in certain foods
    Ⓓ in meteorites that fall to Earth from space

25. Which of the following statements is true?

    Ⓐ Scientists have discovered some viruses that can be seen with the naked eye.

    Ⓑ Viruses are larger and more complex than bacteria.

    Ⓒ Viruses will destroy any plant or animal cell that they enter.

    Ⓓ Viruses are made up of bundles of DNA or RNA.

Stop! End of Session 1, Part 1

A note about the rest of the test:

This part of the test asks you to write about what you have listened to or read. Your writing will NOT be scored on your personal opinions. It WILL be scored on:

- how clearly you organize and express your ideas
- how accurately and completely you answer the questions
- how well you support your ideas with examples
- how interesting and enjoyable your writing is
- how correctly you use grammar, spelling, punctuation, and paragraphs

 Whenever you see this symbol, be sure to plan and check your writing.

Session 1
Part 2: Listening

Directions *In this part of the test, you will listen to an article called "The Wizard of Menlo Park," by Helen Canton. Then you will answer some questions to show how well you understood what was read. You will listen to the article twice. As you listen carefully, you may take notes on the article anytime you wish. You may use these notes to answer the questions that follow. Use the space below and on the next page for your notes.*

This article is about one of the most famous inventors of all time, Thomas Edison. Here are the spellings and meanings of some words from the article that may be unfamiliar to you:

disintegrated	fell apart; came apart
filament	a thin strand of thread, fiber, or wire
phonograph	a machine that reproduces sound by having a needle rest on a rotating grooved disc; an old-fashioned record player
patent	a government document that gives only the inventor the right to produce, use, and sell his or her invention
tungsten	a very hard, heat-resistant metal

Notes

*Note to Teachers: This listening selection appears in the Teacher's Guide for *AIM Higher! New York ELA Review.*

Notes

26. In the boxes below, list four inventions that Edison contributed to or helped to perfect.

Edison contributed to inventions such as...
1.
2.
3.
4.

27. Thomas Edison's childhood experiences were different from most children's. In what ways might Edison's unusual childhood have helped him to become a successful inventor?

_____

_____

_____

_____

_____

_____

GO ON

28. Edison was quoted as saying, "I have not failed, I have just found ten thousands ways that won't work." What do you think Edison meant by this?

_____

_____

_____

_____

_____

Planning Page

You may PLAN your writing for question 29 here if you wish, but do NOT write your final answer on this page. Your writing on this Planning Page will NOT count toward your final score. Write your final answer on the next two pages.

Notes

GO ON

29. Thomas Edison once said, "Genius is 1 percent inspiration, 99 percent perspiration." What does this statement mean? How do Edison's experiences support this statement? Do you agree with this statement?

In your answer, be sure to include

- an explanation of what Edison's statement means
- details from Edison's life that support this statement
- whether you agree with this statement

Check your writing for correct spelling, grammar, and punctuation.

_____

_____

_____

_____

_____

_____

_____

_____

_____

_____

_____

_____

_____

_____

_____

_____

_____

_____

_____

_____

_____

_____

_____

_____

_____

_____

_____

_____

_____

_____

_____

_____

 **Stop! End of Session 1, Part 2**

Session 2

This session contains two parts. In Part 1, you will read two passages and write about them. In Part 2, you will write an essay.

Session 2
Part 1: Reading

Directions In this part of the test, you are going to read a story called "Lester's Lesson," by Sterling Moore. You will also read a poem called "What Freedom Means," by Robin Lamb. You will answer questions and write about what you have read. You may look back at the story and the poem as often as you like.

Lester's Lesson
by Sterling Moore

When Kiki's English teacher, Mrs. Conners, announced the partners for the next group project, Kiki groaned. Not Lester! Anybody but Lester, she thought. Lester was the class outcast: a scrawny little kid with enormous ears, who bounced on the balls of his feet when he walked. The strange thing was that Lester didn't seem bothered by the other kids' teasing. He ignored them when they called him names and made fun of him. He never hesitated to answer questions or to get up in front of the class. The way he acted, you'd think he was the most popular kid in school.

Kiki, on the other hand, was terrified of being teased. She knew that, at lunch, she would hear endless jokes about how she and Lester were sitting in a tree, K-I-S-S-I-N-G. Her face grew red just thinking about it. Ever since she had started middle school, she woke up each morning with a queasy feeling in the pit of her stomach, dreading the day ahead. Her palms would sweat as she got on the bus, for fear that she might trip or not be able to find a seat. Her worst nightmare was that the other kids would laugh at her.

When the bell rang, Kiki waited until the other kids were gone. Then she approached the teacher.

"Mrs. Conners," she whispered, "may I *please* switch partners?"

Mrs. Conners looked up from her book. "Why, Kiki?"

"Because…" Kiki thought it was pretty obvious. "Well, I'd rather work with a girl."

"I can't just let everyone pick and choose the partner they want to work with," Mrs. Conners replied. "I'd have to rearrange the whole list. Besides, you need to learn how to work with boys, too. They don't bite." She smiled and went back to her book.

Kiki walked reluctantly toward the lunchroom, bracing herself for the teasing that was sure to come. It was even worse than she had imagined. For the rest of the school day, kids whispered comments like "Kiki loves Lester," and passed her notes with pictures of Lester and her holding hands.

The next day in English, everyone was paired up with his or her partner. They were supposed to write a skit of a scene from Greek mythology. Kiki cringed at thought of performing in front of the class, especially with Lester.

"So, what scene should we do?" Lester asked.

Kiki glared at him. "I don't care," she said sullenly. She was sure that everyone in the class was watching her; she didn't want to look as if she liked working with Lester.

"How about a scene from Theseus," Lester suggested.

"Whatever," Kiki said, staring out the window. "As long as I don't have to say anything."

Lester said, "Fine," with a twinkle in his eye. He took out his notebook, bent over it, and began scribbling away. Kiki did her best to pretend that she was someplace else.

By the next day, Lester had written the entire script. "Here's your copy," he said.

Kiki glanced at the script with a yawn. The only two characters were Theseus and the Minotaur. "Wait," she said, a little louder than she'd meant to. "I have to be the Minotaur? He's a hideous beast."

"Yeah, but you don't have to say anything," Lester replied with a grin. "All you have to do is lie there and pretend to be asleep until I kill you."

"But I don't want to be a beast," Kiki protested.

"OK," Lester said, "You can be Ariadne."

"You mean the princess who helps Theseus kill the Minotaur?" Kiki asked.

"Yeah," Lester said with a grin. "We can easily add her lines."

"Let me get this straight," Kiki said. "I can either be a hideous beast, or I can be a

beautiful princess who falls in love with *you?*"

"Yup," said Lester, smiling.

Kiki laid her head on her arms. "I'm going to be the laughing stock of the whole sixth grade," she groaned pitifully.

"No," Lester corrected her, "that's my job."

Kiki gave him a puzzled look. She couldn't believe he was so willing to admit it. "Doesn't it bother you?" she asked quietly.

"Nah," Lester said with a shrug. "You know, Theseus was a scrawny little kid. The other kids made fun of him all the time. But he was smart and brave, and look where he ended up: He became a king, while those other kids became shepherds and shopkeepers and boring stuff like that." He paused and then leaned in a little closer to Kiki and whispered, "They only make fun of me to convince themselves that they're better. But here's a little secret that my sister told me: 'No one can make you feel inferior without your consent.'"

"What does that mean?" Kiki asked.

"It means they can't make you feel bad unless you let 'em."

Kiki liked the sound of that. She sat up a little straighter and looked around the room at her classmates. She noticed that perfect Mary McConnelly's hair was sticking up in the back and that Jessica Trudale's shirt didn't match her pants.

She turned back to Lester, whose ears didn't look quite so big. "So, what will Ariadne say?" she asked.

Kiki and Lester revised the script and then practiced their parts. By the next day, they had memorized all their lines. They even created a fake Minotaur. Lester played Theseus so enthusiastically that Kiki couldn't help but get swept up in her role. When Lester leaped onto the Minotaur and thrust his sword into the beast, everyone clapped and cheered. Mrs. Conners gave them both an A.

That afternoon, when Kiki got on the bus, she didn't worry one bit about tripping or not finding a seat. ○

30. In the boxes below, list three similarities between Lester and Theseus.

Similarities between Lester and Theseus
1.
2.
3.

31. What secret does Lester tell Kiki, and how does she seem to change after hearing it?

_____

_____

_____

_____

_____

_____

What Freedom Means
by Robin Lamb

It means that you are not a rock
Falling from space
Faster and faster
Burning up in the atmosphere
Until nothing is left
Except some smoke
And a child's "Look, Daddy!"

It means you can decide,
For example,
To fall or not to fall
In or out
Of love.
Yes, even that doesn't have to be
Something that just happens to you,
Like being hit by a train.

It means that however bad things get
You can choose to laugh,
So that people say, "What's he laughing about?"
Thinking that you've got a secret.
Which you do:
You're free. ○

GO ON

32. Explain what freedom means, according to the poem.

_____

_____

_____

_____

_____

_____

Planning Page

You may PLAN your writing for question 33 here if you wish, but do NOT write your final answer on this page. Your writing on this Planning Page will NOT count toward your final score. Write your final answer on the next two pages.

Notes

33. How is Lester's secret similar to the secret mentioned in the poem? What main idea or theme is shared by the story and the poem?

In your answer, be sure to include

- an explanation of how Lester's secret is similar to the secret in the poem

- an explanation of the main idea or theme that the story and the poem have in common

- details from BOTH the story and the poem

 Check your writing for correct spelling, grammar, and punctuation.

_____

_____

_____

_____

_____

_____

_____

_____

_____

_____

_____

_____

_____

_____

_____

_____

_____

_____

_____

_____

_____

_____

_____

_____

_____

_____

_____

_____

_____

_____

 Stop! End of Session 2, Part 1

Session 2
Part 2: Writing

Directions In this part of the test, you will be writing an original essay.
Follow the directions on the next two pages and begin your writing on page 40.

Planning Page

You may PLAN your writing for question 34 here if you wish, but do NOT write your final answer on this page. Your writing on this Planning Page will NOT count toward your final score. Write your final answer on the next three pages.

Notes

GO ON

34.

> What is your definition of freedom? Explain what you think freedom means. Use examples and details from your own life—or from what you have read, seen, or heard—to make your definition clear.
>
> In your essay, be sure to include
>
> - your definition of freedom
> - examples from your own life, to make your definition clear
> - details to make your writing interesting

 Check your writing for correct spelling, grammar, and punctuation.

_____

_____

_____

_____

_____

_____

_____

_____

_____

_____

_____

_____

_____

_____

_____

_____

_____

_____

_____

_____

_____

_____

_____

_____

_____

_____

_____

_____

_____

_____

_____

_____

_____

_____

_____

_____

_____

_____

_____

_____

_____

_____

_____

_____

_____

_____

_____

_____

_____

_____

 Stop! End of Test

Chapter 1
This Is Only a Test

Test-Taking Strategies for Language Arts Students

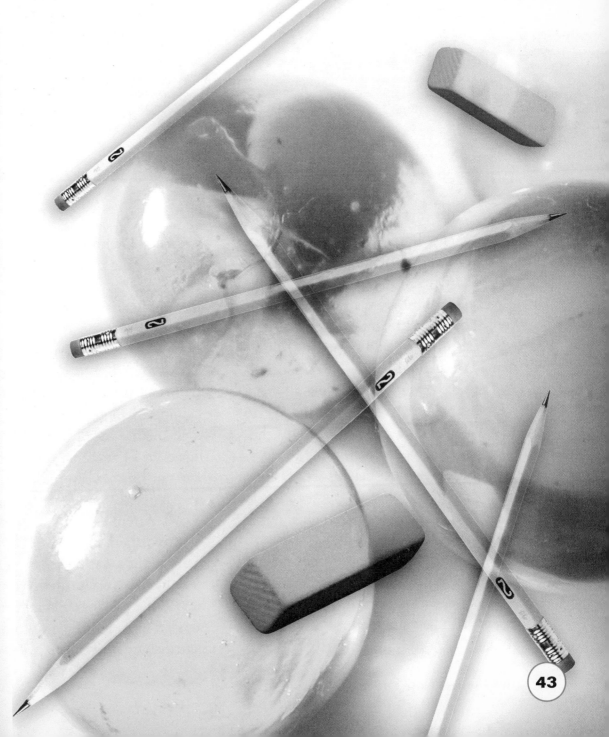

Read this short story. Then try your hand at the exercises that follow the story. You will not be graded on the exercises at this time. At the end of the chapter, you will be directed to return to the exercises to revise and proofread your work.

Stan, The Number-One No. 2

by Drew Johnson

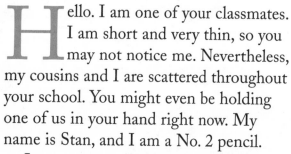

Hello. I am one of your classmates. I am short and very thin, so you may not notice me. Nevertheless, my cousins and I are scattered throughout your school. You might even be holding one of us in your hand right now. My name is Stan, and I am a No. 2 pencil.

Let me start off by thanking all the school supplies who voted me the World's Best Pencil. It is a great honor to be the number-one No. 2 pencil in the world. Some of the younger pencils were asking me about the secret of my success. I would like to take the time now to talk about my long career as a pencil.

I almost did not become a pencil. When I was just a little branch on the family tree, I wanted to be a toothpick. My parents had become toothpicks late in life. So had the rest of my family. Then I overheard a child talking about automatic test-scanning machines. These machines could grade a student's score sheet incredibly fast. In order for the machine to read the score sheet properly, however, the student must use a No. 2 pencil.

All my life, I had wanted to help kids. At first, I thought that would mean helping them get bits of food out of their teeth. Once I heard that child's tale, however, I knew that the life of a toothpick was not for me. I would be a No. 2 pencil, helping children take tests.

My parents were disappointed when I first told them my plans. After a while, though, they warmed to the idea and became very supportive. My mother even helped me pick out special eraser tops, and my dad introduced me to some of the best pencil sharpeners in the area.

Harvey, my first owner, was great fun. When Harvey was taking a test, he used to spin me around and around in his hands. It was like a carnival ride! Unfortunately, Harvey did a little too much spinning. He would never answer a question unless he was absolutely sure he had the right answer. I tried to tell him that he needed more confidence in himself, but he wouldn't listen to me. I suppose this isn't too unusual. Some students have trouble listening to their parents, much less to a piece of wood with a graphite core.

Harvey would have been a good test-taker if he had been a little more sure of himself. Most of the time, the first answer he thought was correct *was* the right answer. Harvey eventually dropped me, and my next owner, Samara, picked me up.

Samara was an excellent test-taker. She was not afraid to trust her instincts or take an educated guess. I remember moving back and forth along the score sheet, as she confidently darkened one oval after another with my sharp head. Samara used to take lots of notes and make a rough outline on scrap paper before she wrote an essay, which helped her to organize her ideas. Of course, this caused me to lose a lot of graphite, but I did not mind. It was for a good cause! Pencils who are afraid to lose their graphite have always disgusted me. Who do they think they are—drumsticks for some rock star? Get with the program.

Samara did so well on her tests that she skipped a grade and left me behind. That was when my last owner, Gavin, found me. Gavin studied quite a bit. How fondly I remember helping him recopy his notes and do homework! Sadly, when it came to test time, Gavin would get too nervous. His palms would sweat so much that I thought I was going to drown. If Gavin had learned to relax, he would have done well on those tests. As it was, he was a little too anxious. I have the bite marks to prove this. Gavin even came close to breaking me one time! I still find it hard to believe that I almost snapped in half because Gavin could not remember how to spell *cantaloupe* properly.

My days of taking tests are coming to an end. I'm so short and stubby now that a student can barely hold me. Two more sharpenings would reduce me to little more than an eraser. I plan to retire to the bottom corner of the desk drawer, where I hope to spend time with my old friends: Reginald, the dried-up glue bottle; Alberto, the bent paper clip; and the broken crayon triplets. Hopefully, we will enjoy ourselves and grow old talking about the good old days, before computers became so popular.

I would like to end this speech with a quick note of advice to the next generation of No. 2s out there:

Whenever there are tests, there will be children who need your help. Tell those children not to be afraid! It's a good feeling when you darken in the circle completely and show the world what you know. ○

Your Turn

Exercise A Recalling and Interpreting *Answer the following questions on your own paper. Use complete sentences.*

1. **A.** RECALLING DETAILS
   When Stan was young, what did he want to be?

   B. INTERPRETING DETAILS
   What made him change his mind?

2. **A.** RECALLING DETAILS
   Who was Stan's first owner?

   B. INTERPRETING DETAILS
   What was this person's biggest problem on tests? How did Stan try to help?

3. **A.** RECALLING DETAILS
   Who gave Stan bite marks?

   B. INTERPRETING DETAILS
   Why did this person bite Stan?

4. **A.** RECALLING DETAILS
   Where is Stan planning to spend his retirement?

   B. INTERPRETING DETAILS
   Why is Stan retiring? What does he intend to do with his time?

Meets
New York
Standards
1.A.1
1.A.3
1.A.4
1.A.6
1.B.1
1.B.4
2.A.1
2.B.1

Throughout this text, standards will appear in a box like this one. The numbers listed in the box are those used to enumerate the standards in the Teacher's Guide.

Exercise B Synthesizing *On your own paper, write a paragraph in response to the questions below.*

Stan, the main character in the story at the beginning of this chapter, knows a lot about taking tests. He talks about his owners and discusses what they did right and what they did wrong. What are some good things to do when taking tests? What should you avoid when taking tests? Explain, using examples from the story.

This Is Only a Test

Wouldn't the world be a better place if there were no tests? Actually, the answer is no. Sure, school would become much, much easier. Think, however, about how you would get to school. Would you drive there? Since no one would have to take a driving test, the streets would be filled with bad, reckless drivers. If you think driving is dangerous now, think about seeing an eight-year-old drive a huge truck across your front lawn!

Maybe it would be safer just to stay in your house. Of course, the architect who designed your house would not have had to take any tests, so you would have to be prepared for the roof to cave in. Also, the people who built your house would not have had to take any tests either, so you could not expect the plumbing or electricity to work or your walls to stand up for long.

Basically, a world without tests would be a place where houses fall apart and driving a car is like entering a demolition derby. The simple fact is that tests are an essential part of the modern life. They are a way to make sure that people have learned the skills and information necessary to do their jobs well. Be thankful for this the next time you visit your doctor, who had to pass tests in order to practice medicine.

You will take many types of test throughout your life. Therefore, it makes sense to learn all the test-taking skills you can. The rest of this lesson will describe some of the tests you will encounter. It will also give good advice about how to get ready for tests of various types.

Types of Test

Tests come in a variety of forms. For example, a music student might give a performance to pass a test. The student might be judged on how well he or she can play a certain piece of music. Tests that you take in school can range from short surprise quizzes to state examinations that take several hours. It is a good idea to figure out an approach for each kind of test. You do not want to prepare for a multiple-choice exam and then find yourself facing an essay test.

Here is a list of some of the types of test you will encounter while you are in school:

Aptitude and Achievement Tests

These are the two major test categories:

Test Type	What Is Tested
Achievement	What you have learned
Aptitude	What you can learn

An **aptitude test** is designed to measure underlying ability, or potential. The IQ (Intelligence Quotient) test is a well-known example of an aptitude test. An aptitude test for horseback riding would not test whether you already knew how to ride a horse. Instead, it would test your hand-eye coordination, balance, ease around animals, and other underlying abilities related to learning how to ride.

An **achievement test** measures what a person has learned. For example, suppose you went to a dude ranch to learn how to ride a horse. At the end of the lessons, you might take an achievement test measuring such skills as putting a saddle on correctly, holding the reins properly, mounting a horse, starting and stopping, turning, and so on. The achievement test would measure how well you had learned the various skills that were taught in the lessons.

There are three main types of achievement test: the classroom test; the standardized (norm-referenced) test; and the criterion-referenced test.

- **Classroom tests.** Most of the tests you take in school fall into this category. Classroom tests are given by teachers. These tests are designed to determine whether you have learned certain concepts and skills taught as part of a class.

- **Standardized tests.** These tests are used to compare the skills of individuals and groups. Standardized tests are also known as **norm-referenced** tests. Examples include the Iowa Test of Basic Skills (ITBS) and the National Assessment of Educational Progress (NAEP) tests. Standardized tests show how your scores compare to those of other students.

More ▶

- **Criterion-referenced tests.** These exams assess a student's ability to meet a set of standards for achievement. In simple terms, standards are lists of skills and concepts that students are supposed to master. Each state usually has its own set of academic standards in each subject area. State standards are often broken down into more narrow units called benchmarks, which tell precisely what a student is supposed to know or be able to do at a certain age or grade level. This book has been created to help you meet or exceed the standards tested by the ELA exam.

Preparing for Tests

A proven, successful approach to most tests is to combine the specific knowledge needed for a certain test with general knowledge about how to take tests well. Many of the later chapters in this book will provide specific strategies and guidelines for succeeding on the ELA exam. On the following page are some general test-preparation guidelines that work well when you are getting ready to take any important test or exam.

Meets
New York
Standards
1.A.1
1.A.5
1.A.6

A Good Approach to Standardized Tests

1. **Practice, practice, practice.** An old joke goes, "The three most important things in real estate are location, location, and location." The three most important things in test preparation are "practice, practice, and practice." Taking practice tests that resemble the actual test is one of the best ways you can improve your scores. The Pretest and Posttest in this book are both practice tests that have been designed for this purpose. They are modeled closely on the actual ELA exam. Taking them will help familiarize you with the types of question found on those exams. You will know what is expected of you if you know the format of a test beforehand.

2. **Have confidence.** In many ways, tests can be a self-fulfilling prophecy. Studies have shown that when students believe they are going to do well on an exam, their scores go up. Think about Gavin, one of the characters in the story at the beginning of the chapter. Gavin knew the answers but lacked confidence. He doubted himself, and his scores suffered for it. Do not let this happen to you. If you believe in yourself and in your abilities, then you will be more likely to do well on tests.

3. **Build your vocabulary.** The bigger your vocabulary, the better your chances are of succeeding on most tests. Some amount of writing and reading is required on most tests. If you have a large vocabulary, you increase your chances of understanding a question and of getting the right answer. Next time you encounter a word you do not know, make sure to write it down. Later, look up the word and write down its meaning. Then try to include that new word in your own writing and speech. This method can build your vocabulary very quickly and effectively. (Chapter 3 will discuss building your vocabulary in greater detail.)

4. **Simulate test conditions.** Try to study in an environment that is similar to a real test-taking situation. Simulate real test conditions if you are going to take a practice test.

5. **Give it a rest.** Students who stay up too late at night studying often do themselves more harm than good. Mental fatigue sets in while they are taking a test. Their scores suffer for it. Make sure you get enough sleep the night before a test. Eat nutritious meals the night and morning before a test. Do not skip breakfast. Rest and eat well, so you can be at your best on the day of the test.

More ▶

6. **Watch your watch.** If a test is timed, make sure you have a watch of your own or can see a clock. Keep track of the time, and pace yourself during the exam. You want at least to attempt to answer every question on a test. Watching the time will help keep you from spending too much time on a single question.

7. **Break out the lucky socks.** Test day is not the best time to worry about high fashion. Comfort is more important, so wear loose-fitting, layered clothing. Wearing several layers of clothes allows you to adapt to the temperature of the room in which you are taking the test.

8. **Do not let any single question frustrate you.** Almost inevitably, there will be one or more questions on a test that most students will not understand. Instead of getting mad or going into a panic, remember that your goal is to get the *best* score that you can. You do not need a *perfect* score. When you come across a tough question, reread it and try to figure out what is being asked. Then use the strategies discussed in this book to make your best guess. On hard questions, don't get discouraged: Keep in mind that everybody else taking the test is in the same boat.

9. **Relax.** Mental fatigue will settle in at some point whenever you are taking a long exam. If you feel your brain starting to ache, take a minute or two to relax and rest. Stretch your arms and legs if possible. Close your eyes for a moment and imagine a calm, peaceful scene. You're at the beach! In your mind, feel free to dive into the calm, blue waters, or just relax and take in the view. Dive back into the test once you feel rested.

10. **Exercise your skills over a period of time.** Many of the skills tested by state exams—such as the ability to read and write well—are developed over a long time. Begin practicing your reading and writing skills today. For example, every week, try to read one or two long magazine articles. It is perfectly acceptable to read articles in magazines about sports, hobbies, music, or popular culture. The important thing is that you read regularly on your own in order to build your reading skills.

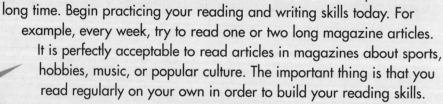

You can practice your writing skills by beginning a journal. Write in it every day. The chart of journal ideas on the next page will give you some ideas for entries of different types that you can make a regular part of your journal.

Journal Ideas

Dear Diary. Simply tell what happened in your day.

Feelings First. Describe your changing feelings about people, places, things, and events around you.

Great Expectations. Describe your goals, dreams, wishes, and hopes for the future.

Imaginings. Let yourself go. Describe daydreams and wild imaginings that answer "what if" questions like *What if dogs could read minds?* or *What if kids ran schools?*

News Views. Be a pundit! Give your reactions to and opinions about current events.

Critically Speaking. Write your own mini-reviews of movies, television shows, sporting events, CDs, and computer games.

Personal Portraits. Create character sketches of people you know. (Be kind!)

The Fame Game. Create character sketches of famous people (celebrities, historical figures, etc.).

Learning Log. Tell about the new things that you've learned in school and in life.

On the Agenda. Make to-do lists for tomorrow, next week, ten years from now, or fifty years from now.

Dream Team. Record your dreams. (You'll remember them more easily if you lie awake in bed in the morning for a bit, thinking about what they were.)

Credos. Tell what you believe in strongly and why.

Kudos. If you were handing out prizes, to whom would you give them and why? Explain.

Eye Catching. Describe the marvelous or weird things that you notice around you during the day—especially those unusual things that people might overlook, like a sandwich sitting on a mailbox or a big, burly weight-lifter type buying a home-and-garden magazine.

Suggestion Box. Describe ways to make the world a better place.

Types of Test Question

Two of the most common question types are multiple-choice questions and extended-response questions. **Multiple-choice questions** ask a question and then provide possible answer choices. Your task is to pick the best possible response. **Written-response questions** do not provide possible answers: They ask a question and you have to provide the answer.

Written-response questions are generally more difficult than multiple-choice questions. This can be shown by comparing the following two questions:

1. Name one of the bones in the human forearm. What are some of the other bones located around it? Where are these other bones in relation to the forearm bone that you named?

Written-Response Question

Multiple-Choice Question

2. Which bone is located in the human forearm?

Ⓐ ulna

Ⓑ skull

Ⓒ tendon

Ⓓ humerus

These questions are quite similar. However, it should be easy to see that you have a much better chance of answering the multiple-choice question correctly than the written-response question. If you do not know the answer to Question 1, your chances of guessing correctly are very, very slim. Your goal for Question 2 is to pick the correct answer choice, so you have a one-in-four chance of guessing correctly.

This means you already have a 25 percent chance of picking the right answer, even if you know nothing about the subject. These are already better odds than you had with Question 1. With a little work, you can improve your chances even more. Look at the four choices, and eliminate any choices

you know are incorrect. You should realize that your skull is in your head, not your forearm. This means that choice B is incorrect. Now you have a one-in-three chance of getting the question right. Furthermore, you might know that the word *tendon* describes a kind of soft tissue found in the body. It is not a bone at all. This means that the answer is either A or D. Which is it?

Consider this: Having eliminated two wrong answers, you now have a fifty-fifty chance of getting Question 2 correct. Compare these odds with the odds of guessing correctly the answer to Question 1. Now you can see why multiple-choice questions are generally easier than written-response questions.

For those of you who just have to know the correct answer, take some time to look up *ulna* and *humerus* in a dictionary. Doing so will help build your vocabulary!

Most multiple-choice questions can be separated into two parts, a leader line and answers. The **leader line** is the opening part; it is often a question. In this case, the leader line is "Which bone is located...." **Answers** are simply the choices from which you have to pick the best answer. Of these answers, all but one, in most cases, are **distractors**—answers that are incorrect. It is important to take time to make sure that you understand the leader line before you proceed to look at the answers. Doing so prevents mistakes caused by rushing and not reading the question properly. Eliminating distractors is another good strategy for approaching multiple-choice questions.

A good approach to creating answers to written-response questions will be covered in later chapters. For now, look over these tips for handling multiple-choice questions:

Meets
New York
Standards
1.A.1
1.A.3
1.A.4
1.A.5
1.A.6

How to Approach Multiple-Choice Questions

1. If you do not immediately know the answer to a question, go on to the other questions. You can come back later to the one you could not answer.

2. Pay particular attention to key words in directions, such as MOST LIKELY or LEAST.

3. Eliminate answers that are obviously wrong first. Then choose the answer that seems most likely from the ones that remain. (This technique, often called *process of elimination,* was used to answer the sample multiple-choice question.)

4. Remember that on multiple-choice tests, you are supposed to choose the *best* answer to the question. If one answer is partly right but another is completely right, choose the one that is completely right.

5. For some tests, wrong answers and answers left blank are given the same score. If there is no additional penalty for a wrong answer, take a chance: Make your best guess when you are not sure of an answer. Eliminate any answers you know to be wrong, and then choose the best answer from those that remain. You will have at least some chance of choosing the correct answer.

Your Turn

Meets
New York
Standards
1.A.1
1.A.3
1.A.5
1.A.6

Exercise *Fill in the circle next to the correct answer to each multiple-choice question.*

1. All tests can be divided into what two categories?
    - (A) multiple-choice and achievement tests
    - (B) standardized and achievement tests
    - (C) criterion-referenced and achievement tests
    - (D) aptitude and achievement tests

2. Which of the following is an example of a norm-referenced test?
    - (A) a pop quiz
    - (B) the ELA exam
    - (C) the ITBS
    - (D) a classroom test

3. An essay question is an example of a
    - (A) written-response question.
    - (B) criterion-referenced test.
    - (C) multiple-choice question.
    - (D) effective way to practice reading skills.

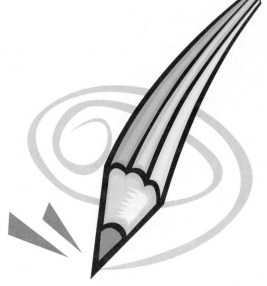

4. Imagine that you are taking a multiple-choice test. The first question seems very difficult to you. If this is the case, you should
    - (A) leave the question blank.
    - (B) skip the question but then come back to it later.
    - (C) spend as much time as necessary to get that question right.
    - (D) keep in mind that difficult questions are often tricky. Pick the one answer choice that you eliminated; it is probably correct.

Return to the exercises at the beginning of the chapter, revise your work as necessary, and submit the exercises to your teacher for grading.

Chapter 2

On Closer Examination

Understanding Your State Test

On Closer Examination

Can just anyone decide to practice medicine? Could you, for example, just rent an office and put out a sign with your name, followed by the letters M.D.? Of course not—not unless you have been to medical school, have done an internship, and have passed your medical boards (a series of exams). Most doctors have also completed a residency program to practice a particular specialty. So, it is not the case that just anyone can become a doctor. To become a doctor, you have to show that you have met certain standards. Having standards for doctors protects people from untrained or poorly trained physicians who might do them harm.

In a similar way, states across the country have created standards for students in kindergarten through twelfth grade. These standards are lists of what students should know and be able to do in certain subjects at each grade level. Here are the standards for English language arts created by the state of New York:

Standard 1 Students will read, write, listen, and speak for information and understanding.

Standard 2 Students will read, write, listen, and speak for literary response and expression.

Standard 3 Students will read, write, listen, and speak for critical analysis and evaluation.

Standard 4 Students will read, write, listen, and speak for social interaction.

Passage and Question Types on the ELA Exam

How does the state of New York find out whether its students are meeting these standards? The state does so by administering the **English Language Arts,** or **ELA,** examinations. These exams test reading, writing, and listening skills at particular grade levels. When you take one of these exams, you read short literary and informational passages. You also listen to some passages that are read aloud.

In response to these, you answer various types of question. Here are the question types that you will find on the ELA exam:

A **multiple-choice question** requires you to select the best answer to a question from the group of possible answer choices provided.

A **short-response question** requires you to write a brief response or to complete a graphic organizer, such as a tree diagram or chart.

An **extended-response question** requires you to answer in a longer piece of writing, generally one that is more than a single paragraph in length.

An **independent writing question** requires you to write an essay—a multiparagraph piece with an introduction, body, and conclusion.

The Structure of the ELA Exam

The following chart describes the typical structure of an ELA exam.

Session 1

Part 1
Reading
—Four to six informational and literary passages, each followed by multiple-choice questions (twenty-five questions overall)
—Covers Standards 1, 2, and 3

Part 2
Listening
—One informational passage or two short linked informational passages, followed by three short-response questions and one extended-response question
—Covers Standard 1

Session 2

Part 1
Reading and Writing
—Two linked literary or informational passages, three short-response questions, and one extended-response question
—Covers Standard 3

Part 2
Independent Writing
—One essay question, thematically related to the reading passages
—Covers Standard 1

This book will give you an opportunity to learn and to practice the skills necessary for success on the ELA exam. These skills include

- reading informational and literary passages with understanding,
- taking notes on what you read and hear,
- answering multiple-choice and short-response questions,
- writing extended responses, and
- writing essays.

Before you begin your ELA practice, however, it is important for you to understand one thing: The ELA exam tests reading, writing, and listening skills that are developed over a long time. The very best way to practice for the ELA exam is to read, write, and listen often. In other words, you need to practice and to hone your skills throughout the school year. This book will help you a lot. However, you have to make up your mind to help yourself by making a commitment to the work that you do for all of your classes. Beyond that, it is important to read and write on your own, for enjoyment. Keeping a journal and reading magazines and newspapers are excellent ways to keep your writing and reading skills at a high level.

Chapter 3
Words for the Wise

Developing Your Vocabulary

Mountain Biking: How to Hit the Dirt without Hitting the Dirt

by Lewis Scott

Mountain biking has emerged as one of the most popular sports of recent years. Basically, the sport involves taking a specially made bicycle with wide tires and, quite often, shock absorbers, off road, onto trails and across country. What does it take to get into this exciting new sport?

First, a mountain biker needs a well-tuned bike with good tires. In addition, a mountain biker needs quite a bit of safety equipment. It is vital for a mountain biker to have a well-fitting helmet with a high impact rating. Mountain biking can be dangerous. Even the best mountain bikers—those involved in professional competitions—sometimes have accidents. They fall off their bikes and find themselves supine—flat on their backs. Mountain bikers without helmets can suffer serious head injuries that may lead to paralysis or death. So, a good helmet is the most important piece of equipment of all.

In addition to a helmet, there are other accouterments that can help to protect the mountain biker. These include goggles, wrist guards, elbow pads, knee pads, and a lightweight protective vest. Mountain bike trails are usually very narrow. Many are rough, steep, twisted, and covered with obstacles and loose debris. Often there are branches and vines hanging in the way of the trail. The additional gear doesn't just make a mountain biker look "cool": It can help prevent the scrapes, cuts, and bruises that can happen when a biker hits branches, roots, rocks, or other objects, or the ground at high speeds.

Speaking of speed, many beginning mountain bikers try to go very slowly in order to avoid accidents. This does not work as well as one might think. Why? The answer is that moving along at a decent speed gives stability to a bike: If you go too slowly, you'll wobble. On the other hand, going fast gives a biker less time to make decisions. The trick to riding well is to find a happy medium—to travel fast enough to stay upright but slow enough to have time to react to surprises along the trail. Even if you travel at moderate speeds and wear lots of safety equipment, however, you can get into trouble on a mountain bike. Mountain biking is definitely something that you should do only with your parents' permission and at your own risk.

Still interested in being a mountain biker? Great! Wait a moment, however, before you head off to the woods. There are some useful biking skills you should learn before attempting to bike a trail. You could hope to acquire these skills through serendipity, but most people are not lucky enough to learn them by chance alone. You will need to practice on a normal street. One important skill a mountain biker needs is the ability to bump over objects. This involves lifting your front wheel so that it clears the object and then letting your back wheel bump over the object. Another useful skill, though more dangerous, is hopping. Hopping involves lifting both wheels off the ground while the bike is in motion. A mountain path is often studded with obstacles such as rocks and tree roots; it may also be littered with branches. If you do not bump or hop over these objects, you might crash your bike.

Many bike trails are difficult even without roots or large objects in the way. Fortunately, you do not have to take a new path without knowing what to expect. You can always reconnoiter the path on foot first. This will let you know where the toughest parts of the trail are—the place where the path goes through a creek or down a steep slope, for example.

With all the dangers involved, why would anyone want to take up mountain biking? This is a reasonable question. Not everyone likes the sport. Then again, the same can be said for riding a skateboard. Some people love the excitement of riding a skateboard. Other people would never step onto one. Both riding a skateboard and mountain biking can be quite thrilling. Mountain biking is a freeform exercise, since every ride is different in some way. The sport is physically challenging, and you also have to make tough decisions on the spot. Furthermore, you can never be completely sure what challenge awaits you around a turn on a mountain bike trail. That's part of what makes the sport so exciting. ○

Your Turn

Exercise A *Fill in the circle next to the correct answer to each multiple-choice question. Use clues from the selection to help you determine the meanings of the italicized words.*

1. Which of the following phrases is closest in meaning to *reconnoiter?*
   - Ⓐ scout ahead
   - Ⓑ end a journey
   - Ⓒ change direction
   - Ⓓ take a chance

2. An *accouterment* is
   - Ⓐ a pants suit.
   - Ⓑ an equipment accessory.
   - Ⓒ a piece of practical advice.
   - Ⓓ a helpful friend.

3. *Freeform* and _____ have similar meanings.
   - Ⓐ standard
   - Ⓑ flexible
   - Ⓒ predictable
   - Ⓓ rigid

4. What does *supine* mean?
   - Ⓐ on the ground
   - Ⓑ on a bicycle
   - Ⓒ seriously injured
   - Ⓓ on your back

5. *Serendipity* is similar to
   - Ⓐ hard work.
   - Ⓑ a bad break.
   - Ⓒ a lucky accident.
   - Ⓓ a silly song.

Exercise B *Answer the following questions on the lines provided.*

1. Look up the word *serendipity* in a dictionary. What is the meaning of the word?

   _____

   _____

2. What is the origin of the word *serendipity?* Explain.

   _____

   _____

   _____

3. Briefly describe an experience you had that involved serendipity.

   _____

   _____

   _____

   _____

   _____

   _____

Meets
New York
Standards
1.A.1
1.A.2
1.A.3
1.A.5
1.A.6
1.B.1
1.B.2
1.B.4

Developing Your Vocabulary (65)

Words for the Wise

When you take the ELA exam, you will have to read a number of selections. Some passages will be fiction. Some will be nonfiction. Sometimes, when you are reading, you may come across a word that you do not recognize. In this chapter, you will learn how to decode, or make sense of, unfamiliar words that you encounter in your reading.

Using Context Clues

Often, when you come across an unfamiliar word, you can figure out its meaning based on the context of the word. The **context** is simply all of the words and phrases that immediately surround the word. These words and phrases will give you hints about what the unfamiliar word means. The hints are called **context clues**.

There are several types of context clue. Here are some of the most important ones.

Restatement

A **restatement** occurs when the same idea is said over again in different words. Restatement is sometimes called **direct definition**. Think about this sentence from the opening selection about mountain biking:

> They fall off their bikes and find themselves *supine*—flat on their backs.

In that sentence, the word *supine* is restated by the phrase "flat on their backs." *Supine* means "lying on one's back, facing upward."

Comparison and Contrast

A **comparison** shows how two ideas or things are alike. A **contrast** shows how they are different. Sometimes a writer will use comparison or contrast as a context clue. Think about these sentences:

> I argued *vociferously* against moving to a new town. My little brother also argued loudly and strongly for staying put.

The word *also*, in the second sentence, is a clue that two things are being compared. What the little brother

ontext clues

did (arguing loudly and strongly) is like what the speaker did (arguing vociferously). So, *vociferously* must mean "loudly and strongly." Some words and phrases that often signal comparison are *like, same, same as, similarly, likewise, in comparison,* and *another*.

Now think about this sentence:

Gandalf the Gray was quite sagacious; Bilbo, on the other hand, could be quite foolish.

The phrase *on the other hand* signals a contrast. Bilbo is foolish. He is unlike Gandalf. Gandalf is *sagacious.* Therefore, *sagacious* must mean "wise"—the opposite of *foolish.* Some words and phrases that often signal contrast are *unlike, different, differ, on the other hand,* and *in contrast.*

Examples

Examples are specific instances chosen to illustrate a general type of thing. Consider these sentences:

In addition to a helmet, there are other *accouterments* that can help to protect the mountain biker. These include goggles, wrist guards, elbow pads, knee pads, and lightweight protective vests.

The examples—goggles, knee pads, and so on—help to give you an idea of what *accouterments* are. They are accessory items of equipment or clothing.

Synonyms and Antonyms

Sometimes synonyms or antonyms are used as context clues. A **synonym** is a word that has a similar meaning. An **antonym** is a word that has an opposite meaning. Think about these sentences:

This hotel is quite *sumptuous.* The other one is also *magnificent.*

Dareb thinks that peas are *vile,* but I think that they are *great.*

In the first example, the word *also* signals that *magnificent* is a synonym for *sumptuous.* In the second, the word *but* alerts readers that *great* is an antonym for *vile.* So, *sumptuous* means "magnificent," and *vile* means something like "terrible," the opposite of "great."

Inference

Sometimes, to figure out the meaning of an unfamiliar word, you have to make an educated guess, or **inference.** To do this, you choose a meaning that makes sense based on everything else that you can figure out from the context of the unfamiliar word. Consider this example:

When it came time for his dentist appointment, Roger proved to be quite *recalcitrant.* He refused to leave the chair that he was in, and his parents ended up having to drag him to the car.

Notice the actions described in the passage. The boy refuses to leave his chair. His parents have to drag him to the car. The boy is acting stubborn and resistant. Therefore, *recalcitrant* must mean "stubbornly resistant."

Meets
New York
Standards
1.A.1
1.A.2
1.A.3
1.A.5
1.A.6

Your Turn

Exercise A *As you read each sample passage, pay attention to the context clues. Then fill in the letter of the correct answer to each multiple-choice question.*

1. Most people thought that Jay's newspaper column was *trite*, but I thought that it was really original.

   What does *trite* mean?
   - Ⓐ unusual
   - Ⓑ unoriginal
   - Ⓒ boring
   - Ⓓ fun to read

2. The *milliner's* shop displayed all of her recent creations. There were berets, dress hats, informal caps, and even a cowgirl hat.

   What does *milliner* mean?
   - Ⓐ a member of the Chamber of Commerce
   - Ⓑ a small shopkeeper
   - Ⓒ a seller of women's clothing
   - Ⓓ a maker of women's hats

3. It is *implausible* that there is life on Venus. The idea that there might currently be life on Mars is also unlikely.

   What does *implausible* mean?
   - Ⓐ likely
   - Ⓑ definite
   - Ⓒ unlikely
   - Ⓓ possible

4. Because of the trade made possible by the Erie Canal, New York City *superseded* Philadelphia as the most important city in the East.

   What does *supersede* mean?
   - Ⓐ to take the place of
   - Ⓑ to crush in battle
   - Ⓒ to act snobby toward
   - Ⓓ to trade with

5. Some common *canines* are collies, German shepherds, and golden retrievers.

What is a *canine?*

Ⓐ a bird   Ⓑ a cat   Ⓒ a bear   Ⓓ a dog

Meets
New York
Standards
1.A.1
1.A.2
1.A.3
1.A.5
1.A.6

6. David was a very *belligerent* boy; he was always getting into arguments.

What does *belligerent* mean?

Ⓐ kind   Ⓑ numb   Ⓒ quarrelsome   Ⓓ crooked

7. Ms. Robinson made every effort to *placate* the angry customer. Mr. Johnson's words, however, only irritated the customer more.

What does *placate* mean?

Ⓐ to calm down   Ⓑ to annoy   Ⓒ to confuse   Ⓓ to identify

8. Badger was a clever, *wily* old character. He was always tricking people into doing what he wanted them to do and pulling fast ones on all the villagers.

What does *wily* mean?

Ⓐ cute   Ⓑ tricky   Ⓒ rich   Ⓓ trusting

9. Indira Gandhi, a prime minister of India, once said, "You cannot shake hands with a *clenched* fist." She was saying that there cannot be peace between people when they approach each other ready to fight.

What does *clenched* mean?

Ⓐ dirty   Ⓑ tightly closed   Ⓒ cold   Ⓓ wide open

10. The moon's actual appearance is *mercurial*, changing all the time. It looks like a full circle about once a month, and the rest of the time it looks like only part of a circle, depending on the way it is hit by light from the sun.

What does *mercurial* mean?

Ⓐ always changing
Ⓑ never changing
Ⓒ very small
Ⓓ very large

Your Turn

Exercise B *Read the following short passages. For each passage, explain, on the lines provided, what you think the italicized word means.*

1. Despite all the time and effort she put into protecting her home—building a sea wall, reinforcing the roof, installing storm shutters—she knew that her house was still not *immune* to the destructive forces of a hurricane.

    _____

    _____

    _____

2. "The minister was not in the mood that morning to turn the other fender. He insisted that the accident be reported to the police and that neither vehicle be moved until an officer arrived. The suspects took a *dissenting* position and insisted on driving away."
    —Tony Hillerman, "The Great Taos Bank Robbery"

    _____

    _____

    _____

3. "They were such *resplendent* uniforms, brave with shining buttons and dazzling with twined gold braid on cuffs and collars.... Scarlet and gold sashes swung to and fro, sabers glittered and banged against shining boots, spurs rattled and jingled."
    —Margaret Mitchell, *Gone with the Wind*

    _____

    _____

    _____

Developing Your Vocabulary

Using Word Parts

When you were a small child, you doubtless played at some point with building blocks. You could use building blocks to make various objects, such as a tower or a bridge. Similarly, you can use **word parts** to build various kinds of words. Here are some common word parts that you can use:

- A **prefix** is a part that is added to the beginning of a word.

- A **suffix** is a part that is added to the end of a word.

- A **base word** is a complete word to which a prefix or suffix can be added.

- A **root** is a main word part that cannot stand alone as a word. One or more other parts must be added to a root to make a word.

Meets
New York
Standards
1.A.1
1.A.3
1.A.5
1.A.6
1.B.1

Prefixes

When you add a prefix to the beginning of a word, it almost always changes the meaning of the word. For example, the prefix *non–*, when added to the word *Irish (non-Irish)*, changes the meaning of the word to "not Irish."

The following chart gives examples of some common prefixes:

Prefix	Meaning	Example
ambi–	both	*ambi*dextrous (able to use both hands well)
anti–	against	*anti-*American (against America)
astro–	star	*astro*naut (someone who travels among the stars)
auto–	self	*auto*matic (happening by itself)
bi–	two	*bi*lingual (speaking two languages)
circum–	around	*circum*scribe (draw a circle around, go around)
co–	with	*co*-worker (person with whom one works)
ex–	from, out past	*ex*clude (leave out) *ex*-president (past president)
fore–	before, in front of	*fore*tell (predict, or tell beforehand)
hemi–	half	*hemi*sphere (half of a sphere or globe)
hyper–	over, beyond	*hyper*active (overly active)
im–, in–	not, opposite of	*in*frequent (not frequent) *im*possible (not possible)

More ▶

Prefix	Meaning	Example
macro–	large	*macro*scopic (large enough to be seen without a microscope)
mal–	bad	*mal*nutrition (bad or insufficient nutrition)
micro–	small	*micro*scope (device for looking at small objects)
mono–	one	*mono*rail (trail that travels on one track, or rail)
non–	not, opposite of	*non*combatant (one who does not fight)
over–	too much, extra	*over*load (put on too much weight; excess load)
poly–	many	*poly*syllabic (having many syllables)
post–	after	*post*script (note added after, or at the end of, the main part of a letter)
pre–	before, in front of	*pre*war (before the war)
re–	again, back	*re*play (play again)
semi–	part, half	*semi*circle (half of a circle)
sub–	under, below	*sub*marine (below the sea)
trans–	across, over, change	*trans*continental (across the continent) *trans*form (change from one form to another)
tri–	three	*tri*state (across three states)
un–	not, opposite of	*un*hinge (change or remove a piece of something so that it is not hinged)
uni–	one	*uni*cycle (one-wheeled vehicle)

Suffixes

A **suffix** is added to the end of a word. Like a prefix, a suffix almost always changes the meaning of the word to which it is added. Often a suffix changes the part of speech of a word. For example, the suffix *–tion* turns words into nouns, as in *imagine + tion = imagination*. The addition of *–tion* changes the verb *imagine* into a noun, *imagination*.

Suffix	Meaning	Example
–able, –ible	capable of, able to	*workable* (capable of working)
–al	of, like	*magical* (like magic)
–ed	past tense	*laughed* (laughing that took place in the past)
–ess	female	*lioness* (female lion)
–fold	multiplied by	*tenfold* (multiplied by ten)
–ful, full	full of	*soulful* (full of soul)
–ic	like, similar to, having to do with	*angelic* (like an angel)
–ily	in the manner of	*moodily* (in the manner of someone who is moody)
–ish	in the manner of	*childish* (in the manner of a child)
–ism	act, practice, doctrine, or theory of	*terrorism* (act of spreading terror) *communism* (Communist doctrine)
–less	without	*fearless* (without fear)
–ly	in the manner of	*calmly* (in a calm manner)
–ology	study of	*graphology* (study of handwriting)
–s, –es	plural	*games, dishes* (more than one game, dish)
–ward	in direction of	*westward* (in the direction of the west)
–y	full of, containing	*faulty* (containing one or more faults)

More ▶

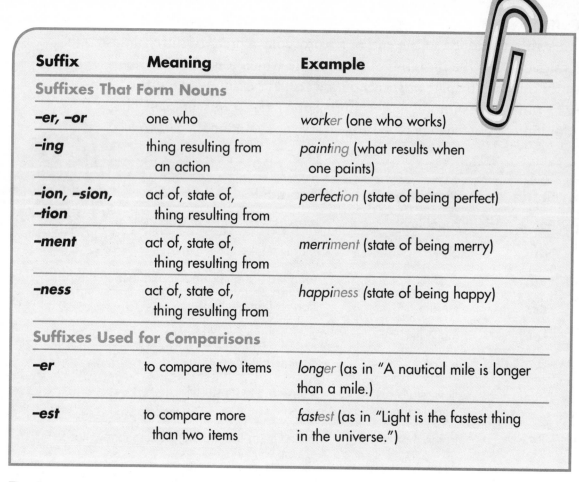

Suffix	Meaning	Example
Suffixes That Form Nouns		
–er, –or	one who	*worker* (one who works)
–ing	thing resulting from an action	*painting* (what results when one paints)
–ion, –sion, –tion	act of, state of, thing resulting from	*perfection* (state of being perfect)
–ment	act of, state of, thing resulting from	*merriment* (state of being merry)
–ness	act of, state of, thing resulting from	*happiness* (state of being happy)
Suffixes Used for Comparisons		
–er	to compare two items	*longer* (as in "A nautical mile is longer than a mile.)
–est	to compare more than two items	*fastest* (as in "Light is the fastest thing in the universe.")

Roots

A **root** is a main word part that cannot stand on its own as a word but that can be used, along with other word parts, to create a new word. The following chart describes some common roots:

Some Common Roots and Word Families		
Root	**Meaning**	**Examples**
anni, annu, enni	year	*anniversary, annual, bicentennial*
anim	living	*animation*
aud	hear, listen	*audible, auditorium*
auto	self	*autobiography*
bibl, biblio	book	*bibliography, bibliophile*
capt	take	*captive, capture*

More ▶

Root	Meaning	Examples
chron, chrono	time	*chronology, geosynchronous*
corp	body	*corporeal, corps, corpus*
cred, creed	know, believe	*credulous, creed, incredible*
dem, demo	people	*democracy, endemic*
duc, duct	carry, lead	*conduct, deduction, induce*
fid, fide	faith, trust	*confidence, fidelity*
fract, frag	break, part	*fracture, fragment*
ge, geo	Earth	*geanticline, geology, geosynchronous*
homo	same	*homogeneous, homonym*
hydro, hydr	water	*hydrant, hydrate, hydraulic, hydropower*
junct	join	*junction, conjunction*
log, logy	word, thought, study	*sociology, neologism, dialogue*
mand	command	*mandate, reprimand*
mort	death	*immortal, mortified*
patr	father	*patron, patriarch*
path	sadness, suffering	*pathological, sympathetic*
phag, phagus	eat, consume	*phagocyte, esophagus, sarcophagus*
phil	love	*philanthropy, philharmonic*
phon, phone, phono	sound	*phonic, microphone, phonograph*
pod, pode	foot, footlike	*podium, pseudopod*
psych, psycho	of the mind	*psychology, psychosomatic*
sci	know	*conscious, omniscient*
sen	old	*senescence, senile, senior*
spec	see	*inspection, spectacle, speculate*

More ▶

Developing Your Vocabulary

Root	Meaning	Examples
tange, tang	touch, feel	*intangible, tangential*
tele	far, across distance	*telegraph, telephone, teleportation*
ten	stretch or hold	*tenacious, tendon*
therm, thermo	heat	*thermal, thermodynamic, thermometer*
viv	alive, life	*revive, vivisection*
voc	call	*vocalize, vocation* (calling)
vore	swallow, devour	*carnivore, voracious*

Very often, the meaning of an unfamiliar word can be discovered by analyzing the word's parts. Consider the word *geochronology*.

geo   +   *chrono*   +   *logy*

= Earth   = time   = study

Geochronology means studying the Earth's history through geologic events.

Word Families

A **word family** is a group of words that have the same root. For example, the root *ocu* means "eye." The following words all share this root:

ocular	"having to do with the eye"
binoculars	"instrument for seeing at a distance"
monocle	"an eyepiece for one eye"
occult	"hidden, unseen"

Your Turn

Exercise A On the line provided, add a prefix to each word or word part to form a complete word with the meaning given in parentheses.

1. _____ + *freeze* (against freezing; a substance that helps keep something from freezing)

2. _____ + *ground* (before or in front of the background)

3. _____ + *sense* (not sensible)

4. _____ + *space* (beyond ordinary space)

5. _____ + *cycle* (a vehicle, or cycle, with three wheels)

6. _____ + *terranean* (under, or below, the Earth)

7. _____ + *word* (to word another way, or say something over again in different words)

8. _____ + *navigate* (to navigate, or travel, around)

9. _____ + *physics* (the physics of the stars)

10. _____ + *tone* (having one tone)

Exercise B Change each one of the following words into a noun by adding a suffix. An example has been provided for you.

EXAMPLE: *sing* + *ing* = *singing*

1. *dream* + _____ = _____

2. *fulfill* + _____ = _____

3. *crabby* + _____ = _____ (Hint: Change the *y* to an *i*.)

4. *communicate* + _____ = _____

Your Turn

Exercise C Draw lines to separate the word parts. Then tell what each word means. An example has been provided for you.

EXAMPLE: fore|gone

MEANING: Gone before; done beforehand

1. eightfold

   MEANING: _____

2. reducible

   MEANING: _____

3. unforgettable

   MEANING: _____

Exercise D For each root listed below, come up with two words that belong to the word family containing that root. Use a dictionary as necessary. Give the meaning of each word.

1. Root: **bio**

   WORD: _____

   MEANING: _____

   WORD: _____

   MEANING: _____

2. Root: **auto**

   WORD: _____

   MEANING: _____

   WORD: _____

   MEANING: _____

Building a Strong Vocabulary

In this chapter, you have learned some excellent ways to increase your vocabulary. You can figure out what words mean by using context clues. You can also determine their meanings by studying the parts that make them up. Here are some other tips for building a strong vocabulary:

Meets
New York
Standards
1.A.1
1.A.2
1.A.3
1.A.5
1.A.6

Increasing Your Vocabulary

- Take responsibility on your own for actively studying and learning new words.

- When you come across a new word, use context clues and/or word parts to figure out what it means.

- Check the meaning in a dictionary.

- Keep a list in one place of all the new words that you come across in your everyday life. You can call this list your Vocabulary Learning Log.

- Study your list of new words at least once a week.

- Make up flash cards to help you to memorize the meanings of the new words.

- Start using the words in your own speech and writing. This will make the new words part of your **active vocabulary.**

The Parts of a Dictionary Entry

A dictionary entry for a word generally contains a lot more than just definitions. The following are some of the standard parts of entries found in dictionaries:

1. **Syllables.** The large dots show where the word (such as **con • flict**) is divided into syllables.

2. **Pronunciation.** The pronunciation of the entry word is given in parentheses following the word. Most dictionaries contain a pronunciation key that tells you what the symbols used in the pronunciation stand for.

3. **Part of speech label.** These labels, such as *v.* for "verb" and *n.* for "noun," identify the part of speech of the word when it is used in different ways, according to the definitions that follow.

4. **Definitions.** Definitions give one or more possible meanings for a word. Most words have more than one definition. The definitions are usually numbered.

5. **Inflected forms.** Inflected forms are alternative forms of the entry word.

6. **Derived forms.** Derived forms are words that are closely related to the entry word and that are made by adding prefixes or suffixes.

7. **Etymology.** An etymology is the history of a word.

8. **Synonyms. Synonyms** are words that are similar in meaning. Dictionary entries may also contain **antonyms,** or words that are opposite in meaning.

9. **Usage labels. Usage labels** explain special uses of a word or tell how the word should or should not be used. The sample entry on the next page contains a usage label showing how the word *conflict* is used in the field of psychology.

definitions
pronunciation
part of speech label
entry word
usage label

Meets
New York
Standards
1.A.1
1.A.3
1.A.6

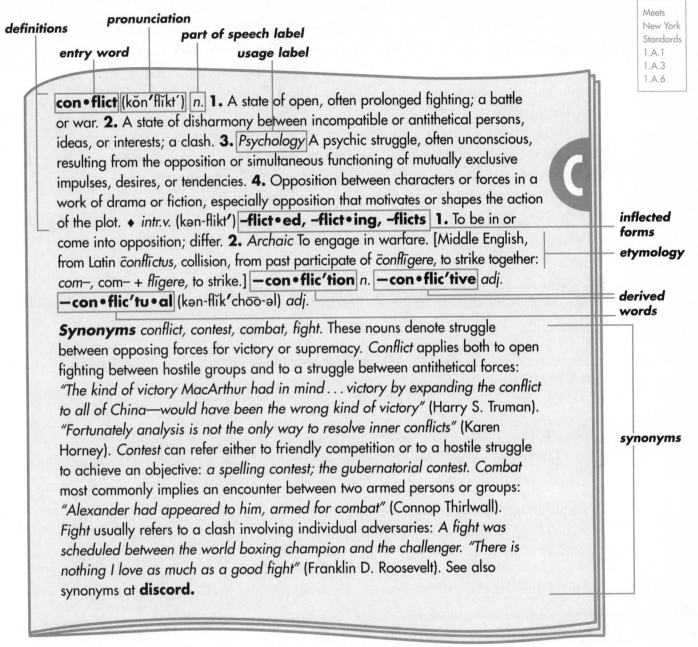

con•flict (kŏn′flĭkt′) *n.* **1.** A state of open, often prolonged fighting; a battle or war. **2.** A state of disharmony between incompatible or antithetical persons, ideas, or interests; a clash. **3.** *Psychology* A psychic struggle, often unconscious, resulting from the opposition or simultaneous functioning of mutually exclusive impulses, desires, or tendencies. **4.** Opposition between characters or forces in a work of drama or fiction, especially opposition that motivates or shapes the action of the plot. ♦ *intr.v.* (kən-flĭkt′) **–flict•ed, –flict•ing, –flicts 1.** To be in or come into opposition; differ. **2.** *Archaic* To engage in warfare. [Middle English, from Latin *cōnflĭctus*, collision, from past participate of *cōnflīgere*, to strike together: *com–*, com– + *flīgere*, to strike.] **—con•flic′tion** *n.* **—con•flic′tive** *adj.* **—con•flic′tu•al** (kən-flĭk′chōō-əl) *adj.*

inflected forms
etymology
derived words

Synonyms *conflict, contest, combat, fight.* These nouns denote struggle between opposing forces for victory or supremacy. *Conflict* applies both to open fighting between hostile groups and to a struggle between antithetical forces: *"The kind of victory MacArthur had in mind . . . victory by expanding the conflict to all of China—would have been the wrong kind of victory"* (Harry S. Truman). *"Fortunately analysis is not the only way to resolve inner conflicts"* (Karen Horney). *Contest* can refer either to friendly competition or to a hostile struggle to achieve an objective: *a spelling contest; the gubernatorial contest. Combat* most commonly implies an encounter between two armed persons or groups: *"Alexander had appeared to him, armed for combat"* (Connop Thirlwall). *Fight* usually refers to a clash involving individual adversaries: *A fight was scheduled between the world boxing champion and the challenger. "There is nothing I love as much as a good fight"* (Franklin D. Roosevelt). See also synonyms at **discord.**

synonyms

Copyright from *The American Heritage Dictionary of the English Language,* 4th Edition. Used by permission.

Developing Your Vocabulary

The Multiple Meanings of Words

"When making pancakes or playing baseball, you need to start with a good batter." That sentence is an example of a pun because it makes use of the fact that *batter* means more than one thing. The word can mean "a liquid made with flour and water," or it can mean "a player who attempts to strike a ball with a bat."

If you look at an entry in a dictionary, you will notice that for many words there are several numbered definitions. That's because many words have more than one meaning. For example, the term *hot dog* can mean "a frankfurter served on a long, soft roll," or it can mean "someone who tries to show off." Here are some of the many meanings of the word *cold*.

1. chilly (adjective)

   In this part of the country, it gets cold in November.

2. without warmth or feeling (adjective)

   I tried to make friends with her, but she is too cold.

3. of a color that suggests a cold thing (adjective)

   The room was painted a cold grayish blue, so we had it repainted a bright yellow.

4. precise, actual, real (adjective)

   The judge made her ruling based on the cold, hard facts of the case.

5. no longer strong or fresh (adjective)

   After a day had gone by, the scent had grown cold, and the dogs had to be called off.

6. completely (adverb)

   The boxer was out cold.

7. with mastery (adverb)

   The actor knew her lines cold.

8. an illness characterized by coughs and congestion (noun)

   Hector has a bad cold.

9. weather that is not warm, a low temperature (noun)

   Don't go out in the cold without your coat.

Notice that words with multiple meanings can sometimes be used as different parts of speech. In the examples above, the word *cold* is used as an adjective, an adverb, and as a noun. Notice also that when a word has multiple meanings, the meanings are often related.

Some words have special meanings when used with regard to particular activities. For example, the word *bond* usually means anything that holds or fastens things together. For example, you might have a bond with your friends or your parents or your brothers or sisters. In chemistry, a *bond* is the electrical attraction between atoms or groups of atoms. It is what holds molecules together.

A *bond* can also be a type of promise or obligation. In business, a *bond* is a piece of paper that represents an agreement between the investors who buy the bond and the company or government that issues it: As part of this agreement, the business or government promises to pay back a certain amount of money to bondholders (investors) on a certain date. In dictionaries, special labels are often used to signal meanings particular to fields of endeavor. So, for example, a dictionary entry might read, "**bond**...*Chem.* The electrical attraction between atoms or groups of atoms." The abbreviation *Chem.* means that in the field of chemistry, the word can have the meaning indicated.

Meets New York Standards 1.A.1 1.A.2 1.A.3 1.A.5 1.A.6

JANE'S BOND Ultra-Hold

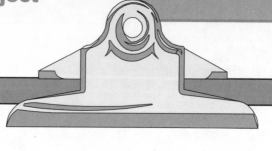

Use the word parts from the lists on pages 71–76 to create as many words as possible. Write the words on your own paper along with their definitions. Use a dictionary to look up each of the words that you create to make sure it is an actual word and to check that your definition is accurate. An example is provided below.

EXAMPLE: geo + thermal = <u>heat coming from inside the Earth</u>

Return to the exercises at the beginning of the chapter, revise your work as necessary, and submit the exercises to your teacher for grading.

Chapter 4
Talking Back to Books

Active Reading

Read this article about dinosaurs. Then try your hand at the exercises that follow the article. You will not be graded on the exercises at this time. At the end of the chapter, you will be directed to to return to these exercises to revise and correct your work.

Dinosaur Profiles

by Will Tripp

Ever since the first dinosaur bones were discovered in 1763, people have been excited by these prehistoric giants. For about two hundred years, it was believed that dinosaurs were similar to modern-day lizards. Any reptile that large, many people thought, must have been slow and lumbering. Then, in the 1960s, a scientist posed the theory that dinosaurs might have been much more active than previously thought. People began to imagine dinosaurs such as *Tyrannosaurus rex* as fast and fearsome creatures, more like huge birds of prey than lizards. Scientists are still making new discoveries about dinosaurs, but the features that continue to fascinate people the most about them are their size, speed, and **ferocity.**[1]

Big and Tall

The largest dinosaurs were the sauropods. These animals were taller, longer, and heavier than any land animal alive today. The largest sauropods were over one hundred feet long, forty feet high, and weighed up to one hundred tons. That's 200,000 pounds! Such huge animals might sound quite frightening, but they were most likely very gentle. Sauropods

---

[1]**ferocity.** Violent manner

were **herbivores,**[2] so they depended on plant life for food. Their long necks, which made up roughly half of their total length, allowed them to reach leaves high up in tall trees. Because of their enormous size, sauropods were slow creatures. They were **quadrupeds,** which means they walked on four legs. Their huge tails helped to balance their long necks and relatively small (in proportion) bodies. The tail was also probably used to lash at the few predators that would have tried to attack a sauropod. *Brachiosaurus* was the most common type of sauropod. Next to *T. rex*, *Brachiosaurus* is the most widely recognized dinosaur.

Built for Speed

In the movies, *T. rex* has been shown chasing speeding cars. In fact, with such a massive body, *T. rex* might not have been able to run at all, or at least not very fast. Scientists do not know exactly which species of dinosaur was the fastest. From looking at dinosaurs' skeletons and from studying the way modern animals move, scientists who study dinosaur fossils (bones and tracks or imprints) have concluded that the swiftest dinosaurs were probably the ones that looked most like birds. These dinosaurs were **bipeds**[3] with long, skinny legs and small, light bodies. One such

Brachiosaurus, with its long neck, was one of the tallest dinosaurs.

---

[2]**herbivore.** Plant-eating animal
[3]**biped.** Two-footed animal. Bipeds generally travel upright.

dinosaur is called *Ornithomimus,* which means "bird-mimic." This dinosaur was similar in build to the ostrich. It even had the same toothless beak. Like birds, this dinosaur also had hollow bones, which made its body quite light. Scientists think it might have been able to move as fast as an ostrich, reaching top speeds of forty to forty-five miles per hour. That is just over half as fast as the cheetah, the fastest land animal today, which can reach speeds of up to seventy miles an hour.

Fearsome Beasts

The fiercest dinosaurs were the theropods. The best-known theropod is *T. rex.* Theropods varied greatly in size. The largest one found so far, *Giganotosaurus,* was discovered in Argentina in 1994. It was about twelve feet tall at the hip (less than half the height of the sauropods) and weighed about eight tons. Like all theropods, it was a **carnivore.**[4] When scientists dug up the skeleton of this huge dinosaur, they also found the bones of other dinosaurs nearby. These smaller, plant-eating dinosaurs are thought to be victims of *Giganotosaurus.*

---

[4]**carnivore.** Meat-eating animal

Theropods were clearly designed to be predators. They were bipeds, with strong hind legs that could support their full body weight. This left their short front limbs and sharp claws free to grab at prey. Theropods also had long, curved teeth, perfectly suited for ripping and tearing flesh.

Another vicious theropod, *Velociraptor*, was much smaller than *Giganotosaurus* or *T. rex*. While only three feet in height, *Velociraptor*, whose name means "speedy thief," was just as fast as *Ornithomimus* but much more dangerous. These dinosaurs had very sharp claws and about eighty razor-sharp teeth, some more than an inch long. *Velociraptors* probably used their speed to sneak up on their prey. Then, working together in packs, they could tear their victim to shreds with their teeth and retractable claws. A pack of *Velociraptors* could be far more dangerous than a single *T. rex*.

A great deal is known about dinosaurs, yet there is still a lot more to learn. In recent years, scientists have theorized that many dinosaurs died out due to an enormous meteorite that struck the Earth near the Yucatán Peninsula of Mexico about 65 million years ago. More recently, in the Ukraine and on the bottom of the North Sea off the coast of England, scientists have discovered other meteorite craters dating from the same period. These discoveries suggest that a "shower" of meteors might have led to the dinosaurs' extinction. What happened to the dinosaurs remains controversial, however. As scientists continue to uncover more information about these fascinating creatures, our image of how they looked and behaved will doubtless change. They will remain larger than life in our imaginations, however, and people will undoubtedly grow even more fascinated by the unique features of these prehistoric creatures. ○

Exercise A *Fill in the circle next to the correct answer to each multiple-choice question.*

1. What is the main idea of the article?
   - Ⓐ Dinosaurs roamed the Earth millions of years ago.
   - Ⓑ Sauropods are the largest meat-eating dinosaurs.
   - Ⓒ People find dinosaurs fascinating because of their size, speed, and ferocity.
   - Ⓓ *Tyrannosaurus rex* was a carnivore, or meat-eating dinosaur.

2. According to the article, sauropods used their long necks to
   - Ⓐ balance their huge bodies.
   - Ⓑ scratch their backs.
   - Ⓒ look for approaching predators.
   - Ⓓ reach leaves in tall trees.

3. Which of the following isn't a characteristic of *Ornithomimus* mentioned in the article?
   - Ⓐ long, skinny legs
   - Ⓑ hollow bones
   - Ⓒ a scaly back
   - Ⓓ a light body

4. Which of the following is one reason that *Velociraptor* was an effective hunter?
   - Ⓐ It would attack its prey in packs.
   - Ⓑ It was related to *Ornithomimus*.
   - Ⓒ It weighed up to one hundred tons.
   - Ⓓ It could run at up to seventy miles per hour.

5. If sauropods were around today, which of these modern foods do you think they would prefer?
   - Ⓐ hamburger
   - Ⓑ salad
   - Ⓒ spaghetti
   - Ⓓ chicken

Exercise B *On your own paper, write a paragraph in which you summarize the information in the article you have just read. Remember that when you summarize, you restate information in fewer words and in less detail than the author used. In your summary, explain in your own words what the main point, or thesis, of the article is. Also explain the most important points that the author makes in the body paragraphs of the article. (Hint: The headings throughout the article give you clues about the important points the author makes.)*

Talking Back to Books

Meets
New York
Standards
1.A.1
1.A.3
1.A.4
1.A.5
1.A.6
1.B.1
1.B.4

A typical language arts examination consists of reading passages, questions about the reading passages, and writing prompts related to the reading passages. One of the best ways to succeed on these tests is to read actively. In this section, you will learn some reading strategies that will help you to improve your reading skills.

Before Reading: Previewing a Passage

Previewing a reading passage, or looking it over before you read it in depth, can tell you what to expect from the piece and improve your understanding of it. Previewing involves the following four steps: scanning, skimming, calling on your prior knowledge (what you already know) of a subject, and questioning.

1. **Scanning.** When you **scan** a passage, look through it quickly to find specific information, such as the title; author; direction line; headings; any boldfaced, highlighted, or italicized words; illustrations; captions; and special elements such as charts and boxed features. As you locate each of these items, glance at it quickly to get the gist of it. Then go on to the next item.

Elements to Scan in Short Pieces of Nonfiction Writing

Direction Line On reading tests, typically there will be a **direction line** telling you to read a passage. Often, the direction line will identify the type of passage you will be reading and tell you what you should do when you finish reading. For example, "Read the article and then answer the questions that follow," is a typical direction line.

Title & Subject The **title** is the name of the article. It often tells you what the piece of writing is about, or its **subject.**

Author The name of the **author** usually appears after the title. He or she is the person who wrote the piece.

Headings **Headings** are the subtitles that appear within an article or essay. They mark the major parts of the piece of writing. Headings are important: They often highlight the main ideas in the piece.

Highlighted Words **Highlighted words** are the words the author wants to emphasize. They are especially important words, or **key terms,** that are central to the subject or that are defined in the text. They are usually printed in special type. They might be **boldfaced,** in *italics,* underlined, or in a different color.

More ▶

Illustrations	**Illustrations** are the pictures or graphics that appear within the text. Maps, charts, graphs, diagrams, drawings, and photographs are all examples of illustrations. Some reading passages may be made up mainly of illustrations with accompanying text.
Captions	A caption is usually included with an illustration. The **caption** is text that describes or explains the illustration.
Charts or Boxed Features	**Charts** present information in rows and columns. **Boxed features** are set off from the text and may appear against a shaded or colored background. Boxes usually contain text and/or graphics that illustrate or highlight some aspect of the subject.

Notice the information one student gathered as he scanned the article on dinosaurs at the beginning of this chapter:

One Student's Response

As I scanned the article, I found the direction line telling me to read the article and complete the exercises that follow it. Then I identified the title of the article ("Dinosaur Profiles"), the author (Will Tripp), the headings ("Big and Tall," "Built for Speed," and "Fearsome Beasts"), and some key words (<u>ferocity</u>, <u>herbivores</u>, <u>carnivore</u>, <u>quadrupeds</u>, and <u>biped</u>). There was also an illustration of a brachiosaurus and a caption explaining that this was one of the tallest dinosaurs. Now I know that the subject of the article is dinosaurs and that each of the sections focuses on one of their characteristics: size, speed, and ferocity.

2. Skimming. When you **skim** a piece of writing, glance quickly through the first and last paragraphs of the passage and the first and last sentences of each body paragraph to get an idea of the overall concepts in the text. Do not worry about getting every detail or idea.

Meets
New York
Standards
1.A.1
1.A.3
1.A.5
1.A.6

Elements to Skim in Short Pieces of Nonfiction Writing

Introduction	The **introduction** is at the beginning of the text. It has two purposes: to grab the reader's attention and to introduce the subject of the piece. Along with the body and conclusion, the introduction is one of the three major parts of a piece of writing.
Thesis Statement	The **thesis statement** expresses the central idea of the article or essay. It tells you what the author wants you to learn from the piece. It usually appears in the introduction.
Body	The **body** makes up the bulk of the writing in a piece of nonfiction. The body usually consists of several paragraphs, each focusing on a main idea. Within each paragraph are ideas and details that support and explain that main idea. The body is the second major part of a piece of writing.
Paragraphs	The body of a piece of nonfiction is usually organized in paragraphs. A **paragraph** is a group of related sentences. You can recognize a paragraph because the first line is usually indented.
Topic Sentence/ Clincher Sentence	Often, a paragraph will contain a topic sentence, which may be the first sentence. A **topic sentence** expresses the main idea of a paragraph. A **clincher sentence** may appear at the end of a paragraph to summarize the writer's point.
Conclusion	The third major part of a typical piece of nonfiction writing is the conclusion. The **conclusion** sums up the entire article or essay and often makes a final statement about the subject.

One Student's Response

As I skimmed the article, I found the thesis statement: "Scientists are still making new discoveries about dinosaurs, but the features that continue to fascinate people the most about them are their size, speed, and ferocity." This told me that the writer was going to focus on these three characteristics. As I continued to skim, I noticed from the topic sentences of the body paragraphs that the author was going to discuss the largest dinosaurs, the sauropods; the fastest dinosaurs, which looked like birds; and the fiercest dinosaurs.

3. Calling on Prior Knowledge.

All new learning builds on the knowledge and experiences that you already have. The best way to understand a reading passage fully is to relate it to ideas and experiences that are already familiar to you. As you preview a passage, think about what you already know about the topic and how you feel about it.

One Student's Response

As I scanned and skimmed the article, I thought about what I have already learned about dinosaurs in school and at home. I have read about them in my spare time and seen movies about them, like Jurassic Park, so I have an idea of how they looked. I can relate what I already know about dinosaurs to what the author is saying here. I'm familiar with T. rex and Brachiosaurus, but I have never heard of some of the other dinosaurs the author mentions.

4. Questioning. Steps 1 and 2 (scanning and skimming) will give you an overview of the passage as a whole. Step 3 will help you connect the information in the passage to your personal knowledge and experiences. The next step is to ask yourself questions about the passage that you think might be answered as you read. The following chart shows some useful questions to ask:

Meets
New York
Standards
1.A.1
1.A.3
1.A.4
1.A.5
1.A.6

- What kind of writing is this? Is it persuasive? Informative? Narrative? A lyric poem? A newspaper article?

- What is this reading passage about? What is the author's topic?

- What can I expect this piece to tell me about the topic?

- What is the main idea, or thesis, of the piece?

- What are the major supporting ideas or subtopics in the text?

- What is the author's conclusion?

One Student's Response

I can see that the article is about dinosaurs. Dinosaurs were real, so the piece must be nonfiction. The thesis statement tells me that the author is going to focus on dinosaurs' size, speed, and ferocity. I can turn the headings into questions and ask, "Which dinosaurs were big and tall?" "Which dinosaurs were built for speed?" and "Which dinosaurs were fearsome beasts?" Then I can read to find the answers to my questions.

Your Turn

Use the next reading passage on pages 98–99 to complete Exercises A–D.

Exercise A *Scan* the passage on pages 98–99. Do NOT read it closely. Then, fill in the circle next to the correct answer to each multiple-choice question.

1. What is the title of the passage?
    - Ⓐ "Becoming a Paleontologist"
    - Ⓑ "What Fossils Are"
    - Ⓒ "The Study of Fossils"
    - Ⓓ "Studying Fossils?"

2. Who is the author of the piece?
    - Ⓐ Christina Smith
    - Ⓑ Stuart Walker
    - Ⓒ Malcolm Ivers
    - Ⓓ Will Tripp

3. What is the caption of the illustration on the second page?
    - Ⓐ *Brachiosaurus*, with its long neck, was one of the tallest dinosaurs.
    - Ⓑ Fossils are the remains of plants and animals preserved in rock.
    - Ⓒ The largest dinosaurs were slow, heavy creatures that walked on four legs.
    - Ⓓ Paleontologists are scientists who learn about the past by studying fossils.

Exercise B *Skim the passage on pages 98–99. Do NOT read it closely. Then, fill in the circle next to the correct answer to each multiple-choice question.*

Meets
New York
Standards
1.A.1
1.A.3
1.A.4
1.A.5
1.A.6

1. What is the subject of the piece?
   Ⓐ fossils
   Ⓑ dinosaurs
   Ⓒ scientists
   Ⓓ birds

2. Which would be MOST appropriate as another title for this passage?
   Ⓐ "How to Become a Paleontologist"
   Ⓑ "Paleontology, the Study of Fossils"
   Ⓒ "Where to Unearth Dinosaur Fossils"
   Ⓓ "Fossils of the Northeastern United States"

Exercise C *On the lines below, write two statements giving information you already know about the subject.*

1. _____

   _____

2. _____

   _____

Exercise D *On the lines below, write two questions that you think might be answered by this passage when you read it carefully. Save these questions for the next exercise.*

1. _____

   _____

2. _____

   _____

Exercise E *Now that you have scanned and skimmed this passage (as part of the previous exercises), read it carefully. Next, return to Exercises A–C and correct your answers if necessary. Finally, on your own paper, answer the two questions you wrote for Exercise D.*

The Study of Fossils
by Stuart Walker

What Are Fossils?

Fossils are the remains or imprints of ancient animals or plants. They are usually found embedded in layers of rock or riverbeds. When an animal dies, its body is usually broken down by decay or eaten by other animals. Some parts of animals, however, such as the bones and teeth, are very hard. These parts do not break down easily

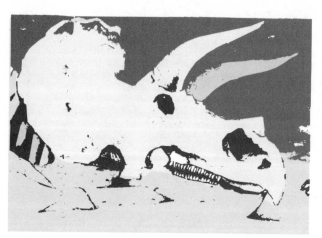

and often get buried deep in the ground. After millions of years, layers of ground turn to rock with the bones and teeth trapped inside. The bones and teeth become fossils. Sometimes, soft tissues become filled with mineral deposits and so are hardened and preserved. At other times, the plant or animal decays, but its

imprint is left in mud that later hardens into rock. When we think of fossils, we tend to think of dinosaurs, but fossils of everything from bacteria to people have been found in every part of the Earth.

Studying Fossils

Paleontology is the study of prehistoric life as it is preserved in fossils. **Paleontologists**, the scientists who study fossils, learn a great deal about the past by examining these ancient remains. For example, they learn from dinosaur fossils how dinosaurs lived and what their **environment** might have been like. Dinosaurs lived on Earth for nearly two hundred million years. Then something went drastically wrong that caused them to die out. There are various theories as to why dinosaurs became extinct. The most likely theory is that a massive meteorite hit the Earth, spreading fires across several continents. These fires might have filled the atmosphere with so much smoke and debris that not much could grow or survive. However, nobody knows for sure what happened. Fossils may help scientists to solve the mystery of what went

More ▶

wrong. Perhaps what scientists discover will help to save us from another catastrophe like the one that killed the dinosaurs.

Becoming a Paleontologist

Fossils may hold the keys to many mysteries, but it is not always easy to find them. It also is not easy to become one of the scientists who studies them full time. To become a paleontologist, one usually must graduate from high school, attend college, and take many science classes. Some of these classes include **biology,** the study of life, and **geology,** the study of Earth's structure. After college, aspiring paleontologists usually go to graduate school and take specialized courses in the study of fossils. In addition, a future paleontologist must usually complete **field studies.** As part of their training, students go on trips to dusty, remote, and sometimes dangerous places where they assist professional experts with excavating (digging up) fossils. Students also learn how to transport and preserve fossils for further study and how to map the locations where they were found.

There are, of course, amateur paleontologists as well—people who do some work in the field and are largely self-taught. Some amateurs,

Paleontologists are scientists who learn about the past by studying fossils.

in fact, have made important contributions to the science of paleontology. The skeleton of *Giganotosaurus,* the largest meat-eating dinosaur found to date, was originally found by an auto mechanic who likes to hunt for dinosaur bones as a hobby.

Searching for fossils can be dirty, time-consuming, and even dangerous, yet there are many people eager to take on the work. Perhaps it is the mysteries of the past contained in these remains of ancient life that people find so interesting. Perhaps it is the hope of new discoveries that may help us to be safe in the future. Whatever their reasons may be, paleontologists continue to dig into the Earth's surface to uncover new clues about the past. O

Active Reading

During Reading: Using Active Reading Strategies

For people who read well, reading is a very active process. An **active reader** thinks about what he or she is reading, pictures what is being described, asks questions while reading, makes predictions about what will happen next, and connects new information to things he or she already knows. Study the active reading strategies below and use them as you read to get the most out of a text.

What to Do While You Are Reading

Active Reading Strategy	Description
Questioning	Form **questions** about what you are reading by asking *who? what? why? where? when?* and *how?* Then read to find answers to your questions.
Visualizing	When you **visualize,** you picture something in your mind. As you read, try to imagine what the people, places, and objects described by the author look like. Picture the actions and events in your "mind's eye."
Predicting	A **prediction** is an "educated guess" about something that might happen in the future. Based on clues in the text and on your own experience, you can make an educated guess about what will come later in the piece.
Making Inferences/ Drawing Conclusions	An **inference** is a conclusion that you come to based on information provided in the text. For example, if a character is described as having a red face after she has spent the day at the beach, you might infer that she has a sunburn or is overheated.
Paraphrasing	A **paraphrase** is a restatement of what you have read in your own words.
Summarizing	A **summary** is a brief statement that sums up the gist, or the essence, of what has come earlier in the text. A summary restates the main ideas in fewer words than a paraphrase. Noticing themes and main ideas as you read will help you to summarize what the text is about.
Evaluating	An **evaluation** is a judgment that you make about something in a piece. For example, you might evaluate a writer's ideas, deciding whether you agree with them or not.
Connecting and Extending	A **connection** is a thought that relates something you are reading to something in your own life. An **extension** is a thought that connects something you are reading to something else in the world outside the text.

After Reading: Reflecting and Responding

In this chapter, you have been learning about **the process of reading.** This process is divided into three parts—into what takes place before, during, and after your reading. The following chart lists some things you can do after reading, to help you get more out of what you have read.

Meets
New York
Standards
1.A.1
1.A.2
1.A.3
1.A.4
1.A.5
1.A.6
1.B.1
3.A.1
3.A.4
3.B.1
4.A.1

Some Possible After-Reading Activities

Reflecting. Reflecting is the process of thinking about what you have read. Here are some possible reflecting activities:

1. Answer your prereading questions. These are the questions that you came up with when you previewed the passage before reading it.

2. Look over and think about any notes that you took during reading.

3. Think about how the reading connects to your own life or to other things in the world.

4. **Evaluate** the reading. In other words, pass judgment on it. What did you like? What did you not like? Why?

Responding. Responding is the process of doing something active in reaction to the reading. Here are some possibilities:

1. Talk about the reading with others.

2. Write about the reading. For example, you might write a brief review or create a summary of the reading as an entry in your learning log.

3. Create a piece of artwork or music related to the reading.

4. If you liked the reading, recommend it to others.

Exercise A *Read the passage below about a fossil hunter who made an important discovery. As you read, use the active reading strategies listed in the chart on the previous page. Write down your comments, questions, and reactions on the lines provided below. Some examples are shown to help you get started.*

Willo, the Dinosaur with Heart
by Melissa Crawford

An Amazing Discovery

Sixty million years ago, in what is now South Dakota, a big dinosaur took its last stomp. Over time, its remains became fossilized. In 1993, a fossil collector named Mike Hammer unearthed this dinosaur and gave it the name "Willo."

Finding a dinosaur specimen is always exciting for paleontologists, but with the discovery of Willo came an unexpected surprise. Inside the chest of this dinosaur was a fossilized heart! Willo's heart was shipped to a team of scientific researchers in North Carolina for further study. They could hardly believe their luck. They were used to seeing fossils of bones and teeth from prehistoric animals. Those fossils are common because they are made of hard materials that can be preserved in layers of rock for thousands or even millions of years. It is extremely rare, however, for anyone to find the remains of an organ from inside an animal's body, especially the body of a prehistoric animal. A heart, kidney, or other organ is made of soft tissue that usually decays (breaks down) long before it could be preserved as a fossil. Willo's was the first dinosaur

More ▶

Comments or Questions

_____

_____

_____

_____

_____

Questioning: I wonder why he named this dinosaur Willo.

_____

_____

_____

_____

_____

_____

_____

Questioning: Why was this dinosaur's heart preserved for so many years when others are not?

heart ever to be found. When the scientists studied the heart more closely, they noticed something even more amazing: Willo's heart appeared to have four internal sections, or chambers.

Are Dinosaurs Warm-blooded or Cold-blooded?

For years, scientists have been wondering whether dinosaurs were warm-blooded, like birds and mammals, or cold-blooded, like fish, amphibians, and reptiles. At one time, people thought that dinosaurs were prehistoric reptiles. In fact, the word *dinosaur* comes from a Greek word meaning "monstrous lizard." For roughly two hundred years after the first dinosaur bones were discovered in 1763, it was widely believed that dinosaurs, like reptiles, were cold-blooded. Then, in 1968, Robert T. Bakker (who was a college student at Yale)[1] proposed the theory that dinosaurs were probably more active than scientists previously thought. He even raised the possibility that dinosaurs might have been warm-blooded. The debate has been going on ever since.

Most cold-blooded creatures have simple hearts with only two or three chambers. Could Willo's four-chambered heart prove that dinosaurs were warm-blooded? Is it far-fetched to consider the possibility that dinosaurs might have been more closely related to birds and mammals than to reptiles? Scientists do not have the answers to these questions yet. Let's examine the evidence they have so far. **More ▶**

Predicting: Scientists are going to have to find a lot more fossils in order to figure this out.

Meets New York Standards
1.A.1
1.A.3
1.A.4
1.A.5
1.A.6
3.A.1
3.A.4

[1]Bakker went on to get his Ph.D. from Harvard. He became a famous paleontologist.

Hipbones and Prehistoric "Feathers"

Scientists who study dinosaurs generally group them into two types—ornithischians (bird-hipped dinosaurs) and saurischians (lizard-hipped dinosaurs). *Tyrannosaurus rex* and *Velociraptor* are two examples of lizard-hipped dinosaurs. These dinosaurs were carnivores (meat-eaters). Most people think of them as dangerous predators, actively chasing their prey. *Stegosaurus* and *Triceratops* are two examples of bird-hipped dinosaurs. These dinosaurs were herbivores (plant-eaters). Both *Stegosaurus* and *Triceratops* had unusual body armor that protected them, just as a rhinoceros is protected by its horn, or an iguana is protected by its scales. Based on the fossil evidence, none of these dinosaurs looked like the birds we see today. Since 1995, however, a number of fossils of dinosaurs that appeared to have feathers have been found in China. These fossils are controversial[2]: Some scientists think they show a strong link between dinosaurs and birds, but others disagree.

What Kind of Dinosaur Was Willo?

Perhaps the discovery of Willo's heart would not have seemed so startling if he had been a lizard-hipped dinosaur like *T. rex*. Before Willo came along, if a four-chambered heart had turned up in any dinosaur, people would have

More ▶

Connecting: I have seen pictures and models of these dinosaurs, and now I'm confused. If T. rex is built like a lizard, how come it isn't shown crawling on all fours?

Making Inferences: If Stegosaurus is built like a bird, why isn't it shown standing on two hind legs instead of four?

Evaluating: It must have been pretty exciting to find a dinosaur that seemed to have feathers!

[2]**controversial.** Open to debate; provoking disagreement

expected it to turn up in one of the active predators in the lizard-hipped group. (Remember those terrifying packs of *Velociraptors* in *Jurassic Park?*) Willo, however, turned out to be a *Thescelosaurus* (THESS-a-loh-SAWR-us). This type of dinosaur belongs to the bird-hipped group. Could Willo's four-chambered heart provide a possible link between this group of dinosaurs and birds?

The Search for More Evidence

Scientists will need much more fossil evidence—not just one dinosaur heart—before they can decide whether birds and dinosaurs are related. Nonetheless, Willo's heart might provide scientists with important clues about the way at least one dinosaur's body worked. Paleontologists hope to collect more dinosaur specimens from the area where Willo's skeleton was found. They are also planning to study similar places that might turn out to have fossils of other dinosaurs. The more paleontologists can learn about the ways dinosaurs lived and moved, the better they can understand them.

Willo is now on exhibit at the North Carolina Museum of Natural Sciences in Raleigh, North Carolina. By studying Willo and the habitat in which he lived, scientists hope to make more connections between the lives that dinosaurs lived and the lives of birds and mammals today. ○

Connecting: Yes—those Velociraptors really could move fast, especially when they were after something to eat.
Questioning: I wonder whether the real Velociraptors were that vicious millions of years ago.

Meets New York Standards
1.A.1
1.A.3
1.A.4
1.A.5
1.A.6
3.A.1
3.A.4

_____

_____

_____

_____

_____

_____

_____

_____

_____

_____

Paraphrasing/Predicting: If scientists can find fossils of more dinosaurs like Willo, maybe they will be able to figure out whether dinosaurs were warm-blooded and active, like birds.

Your Turn

Exercise B *Read the passage below. Use active reading strategies as you read. Write down at least five comments or questions in the right column. Try to use as many of the active reading strategies listed on page 100 as possible.*

Fossil Fuels
by John Dunn

What Are Fossil Fuels?

Most people think of fossils as the hard remains or imprints of ancient plants or animals. Did you know that coal, oil, and natural gas are also fossils? These substances come from the decayed remains of animals and plants that lived millions of years ago, in what is called the Carboniferous period. After these plants and animals died, their remains became buried under ground. Over millions of years, the remains decomposed (broke down) and turned into coal, oil, and natural gas. Because these fuels come from prehistoric remains, they are called **fossil fuels.**

Uses of Fossil Fuels

Fossil fuels have been used for more than 150 years. We burn fossil fuels in our home furnaces and automobiles. Power plants also burn these fuels to produce the electricity we use to run the machines and electronics that we use every day. Schools, hospitals, factories, office buildings, and stores all use electricity. Many of these buildings also rely on fossil

More ▶

Comments or Questions

fuels for heat and air conditioning. Eighty-five percent of the electricity Americans use is produced by the burning of fossil fuels. Electricity powers our televisions, refrigerators, lights, computers, and other electronic devices that we depend on every day. Oil is refined into diesel oil or gasoline, the fuels that power our cars, planes, trains, trucks, and boats. We use oil, as well as natural gas, to heat our homes and cook our food. Clearly, our modern way of life is dependent on fossil fuels.

Problems with Fossil Fuels

Unfortunately, burning fossil fuels creates problems, including air pollution. Many power plants burn coal or oil to produce electricity. Burning these fossil fuels releases soot as well as waste gases that pollute the air. When people burn gas by driving their cars, they also produce soot and waste gases that become part of the air we breathe. The gases trap heat in the atmosphere. The widespread burning of fossil fuels has thus created problems, including the fact that the average temperature on Earth is increasing. Scientists predict that this process, called **global warming,** will cause a wide range of serious environmental problems if it continues at its current rate.

More ▶

Meets
New York
Standards
1.A.1
1.A.3
1.A.4
1.A.5
1.A.6
3.A.1
3.A.4

Meets
New York
Standards
1.A.1
1.A.3
1.A.4
1.A.5
1.A.6
3.A.1
3.A.4

Another problem with our reliance on fossil fuels is that there is a limited amount of these substances in the Earth. Many fuel-dependent machines, such as cars and other vehicles, are designed to run only on gasoline made from oil. If we continue to depend so heavily on fossil fuels, eventually we will use up the Earth's supply.

Alternative Sources of Power

Fossil fuels may be useful and convenient now, but there are many problems linked to their use. The most pressing issue is the pollution caused by the burning of fossil fuels, which is causing global warming. In addition, there are serious concerns about how long the supply of fossil fuels will last. Alternative sources of energy, such as solar, wind, water, and nuclear power, are already in use. These sources, however, produce only a small fraction of the power we need. It is very important that people find ways to conserve energy. Scientists and engineers must also research and develop alternative sources of power as soon as possible, so that we can preserve the environment and continue to have reliable sources of power. ○

Return to the exercises at the beginning of the chapter, revise your work as necessary, and submit the exercises to your teacher for grading.

Chapter 5

I Think I've Got It!

Reading Comprehension

From Trash to Treasure

by Harry Mills

The abandoned lot on Third Avenue was overflowing with junk and weeds. Rusting radiators and abandoned refrigerators, scraps of paper and plastic wrappers, cardboard, old tires, and rotting food were strewn about the lot. As I passed this mess each day on the way to school, I wondered how other people in the neighborhood felt about living near a dirty, smelly lot. I didn't like it at all.

One day in early spring, my social studies teacher, Mr. McCord, asked us to think about ways to improve our community.

"Let's start a recycling program!" suggested Myleen.

"Why don't we paint a mural?" asked Bill.

I knew what I wanted to do: "Let's clean up that vacant lot on Third Avenue!"

Mr. McCord put his hand to his chin, the way he always did when he was thinking hard. "What would we do with the lot after it's cleaned up?" he asked.

The kids in my class had several suggestions. Derrick wanted to turn the lot into a baseball field. Gina thought it would be a good idea to turn it into a playground.

Then I had an idea: "Let's turn the lot into a garden," I suggested.

"What kind of garden, Antoine?" asked Mr. McCord.

I thought for a few moments. "We could plant a vegetable garden and sell the vegetables we grow for a profit. We could use the profits to buy supplies to take care of the garden. If there's any money left over, we could use it to help fund other neighborhood projects."

"That's a great idea," Mr. McCord said enthusiastically, "but first we have to find out who owns the lot. I will look into it."

The next day Mr. McCord came into the classroom with a huge grin.

"Well, I think we're in luck," he began. "The city owns the lot. As part of the "Improve Our Communities" program, the city is willing to sell the lot to the school for only one dollar, as long as we agree to clean it up and put it to a use that benefits the school and the whole community. I think we can safely say that providing fresh vegetables and improving the appearance of the neighborhood would benefit the whole community. I've also talked with the principal about it; he thinks it is a great idea. He even gave me the dollar to pay for the lot." The class cheered wildly, and a few kids patted me on the back.

Over the next few weeks, our class held a series of meetings after school to plan the project. We met with the local community board and got permission to start the garden. Then we traded ideas about ways to pay for the cleanup and for the supplies we would need to start the garden. We asked local merchants for donations. They were happy to donate money once they learned what our class was trying to do. After several weeks of collecting donations, we had raised enough money. Finally, we set a date for beginning the cleanup of the lot.

One sunny Saturday morning, my class—along with other volunteers from the community—met at the lot to begin the cleanup. We rented a huge dumpster and loaded it with junk. By the end of the day, all the trash was cleared. The next day we met again and put up a chain-link fence around the lot. It was hard work, but the lot already looked much better. During the week, some workers from the state Department of Environmental Protection collected samples of soil from the lot for testing to make sure it was safe for growing food.

Meanwhile, we were busy in class trying to figure out how many seeds we would need. First, we had to measure the total square footage of the lot. We drew the lot on a huge piece of poster board in the classroom and divided the lot into sections—one for each type of vegetable. After figuring out how much space we had available for each type of vegetable, we had to figure out how many seeds of each type we would need. Each vegetable requires a different amount of space between the seeds. For example, carrot seeds can be planted very close together, whereas squash seeds need to be planted about ten feet apart. Figuring out the number of seeds we needed was one of the most complicated math problems I have ever done, but I have never enjoyed doing math so much.

The next weekend, the real fun began. We began to prepare the soil for planting. First, we tilled the soil with hoes and shovels. Mr. McCord said this would loosen the soil and fill it with air pockets, which would help the plants to grow. Then, we marked off the sections for the different vegetables we would plant. We watered the soil and began planting seeds for cucumbers, squash, peas, beans, carrots, beets, and green peppers. By Sunday night we were done. Boy, were we tired!

Even though the seeds were planted, we still had a lot of work to do. We had to keep the soil damp, but not too damp. We watered the garden lightly every morning before school. We rechecked the soil after school, and if it felt dry, we watered it lightly again. By the third or fourth day, little shoots had sprung up in the pea and bean sections. Then we cut back to watering the ground once a day. Soon tiny shoots were sprouting up in the other sections as well. Each day, I passed by the garden to check on the vegetables. Before long, I began to see flowers on some of the plants. Soon, the vegetables would start growing and we would have to pull up weeds. The only thing left to do was wait!

By the time school was about to end for the summer, we were busier than ever in the garden. Almost the whole class, except for kids who were going away, agreed to keep working in the garden throughout the summer. We set up a schedule to make sure someone would be there each day to water and weed the garden. Before long, we began harvesting the vegetables and selling them to the local bodegas.[1] There were so many vegetables that we even set up a stand near the garden to sell produce to people in the neighborhood.

By the time school started again, we had sold most of the vegetables. We made enough money to pay for supplies so that students could plant another garden the next year. We even had enough money left over to donate to several charities in the community.

Just yesterday, I passed by the garden on the way home from school. Several of my classmates were working to harvest the last vegetables of the season. I paused by the fence to wave to my friends. A woman from Third Avenue stood next to me.

"My," she said, "I really have to thank you for what you all have done for the community. That lot has gone from trash to treasure!"

I swelled up with pride. It felt great to do something for my community. As I continued walking home, I took a look around to see what else I might do to improve my neighborhood. O

[1]**bodega.** Spanish word for a small grocery or convenience store

Your Turn

Exercise A *Fill in the circle next to the correct answer to each multiple-choice question.*

Meets New York Standards
1.A.1
1.A.3
1.A.4
1.A.6
2.A.1

1. What is this story MOSTLY about?

    (A) how to grow a vegetable garden in a small city lot

    (B) how a group of students improved their community

    (C) how to make money for charity over the summer

    (D) how to clean up an abandoned lot in a weekend

2. What statement BEST expresses the theme of this story?

    (A) Planting a vegetable garden requires a lot of patience.

    (B) Gardening is hard work that is not worth the time.

    (C) Helping your community can be a rewarding experience.

    (D) Selling vegetables is more fun than pulling weeds.

3. How do the volunteers clean up the abandoned lot?

    (A) They hire a team of workers to do it.

    (B) They rent a huge dumpster and load it with junk.

    (C) They put up a chain-link fence around the lot.

    (D) They sell everything in the lot to a junkyard.

4. Which of the following is one of the suggestions offered by class members to help improve their community?

    (A) Let's set up a crime patrol.

    (B) Let's start a soup kitchen.

    (C) Let's paint a mural.

    (D) Let's start a jobs program.

5. Which event happens FIRST?

    (A) Antoine suggests that the class create a community garden.

    (B) Mr. McCord announces that the principal has approved the project.

    (C) Antoine suggests that the class clean up the abandoned lot.

    (D) Scientists test soil samples from the abandoned lot.

6. On the weekend when the actual planting begins, which event happens LAST?

    (A) The students till the soil.

    (B) The students help put up a fence.

    (C) The students plant seeds.

    (D) The students water the soil.

More ▶

7. Which event causes Antoine to suggest planting a community garden?

Ⓐ A local merchant asks Antoine to clean up the lot.

Ⓑ Antoine needs to raise money for community projects.

Ⓒ Antoine's teacher asks the students for suggestions to help improve their community.

Ⓓ Antoine's teacher asks what the class would do with the abandoned lot after cleaning it up.

8. What happens as a result of the vegetable garden project?

Ⓐ The abandoned lot is dirty and full of weeds.

Ⓑ Antoine is proud of himself.

Ⓒ Parents contribute money to the project.

Ⓓ The community members hold a series of meetings.

9. What is Antoine MOST LIKELY to do after the events in the story?

Ⓐ He will think of something else that he can do to improve his community.

Ⓑ He will eat a lot of vegetables and become a star athlete.

Ⓒ He will help his classmates paint a mural on the wall behind the garden.

Ⓓ When he grows up, he will move to the country and become a farmer.

10. Based on details provided in the story, what kind of person is Antoine?

Ⓐ unkind and rude

Ⓑ caring and hardworking

Ⓒ selfish and lazy

Ⓓ imaginative but scatterbrained

Exercise B   *The last question in the previous exercise asks you what kind of person Antoine is. Think about your answer and look for evidence—details and examples from the story—to support it. In other words, what actions does Antoine take in the story that show he is that kind of person? On the lines provided below, write a paragraph that answers these questions.*

Meets
New York
Standards
1.A.1
1.A.3
1.A.4
1.A.6
1.B.1
1.B.4
2.A.1
3.A.1
3.B.1
3.B.2

I Think I've Got It!

Comprehension means making sense of what you read or hear. Reading comprehension happens when readers think actively about what they are reading, are able to make sense of the text, and remember details about what they have read. Reading comprehension is the outcome of good reading habits. In the pages that follow, you will learn some strategies to help you improve your reading comprehension. These are strategies that anyone can learn and apply. How do they work? The strategies help you to focus on the important parts of a passage. They also help you to draw conclusions about what you read and to make judgments about what is important to remember. One good way to start is by learning how to identify the author's main idea.

Answering Questions about Main Ideas

The **main idea** is the major point that the author of the piece is trying to get across. A main idea contains two parts: the topic the author is writing about, and what the author has to say about that topic. For example, you might read a story about building a community. The author's main point about that topic might be that "building a community requires that people work well with each other." Test

questions that ask about the main idea are often phrased in the following ways:

• What is the main idea of this story?

• What is this story mostly about?

• What is the author's purpose in writing this story?

• Which of the following titles is most appropriate for this story?

• What is the theme of this story?

When a question asks you to identify the theme, look for the author's main point.

When you are asked to identify the writer's main idea, go back and skim the entire passage. When you **skim,** you look quickly over the text. Pay attention to the title, the first and last paragraphs, and any headings or key words, which are often in **boldface.** Skim the first and last sentences of paragraphs. You can use one or more of the following strategies to help you answer questions about main ideas:

Meets New York Standards
1.A.1
1.A.3
1.A.4
1.A.5
1.A.6

Strategies for Answering Questions about the Main Idea

- Look at the question carefully for words that tell you it is asking about the passage as a whole. Here are some key words and phrases that often appear in questions of this type: *main idea, subject, theme, lesson, mostly about,* and *as a whole.*

- Rule out any answers that are obviously incorrect. Then focus on the remaining choices.

- Make sure that the answer you choose refers to the *whole* passage, not just part of it.

- Remember that an answer may be true, but it may not express the main idea.

Take another look at this multiple-choice question about "From Trash to Treasure":

1. What is this story MOSTLY about?
   (A) how to grow a vegetable garden in a small city lot
   (B) how a group of students improved their community
   (C) how to make money for charity over the summer
   (D) how to clean up an abandoned lot in a weekend

Here is how one student thought through the answer to Question 1:

One Student's Response

When I read the words "mostly about," I knew this question was asking about the main idea. I read all the answer choices and then skimmed the story. I reread the beginning and ending paragraphs. I also read the first and last sentences of each paragraph. All the answer choices seemed to come up in the story, so I didn't know which one to pick at first. Then I realized that I needed to focus on finding an answer that described the whole story, not just a part of it. I figured out that choices A, C, and D do not describe the main point of the story. The students do grow a vegetable garden, clean up an abandoned lot, and make money for charity. However, it is not the author's main purpose to tell readers how to do these things. Choice B seems to describe what the story is <u>mostly</u> about. That answer summarizes the main idea of the story—how a group of students can improve their community.

Now let's take a look at another question about "From Trash to Treasure":

2. What statement BEST expresses the theme of this story?
   Ⓐ Planting a vegetable garden requires a lot of patience.
   Ⓑ Gardening is hard work that is not worth the time.
   Ⓒ Helping your community can be a rewarding experience.
   Ⓓ Selling vegetables is more fun than pulling weeds.

Here is how one student thought through the answer to Question 2:

Meets
New York
Standards
1.A.1
1.A.3
1.A.4
1.A.5
1.A.6

One Student's Response

I knew this question referred to the main idea because it asked about the <u>theme</u>, which is one of the words used to refer to the main idea. First I ruled out D, because no one in the story talks about whether selling vegetables is more fun than pulling weeds. Next I figured out that B was wrong, because the characters do think that taking care of the garden is worth the time, even though it is hard work. Choice A refers to only one part of the story. The main character does talk about how they have to wait for the plants to sprout, but this is not the main point of the story. The only choice left was C. I skimmed the story again and saw that, at the end, the main character feels very proud. Clearly, he thinks that helping his community is a rewarding experience. I felt confident that C was the correct answer, because it says, "Helping your community can be a rewarding experience."

Answering Questions about Supporting Details

Some questions ask about a specific detail or fact from a reading passage. **Supporting details** are facts, examples, or statements in the passage that help to support, or back up, a main idea. Supporting details give information about a person, character, event, place, topic, or idea. For example, an author might state this main idea: "Building model airplanes is a productive and rewarding hobby." Then the author might back up this statement with details that support it: "Building model airplanes is productive because it helps develop important life skills such as planning ahead, following directions, and having patience. When you are done, you have something fun to play with as a reward for all your hard work." A supporting-detail question might then ask you, "According to the passage, which of the following life skills can one develop by building model airplanes?"

(A) cooperation skills

(B) memorization skills

(C) doing mental math

(D) having patience

One way you can find answers to questions about supporting details is to identify a key word or key phrase in the question. A **key word** or **key phrase** is an important word or phrase from the question. You can scan the passage for the key word or phrase to help you find the correct answer to the question. Once you find the key word or phrase, read the sentences around it carefully to find the answer to the question. You can also scan the text for a key word or phrase from one of the answer choices.

Reading Comprehension

This is a good strategy to use when you are trying to decide between two answer choices or when you want to check to make sure that the answer you have chosen is correct. Use the following strategies to help answer questions about supporting details:

Strategies for Answering Questions about Supporting Details

- Choose a key word or phrase from the question or from one or more of the answers.

- Scan the text for the key word or phrase. When you find it, read carefully around the word or phrase to find the answer you need.

- Use your finger, an index card, or a ruler to keep your place as you scan down a page.

Here is a question about details from the story "From Trash to Treasure."

3. How do the volunteers clean up the abandoned lot?
    (A) They hire a team of workers to do it.
    (B) They rent a huge dumpster and load it with junk.
    (C) They put up a chain-link fence around the lot.
    (D) They sell everything in the lot to a junkyard.

Here is how one student thought through the answer to Question 3:

One Student's Response

I could tell this question was related to a supporting detail because it asked about a specific fact—how the volunteers clean up the abandoned lot. First, I looked through the answer choices to see if any of the answers could be eliminated. All of the answers except C were possible: Choices A, B, and D all describe ways that an abandoned lot could be cleaned. I eliminated C because building a chain-link fence protects the property but doesn't have anything to do with cleaning it up. I then scanned the story for the key words clean up to find the part in the story where the students clean up the lot. I came across the word cleanup twice. The second time the word cleanup appeared in the story, it was followed by this sentence: "We rented a huge dumpster and loaded it with junk." Then I knew that B was the correct answer.

Now let's consider another example of a question about supporting details:

4. Which of the following is one of the suggestions offered by class members to help improve their community?

   Ⓐ Let's set up a crime patrol.

   Ⓑ Let's start a soup kitchen.

   Ⓒ Let's paint a mural.

   Ⓓ Let's start a jobs program.

Here is how one student thought through the answer to Question 4:

One Student's Response

   To answer this question about a supporting detail, I first chose some key words from the question. These words were <u>improve</u> and <u>community</u>. I then scanned the passage until I found these words, in the second paragraph. Next, I looked at the list of suggestions that the kids made. The only suggestion that appeared both in the story and in the answers was C, <u>paint a mural</u>.

Answering Questions about Sequence

Sequence is the order in which events take place. In many stories, the events are described in **chronological (time) order.** This means that the events in the story are described in the same order in which they happen. However, authors do not always describe events in chronological order. Sometimes an author will begin a story in the middle of events and then go back to describe what took place at an earlier point in time. This technique is called **flashback.** Authors also use a technique called **foreshadowing** to hint at events that will happen later on. The text may contain clues about when different events take place. The author may include dates or times, or use words that signal time order, such as *first, next, last, before, after,* or *finally.*

Reading comprehension questions often ask about the sequence of events. Effective readers can trace the events of a story from beginning to end, even if some of the events are presented out of order. To answer sequence questions correctly, pay attention to the order of events as you read. Ask yourself, "Do the events occur in chronological order, or in some other sequence?" Create a timeline or make a list of events to help you keep track of their sequence as you read. Also note any key words that identify time.

Strategies for Answering Questions about Sequence

- Remember that events are often, but not always, told in the order in which they happen. Be alert to variations in this order, such as flashback or foreshadowing.

- Look for key words like *first, next, last, then, before, after,* and *finally.* These words signal when things happen.

- Look for dates or times that tell when things occur in the story.

- Create a timeline or list of events to keep track of the sequence of events in a story.

The fifth question about "From Trash to Treasure" asks you to identify the order of events in the story.

5. Which event happens FIRST?

   Ⓐ Antoine suggests that the class create a community garden.
   Ⓑ Mr. McCord announces that the principal has approved the project.
   Ⓒ Antoine suggests that the class clean up the abandoned lot.
   Ⓓ Scientists test soil samples from the abandoned lot.

Here is how one student thought through the answer to Question 5:

One Student's Response

The word <u>first</u> in this question told me that it was a sequence question. I began by looking over the answer choices to see if I could eliminate any of the answers. The principal approves the project and people come to test the soil <u>after</u> the class makes suggestions, so I knew right away that B and D were not possible answers. That left me with A and C as possibilities. When I skimmed the part of the story where the kids discuss what they can do to improve their community, I saw that Antoine suggests cleaning up the lot (C) <u>before</u> he suggests creating a garden (A), so I knew that C was the correct answer.

Now let's consider another example of a sequence question:

6. On the weekend when the actual planting begins, which event happens LAST?

   Ⓐ The students till the soil.

   Ⓑ The students help put up a fence.

   Ⓒ The students plant seeds.

   Ⓓ The students water the soil.

Here is how one student thought through the answer to Question 6:

One Student's Response

I knew that this question was about sequence because the word <u>last</u> is a key word for sequence. To answer this question, I scanned the story for the following key words in the answer choices: <u>fence</u>, <u>till</u>, <u>seeds</u>, and <u>water</u>. First, I came across the words <u>chain-link fence</u>. The students build the fence first, so I knew that B was wrong. Next I came across the word <u>tilled</u>, so I eliminated A. Then I found the sentence "We <u>watered</u> the soil and began planting <u>seeds</u>. <u>Seeds</u> came last, so I was confident that C was the correct answer.

Answering Questions about Cause and Effect

Causes and effects are events that are related to one another. A **cause** is something that makes or helps to make another event happen. An **effect** is the event that happens as a result of the cause. When you read a story or piece of nonfiction, pay attention to cause-and-effect relationships. Look for the reason(s) why something happens and notice what happens as a result of the event(s). For example, a big snowstorm (the cause) results in the cancellation of school (the effect).

Cause and effect is closely related to sequence because a cause comes before its effect. But be careful! One event can follow closely after another without having been caused by the first event. For example, suppose that a girl dropped her pencil and then the bell rang. The bell rang *after* she dropped her pencil, not *because* she dropped it.

When looking for cause-and-effect relationships, keep in mind that a cause can have several effects and an effect can have several causes. Sometimes a single cause is enough to bring about an effect, but often this is not so. For example, suppose that an ice storm occurs while Mr. Jones is away on vacation. Because Mr. Jones is away, he is not able to spread sand on the sidewalk in front of his house. His neighbor Jake takes his dog for a walk.

Reading Comprehension (123)

The dog, who has been cooped up inside because of the storm, takes off running, dragging Jake behind him. When Jake gets to the sidewalk in front of Mr. Jones's house, he slips and falls. Jake's fall is caused by a series of events: the ice storm, Mr. Jones not being able to sand his sidewalk, and Jake's dog forcing Jake to run on the slippery sidewalk.

A particularly interesting example of a cause is motivation. **Motivation** is something that moves a character to act or think in a certain way. Motivation can be **internal** (inside the character) or **external** (outside the character). For example, a boy may decide to join the hockey team because his father wants him to (an external cause). On the other hand, he may decide to join the hockey team because he loves playing ice hockey (an internal cause).

When looking for cause-and-effect relationships, look for words or phrases that signal related events, such as *why, because, therefore, as a result, cause, effect, reason, consequently,* and *so.*

Some test questions ask about causes and effects. Read each question carefully to determine whether it asks about a cause (*Why did this happen?*) or an effect (*What happened as a result of…?*). Look for key words in the passage that indicate cause-and-effect relationships, such as *cause, effect, therefore, why, reason,* and so on.

You can use one or more of the following strategies to help you answer questions about causes and effects:

Strategies for Answering Questions about Cause and Effect

- Determine whether you are looking for a cause or an effect.

- Ask yourself, "Why did this happen?" (**cause**) and "What happened as a result?" (**effect**)

- Look for key words and phrases that signal cause-and-effect relationships, such as *cause, effect, because, why, reason, therefore, consequently, as a result,* and *so.*

- Remember that one event can follow another without being caused by it.

- Read carefully to determine the relationship between two events or facts. Ask yourself whether one causes the other or whether they simply happen at about the same time.

- Look for multiple causes.

Now take another look at the seventh question about "From Trash to Treasure":

Meets
New York
Standards
1.A.1
1.A.3
1.A.4
1.A.5
1.A.6

7. Which event causes Antoine to suggest planting a community garden?

    (A) A local merchant asks Antoine to clean up the lot.

    (B) Antoine needs to raise money for community projects.

    (C) Antoine's teacher asks the students for suggestions to help improve their community.

    (D) Antoine's teacher asks what the class would do with the abandoned lot after cleaning it up.

Here is how one student thought through the answer to Question 7:

One Student's Response

I recognized the key word <u>causes</u>, so I knew this question was asking about a cause-and-effect relationship. First, I looked over the answers to see if I could eliminate any of them. I knew that B was incorrect because Antoine says that any <u>leftover money</u> could be used for neighborhood projects, but he is not thinking about raising money when he first suggests planting a garden. Then I scanned the story to find the place where Antoine suggests planting a vegetable garden. I was pretty sure that no one had asked Antoine to clean up the lot, but I scanned this section of the story for the word <u>merchant</u>. I did not find any mention of a merchant asking Antoine to do this or plant a garden. The other two answers (C and D) seemed like good possibilities, so I decided to read this section of the story closely to see which one of them showed a closer cause-and-effect relationship. I read the part of the story in which Antoine's teacher, Mr. McCord, asks for ideas about ways to help the community. Antoine's suggestion that the students plant a garden is a direct response to Mr. McCord's question, "What would we do with the lot after it's cleaned up?" Therefore, I was sure that D was a better answer than C.

Now let's consider another example of a question about cause and effect:

8. What happens as a result of the vegetable garden project?

    Ⓐ The abandoned lot is dirty and full of weeds.

    Ⓑ Antoine is proud of himself.

    Ⓒ Parents contribute money to the project.

    Ⓓ The community members hold a series of meetings.

Here is how one student thought through the answer to Question 8:

One Student's Response

    I knew this was a cause-and-effect question because it included the key words <u>as a result</u>. To answer this question, I asked myself what happened as a result of planting the garden. I was immediately able to eliminate A because the lot is dirty and full of weeds <u>before</u> the garden is planted, not after. Therefore, this answer cannot be considered an effect. Then I looked at B. I know that at end of the story, Antoine meets a woman standing by the garden fence and she thanks him for the work he and his classmates have done. This praise causes him to "swell up with pride." So, I felt pretty confident that B was the correct answer. Just to make sure, I scanned the story for the words <u>parents</u> and <u>community members</u>. There is no mention of parents anywhere in the story, so I knew C was not the answer. There is one mention of a meeting with the local community board, but it is the class that holds a series of meetings, not community members. Then I was sure that B was the correct answer.

Answering Questions That Require Inferences

The answers to some test questions may not be stated directly in a reading. When you come across this type of question, you must read the passage carefully and to draw your own conclusions about characters or events based on information in the text. This type of question is called an inference question. An **inference** is a reasonable conclusion or generalization based on evidence in the text and your own experiences. It is an informed guess.

One common type of inference question asks you to draw a general conclusion from specific information. For example, suppose the text describes a person looking at sharks, eels, and sea turtles while eating popcorn. If you were asked where the person was, you would probably make an informed guess that the person was at an aquarium. The process of arriving at such a conclusion is called **making an inference.**

Sometimes the author gives general information, and from that information you are asked to draw a specific conclusion that is true. In such cases, this type of reasoning is known as **deduction.** You may also be asked to make a prediction. A **prediction** is a reasonable guess about what you think will happen in the future.

When a test question requires you to make an inference, first rule out any answers that are obviously incorrect. The next step is to rule out other answers that cannot be supported with evidence from the text. Then look at the remaining answers. Choose the answer that is best supported by the text and by your own general knowledge.

Use one or more of the following strategies to help you answer inference questions correctly:

Meets
New York
Standards
1.A.1
1.A.2
1.A.3
1.A.4
1.A.5
1.A.6

Strategies for Answering Questions That Require Inferences

- First, try to rule out as many wrong answers as possible.

- Then look at the choices that are left and skim the text for evidence that supports any of them. Use the facts from the text together with your own knowledge to decide which inference seems most reasonable.

- If more than one answer seems likely, try to determine which one seems to be the *best* answer based on the evidence and your own knowledge.

- Check to make sure that your inferences and predictions are logical, based on your own knowledge and evidence from the text.

Reading Comprehension

The ninth question about "From Trash to Treasure" asks you to make a prediction about the main character:

9. What is Antoine MOST LIKELY to do after the events in the story?

   Ⓐ He will think of something else that he can do to improve his community.

   Ⓑ He will eat a lot of vegetables and become a star athlete.

   Ⓒ He will help his classmates paint a mural on the wall behind the garden.

   Ⓓ When he grows up, he will move to the country and become a farmer.

Here is how one student reviewed the evidence in the story and made an inference about the correct answer to Question 9:

One Student's Response

This question asked me to make a prediction about what Antoine is most likely to do after the events of the story. First, I realized that I could rule out B because there is no mention in the story of Antoine eating vegetables or playing sports. Choice C seemed wrong, too. Painting a mural is mentioned, but the students end up growing the vegetable garden instead. The students could paint a mural, but there is no evidence in the story that suggests they will. Choice D did not seem to be the most likely answer to me. It is hard to say what Antoine will do when he grows up. Choice A seemed like the best answer because Antoine felt very proud about turning the abandoned lot into a garden. I think that the satisfaction he got from the project will encourage him to think of other things he could do to improve his community. Also, the story ends with Antoine thinking about what else he might do to improve his neighborhood.

Now let's consider another example of a question that requires you to make an inference:

10. Based on details provided in the story, what kind of person is Antoine?

   Ⓐ unkind and rude

   Ⓑ caring and hardworking

   Ⓒ selfish and lazy

   Ⓓ imaginative but scatterbrained

Here is how one student thought through the answer to Question 10:

One Student's Response

I could tell this question was asking me to make an inference based on evidence in the story because it said, "Based on details provided in the story…" First, I looked over the answers to see if there were any I could eliminate. I ruled out A because there are no examples of Antoine being unkind or rude anywhere in the story. Choice C seemed wrong, too. No details from the story show that Antoine is selfish and lazy. If anything, his actions in the story show that he is just the opposite—unselfish and hardworking. Answer D also seemed wrong. Antoine does seem imaginative. After all, the whole project was his idea. He does not appear to be scatterbrained, however. In fact, he seems very organized and responsible. Therefore, B seemed like the most reasonable answer to me, because the story shows how Antoine cared about his neighborhood and the people who live in it. Also, the story shows how hard Antoine worked to make the garden a success.

Your Turn

Exercise *Read each of the following short passages. Then fill in the circle next to the correct answer to each multiple-choice question.*

A   Arnold Perry loves a wide variety of sports. He plays different sports depending on the season. In the fall, he plays football. When winter arrives, he plays ice hockey. In the spring, he plays baseball. During the summer, he plays soccer. Soccer is his favorite sport.

1. What is the main idea of this passage?
   - Ⓐ Arnold Perry plays baseball in the spring.
   - Ⓑ Arnold Perry's favorite sport is soccer.
   - Ⓒ Arnold Perry plays a different sport each season.
   - Ⓓ Arnold Perry is a great athlete.

2. Which word BEST describes Arnold Perry?
   - Ⓐ lazy
   - Ⓑ intelligent
   - Ⓒ tired
   - Ⓓ athletic

B   Veronica checked her watch. She knew the bus should have arrived ten minutes ago. "What's taking so long?" she asked. She did not want to be late for school, because she had an important math test to take during first period. Veronica had studied for the test for nearly a week and did not want to miss it. She was eager to take the test while the material was still fresh in her mind. She glanced again at her watch. Then she looked up. To her relief, she saw the bus turning the corner.

1. Which of the following events happens FIRST?
   - Ⓐ Veronica waits for the bus.
   - Ⓑ Veronica studies for the test.
   - Ⓒ Veronica checks her watch.
   - Ⓓ Veronica sees the bus coming.

2. What causes Veronica to keep checking her watch?
   - Ⓐ She is nervous about missing her math test.
   - Ⓑ She wants to know how soon she can eat lunch.
   - Ⓒ She wants to time how long the test will take.
   - Ⓓ She is keeping track of the schedule on this bus route.

C   Dark, heavy clouds loomed in the distance. Mina grabbed her raincoat and put on her hat. She dashed outside and jumped on her bicycle. She pedaled furiously down the dusty road as thunder rumbled overhead. "I hope it doesn't rain before I get to work," she thought to herself. Just as she locked her bike, the first drops of rain began to fall. She hurried inside and arrived at her office safe and dry.

Meets New York Standards
1.A.1
1.A.3
1.A.4
1.A.5
1.A.6

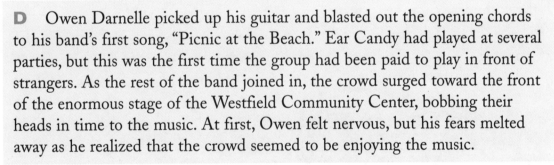

1. When does it begin to rain?
   - Ⓐ before Mina grabs her raincoat
   - Ⓑ during Mina's bicycle ride to work
   - Ⓒ after Mina arrives at her office
   - Ⓓ when Mina is locking her bike

2. What causes Mina to grab her raincoat?
   - Ⓐ She needs to get to work.
   - Ⓑ She wants to be warmer.
   - Ⓒ She sees dark, heavy clouds approaching.
   - Ⓓ She cannot find her umbrella.

D   Owen Darnelle picked up his guitar and blasted out the opening chords to his band's first song, "Picnic at the Beach." Ear Candy had played at several parties, but this was the first time the group had been paid to play in front of strangers. As the rest of the band joined in, the crowd surged toward the front of the enormous stage of the Westfield Community Center, bobbing their heads in time to the music. At first, Owen felt nervous, but his fears melted away as he realized that the crowd seemed to be enjoying the music.

1. What is the name of Owen's band?
   - Ⓐ The Owen Darnelle Band
   - Ⓑ Ear Candy
   - Ⓒ Picnic at the Beach
   - Ⓓ Westfield Community Center

2. What do you think will MOST LIKELY happen to Owen's band in the future?
   - Ⓐ They will play at more parties but will not be paid.
   - Ⓑ The band members will argue, and the group will break up.
   - Ⓒ The band will be paid to play at more shows.
   - Ⓓ The band will win a Grammy award for Best New Band.

More ▶

E   Most people consider watching a movie to be a visual experience. In truth, however, sound is just as important as the images in a movie. You may not be aware of it, but the dialogue, background sounds, and music have a great impact on how people react to movies. The next time you watch a movie, pay attention to the sounds. Notice how they enhance the visual images you see on the screen.

1. What is the main idea of this passage?

    Ⓐ Sound is an important part of the movie-going experience.

    Ⓑ Watching a movie is an exciting visual experience.

    Ⓒ Movie sounds consist of dialogue, background sounds, and music.

    Ⓓ People should ignore the sounds they hear while watching films.

2. According to this passage, which of the following has a great impact on the way people react to movies?

    Ⓐ the ticket price

    Ⓑ the dialogue

    Ⓒ the previews

    Ⓓ the costumes

Return to the exercises at the beginning of the chapter, revise your work as necessary, and submit the exercises to your teacher for grading.

Chapter 6
Picture This!
Notetaking and Graphic Organizers

Read this passage about Viking children. Also study the notes in rough outline form about the passage. Then try your hand at the exercises that follow the passage. You will not be graded on the exercises at this time. At the end of the chapter, you will be directed to return to these exercises to revise and correct your work.

A Viking Childhood

by Theodore Lundst

Viking children lived very different lives than children do today. Parents often sent Viking children away from home when they were only a few years old. Instead of going to school, Viking children went to work on a farm, or they learned a skill, such as how to build a boat. Children were even allowed to travel to new lands. Viking children played with toys and games, but they were forced to grow up quickly. By the age of fifteen, Viking children were treated as adults.

The Viking child's place in the family was not like the place children have today. When a child was born into a Viking family, the father immediately said the child's name aloud. This meant that he recognized the new baby as a member of the family. Some Viking children stayed at home with their parents, but many others were sent to live with another family. Viking parents believed that if their

Rough Outline

Viking children lived differently than children today
   —Many were sent away from home
   —No school
   —Children worked
   —Children played w/games & toys
   —Age 15 = adult

Place in family different from that of children today
   —Some children stayed home w/parents but many were sent away to live w/other families
   —Living away from home prepared children for tough lives

children lived away from home, they would be better prepared for the tough lives they would face as adults.

Viking children did not go to school. They were expected to begin working at a very young age. Children helped on the farm by tending the animals or gathering wood. Children with agile fingers and good eyesight were selected to help create beautiful jewelry that the Viking men and women loved to wear. Young girls helped with the weaving and cooking. Boys went to work with their fathers. They learned to build ships or to make tools. Some children traveled to Viking colonies in England to help build new villages.

Viking children worked hard, but they still had time to play. They kept their toys in small leather bags made by their mothers. Parents gave their children simple wooden toys in the shapes of ships, weapons, and animals. Young boys played with wooden swords or spears with leather-covered tips. Such toys allowed them to learn how to fight without getting hurt. Viking children skated, skied, and played ball games. They also learned to swim, to ride horses, and to sail boats.

In many ways, growing up as a Viking child was different from growing up as a child today. Many Viking children were sent to live away from home, and none of them attended school. They had time to play games and to enjoy their toys, but their childhood did not last long. A Viking childhood ended by age fifteen, when the girls were married and the boys went off to sea or into battle. ○

Children started working at young age
— Some worked on farms
— Some made jewelry
— Girls helped w/weaving & cooking
— Boys learned to make ships & tools
— Some traveled to Viking colonies →
  helped build villages

Hard work, but some time to play
— Kept toys in small bags
— "Make believe" toys helped children
  practice adult skills
— Toy weapons → boys practiced
  fighting
— Children skated, skied, & played ball
  games
— Children learned to swim, ride, & sail

Viking children grew up differently than
children today
— Children worked & didn't go to
  school
— Many were sent away from home
— Some time to play, but not for long
— At age 15, children = adults
— Girls married
— Boys went to war or sea

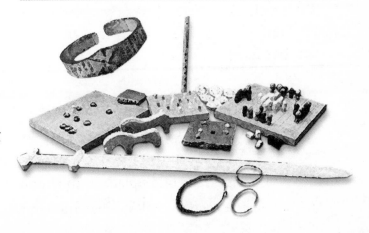

Your Turn

Exercise A *Fill in the circle next to the correct answer to each multiple-choice question.*

1. What is this article MOSTLY about?
   - Ⓐ what the lives of Viking children were like
   - Ⓑ what a Viking wedding ceremony was like
   - Ⓒ why Viking children were sent away from home
   - Ⓓ how a Viking ship was constructed

2. At what age were Viking children considered to be adults?
   - Ⓐ 5
   - Ⓑ 10
   - Ⓒ 15
   - Ⓓ 20

3. Why did many Viking parents send their children away from home at an early age?
   - Ⓐ Parents believed that sending their children away helped to prepare them for the tough life that lay ahead.
   - Ⓑ There were very few schools, so many parents sent their children away to be near a school.
   - Ⓒ Viking children often misbehaved, and parents punished them by sending them away.
   - Ⓓ Many parents could not afford to raise the children, so they sent them to wealthier families.

4. A Viking child who was good with his or her hands would MOST LIKELY
   - Ⓐ sail a ship.
   - Ⓑ get married.
   - Ⓒ make jewelry.
   - Ⓓ make toys.

5. Which of the following topics isn't discussed in the passage?
   - Ⓐ the work that Viking children did
   - Ⓑ Viking children's toys and games
   - Ⓒ a Viking child's place in the family
   - Ⓓ the schools that Viking children attended

Exercise B The main idea of the passage you just read is that Viking children lived very different lives than children do today. Imagine that you are going to write a short essay pointing out three major ways that your daily life differs from that of a Viking child.

Plan your essay by filling in the rough outline form below. (Do NOT write the essay. You are simply being asked to create a rough outline of your ideas.) Use the rough outline on pages 134–35 as a model for your outline. List three major differences. These will become the main ideas in your outline. Then, underneath each main idea, write three details or examples that you could use to support that main idea.

Rough Outline

MAIN IDEA: _____

    DETAIL #1: _____

    DETAIL #2: _____

    DETAIL #3: _____

MAIN IDEA: _____

    DETAIL #1: _____

    DETAIL #2: _____

    DETAIL #3: _____

MAIN IDEA: _____

    DETAIL #1: _____

    DETAIL #2: _____

    DETAIL #3: _____

Picture This!

Graphic organizers are charts, tables, or diagrams that can be used to present and arrange information so that it is easy to understand. Just as you might use a road map when planning a trip, you can use a graphic organizer to help you navigate through your many ideas without getting sidetracked or lost. Graphic organizers serve three main purposes:

- They help you to remember what you have listened to or read.

- They help you to organize ideas for writing.

- They help you to present ideas to others in a clear and visually appealing way.

Good organization is the key to effective writing. Taking notes or using a graphic organizer when you read or listen will help you to remember important information. Organizing your thoughts before you begin to write is crucial to writing well. Having a plan will help you not only when you are writing on your own but also when you need to answer a writing prompt on a test.

Using Rough Outlines

A **rough outline** is one helpful way to organize your ideas before you begin to write. This form of graphic organizer is also particularly useful for taking notes, especially when you are reading nonfiction. It can help you to remember important facts and ideas. The trick in taking notes is to write down as little as possible. Make sure, however, that you write down enough information so that you will be able to understand your notes later.

When you make a rough outline, jot down the main ideas followed by the supporting details. A **main idea** is any important point that an author makes. The **supporting details** are facts and examples that explain or add information about the main idea.

Look back at the essay on Viking children at the beginning of this chapter. Notice that the first sentence in each paragraph of the essay is a main idea. For example, in the first paragraph, *"Viking children lived very different lives than children do today"* is the main idea. The rough outline on page 134 states this main idea in fewer words: *"Viking children lived differently than children today."* Then notice the supporting details that follow the main idea. These details appear beneath the main idea and are introduced by dashes. Continue comparing the paragraphs to the rough outline. Because the rough outline is accurate and complete, the writer was able to use it to write a well-organized essay about the differences between the lives of Viking children and the way most children grow up today.

Here are some tips to keep in mind when making a rough outline:

Rough Outline Form

1. Do not try to write down everything. Write down only the main ideas and the supporting details.

2. Take notes in phrases, not in complete sentences. Begin each phrase with a capital letter.

3. Use a capital letter at the beginning of each main word in a proper noun, such as the name of a person or place.

4. Use abbreviations and symbols such as *Amer.* for *American,* & for *and,* w/ for *with,* = for *is* or *are,* → for *causes* or *becomes.*

5. Begin main ideas at the left margin of the paper.

6. Write supporting details under the main ideas. Use a dash (—) at the beginning of each supporting detail.

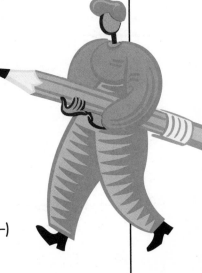

Types of Graphic Organizer

A rough outline may not always be the best way to organize your ideas. Depending upon the kind of information that you want to organize, you may want to use some other type of graphic organizer. In the next few pages, you will see a variety of graphic organizers and will learn how to use the different types.

Compare-and-Contrast T-Chart

A common type of writing assignment is to compare and contrast two subjects. When you **compare** two people, places, or things, you point out their similarities, or the things they have in common. When you **contrast** two subjects, you point out their differences.

The simplest way to compare and contrast information is to prepare a **comparison-and-contrast chart,** which can be set up as a **T-chart.** Suppose you are learning about the Mayan civilization in Central America and you want to compare and contrast the Mayan system of writing with the writing of modern English. You might begin by listing the similarities and differences. A comparison-and-contrast T-chart will help you to take organized notes.

Here is a sample T-chart that shows how these two systems are alike and different:

Ⓐ **Comparison-and-Contrast T-Chart**

Differences and Similarities in Mayan and Modern English Writing

Mayan Writing	Modern English Writing
—Writing used for practical communication, for keeping records, and for ceremonial purposes	—Also uses writing for practical communication, record keeping, and ceremonial purposes
—Used pictures to stand for things and for sounds	—Uses letters to stand for sounds
—Was written on stone and on books (codices) made of bark	—Is written on paper or a computer
—Was read in columns from top to bottom and right to left	—Is read in lines from top to bottom but from left to right
—Only people of high social standing could read & write	—Most people learn to read and write
—Extent of literature unknown due to destruction of books by Spanish	—Vast range of literature, in many genres and about many subjects

---

Here is a piece of writing based on the T-chart comparing and contrasting the two writing systems.

Meets
New York
Standards
1.A.1
1.A.3
1.A.4
1.A.6
1.B.3
1.B.4
1.B.5

The Maya, a group of Native Americans, developed a civilization that thrived in Central America and southern Mexico around A.D. 300 to 900. European explorers first encountered the Maya in the sixteenth century. Like Americans today, the Maya had a system of writing that they used for practical communication and record keeping, as well as for ceremonial purposes. The similarities end there, however, for Mayan writing differed greatly from modern English writing.

Some major differences between Mayan writing and modern English writing include the following: English uses symbols called letters to stand for sounds. The Mayan writing system used some symbols that stood for sounds and some that were pictures of things. People almost always write modern English on paper, though they often write on computers now and sometimes make inscriptions on monuments, gravestones, buildings, and so on. The Maya, in contrast, wrote on books made of bark, called codices, and on great blocks of stone. Modern English is read in lines from left to right, starting at the line at the top of a page and moving down, line after line. Mayan is read in columns from top to bottom, starting with the rightmost column and moving to the left. In modern America and in other English-speaking countries, most people learn to read and write. Among the ancient Maya, in contrast, only people of high social standing learned to read and write. Today, the range of English literature is vast, including writing in many different genres and on many different subjects. Unfortunately, only a few inscriptions and only four Mayan codices survive. Spanish explorers destroyed all the others that they found.

Notetaking and Graphic Organizers

Venn Diagrams

The **Venn diagram** is another way to compare and contrast subjects. To make a Venn diagram, draw a circle for each of your subjects in such a way that the two circles overlap. Label each circle with the name of one of the subjects. List the similarities between the two topics in the space where the circles overlap. Then list the differences in the space specific to each topic, on either side of the overlap.

Below is an example of a Venn diagram based on the information in the passage about Mayan and modern English writing.

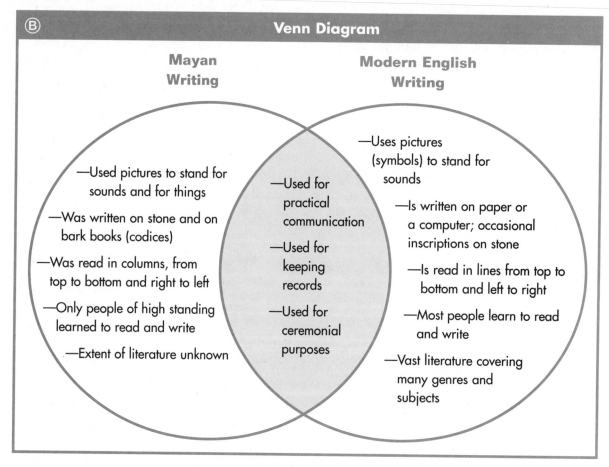

Ⓑ **Venn Diagram**

Mayan Writing

—Used pictures to stand for sounds and for things

—Was written on stone and on bark books (codices)

—Was read in columns, from top to bottom and right to left

—Only people of high standing learned to read and write

—Extent of literature unknown

(Overlap)

—Used for practical communication

—Used for keeping records

—Used for ceremonial purposes

Modern English Writing

—Uses pictures (symbols) to stand for sounds

—Is written on paper or a computer; occasional inscriptions on stone

—Is read in lines from top to bottom and left to right

—Most people learn to read and write

—Vast literature covering many genres and subjects

Pro-and-Con Charts

People often write to convince others to take some action or to adopt a particular point of view. Suppose, for example, that you want to get a pet iguana, but your mother is not crazy about this idea. You could write her a letter explaining why you think she should let you have an iguana. This kind of writing, done to convince others to believe something or to do something, is called **persuasive writing.**

One way to organize information for persuasive writing is to create a **pro-and-con chart.** A **pro** argument is a reason why something is a good idea or activity. A **con** argument is a reason why something is *not* a good idea or

activity. In preparation for writing a letter to your mother, you can make a pro-and-con chart, which is another type of T-chart. Thinking through all the reasons for *and* against getting a pet iguana will help you to express your arguments in favor of the idea clearly. It will also help you to anticipate and respond to your mother's objections.

Suppose that you wanted to explore the pros and cons of using calculators rather than figuring mathematical problems in your head or on paper. You could set up a chart like the one shown below. Then you could use the information in the chart to create a piece of writing that presents both the arguments for and against the use of calculators.

Pro-and-Con Chart

Cause and Effect: Use of Calculators for Doing Math Problems

Pro	Con
—Inexpensive and simple way to ensure faster work done with greater accuracy	—Leads people to forget how to do basic calculations
—Eliminates tedious calculations and busywork	—Undermines becoming comfortable with doing calculation in one's head
—Lowers risk of careless mistakes	—Creates dependence on tool and fosters inability to make quick estimates needed in everyday life
—Allows focus on mathematical principles rather than on rote calculation	

Notetaking and Graphic Organizers

Here is a piece of writing based on the pro-and-con chart on the previous page. Notice how the writer presents the arguments for and against the use of calculators:

When pocket calculators were new in the early 1970s, the price was about fifty dollars for a simple calculator that performed the four basic functions. Today, such a calculator can be bought for less than a dollar. People have welcomed calculators as wonderful labor-saving devices. They have eliminated the need for tedious calculations done by hand and have taken the busywork out of doing math. Furthermore, calculators, unlike people, do not make careless mistakes. Calculators allow users to focus on mathematical principles instead of getting bogged down in time-consuming calculations.

Some people, however, fear that dependence on calculators will lead to mathematical ignorance. If students always use calculators, they may forget how to do basic calculations or may become uncomfortable working with numbers in their heads. This will handicap them when it comes to doing simple calculations in everyday life. Without the calculator, they may not be able to make quick estimates—to estimate for example, the total cost of a series of purchases, the quantity of material needed for a project, or the length of time it will take to arrive at a destination. If people become too dependent on calculators, they may not realize when their tool has given them a wrong answer because they pressed the wrong key. Furthermore, it is in actually working with numbers that one comes to a fuller understanding of mathematical principles. Using calculators might slow or prevent the development of such understanding.

A pro-and-con chart can also help you to evaluate another person's ideas. You might, for example, read an essay that discusses whether a person ought to be punished for his or her actions. A pro-and-con chart can help you keep track of the reasons for and against punishment. Jotting down reasons in a pro-and-con chart can help you to analyze someone else's arguments as well as to organize your own thoughts. Then you can decide whether you agree with someone else's position and explain your reasons.

Cause-and-Effect Charts

Discussions of causes and effects appear in all kinds of writing. For example, an article in a business magazine might describe the causes leading to the success of a particular company. On an exam, you might be asked to write about causes and effects, or you might be asked to answer questions about a reading passage that discusses causes and effects. To organize information about causes and effects, you can create a **cause-and-effect chart:**

Ⓓ Cause-and-Effect Chart	
Cause and Effect: Causes of World War I	
Causes	**Effects**
—War between Prussia (Germany) and France (1871)	—World War I begins (1914)
—Europe split between two hostile groups, joined by alliances (1882)	—Most costly war in history
—Kaiser Wilhelm's attempts to expand German Empire (1890)	—More than 20 million die
—Assassination of Archduke Franz Ferdinand of Austria-Hungary by Serbian nationalist group (1914)	
—Groups on either side of conflict between Austria-Hungary and Serbia declare war on one another	

Below is an example of how the information in the chart above can be used to write a response to an exam question that asks students to explain the causes of World War I:

> World War I, also known as "The Great War," was the most costly war in history up to that point. About twenty million people lost their lives in the conflict. It was the first time that aircraft, machine guns, poison gas, and other devices of modern war were used on a large scale. What led to such a brutal and devastating war?
>
> The roots of World War I go back to the nineteenth century. In 1871, Prussia (later part of the German empire) crushed France in a quick war, took two valuable provinces, and made France pay millions of francs. By 1882, Chancellor Otto von Bismarck of Germany, fearing that France would one day retaliate, had formed an alliance with Austria-Hungary. The two European empires promised to help each other in case of war. France feared Germany, too, and made alliances with Russia and Great Britain.
>
> **More ▶**

In 1890, Kaiser (Emperor) Wilhelm II removed Bismarck from his position as German chancellor. Then Kaiser Wilhelm launched a campaign to expand the German empire. His attempt to control Morocco in 1905 almost led to war with Britain and France. It wasn't until 1914, however, and the assassination of Archduke Ferdinand of Austria-Hungary that war finally broke out. Countries began to take sides: Austria-Hungary declared war on Serbia, Russia declared its support for Serbia, and France stepped forward to support Russia. Germany retaliated by declaring war on Russia, and then on France. Great Britain declared war on Germany because they invaded Belgium en route to their attack on France. World War I was underway. The war eventually involved more than thirty countries, including the United States. The first world war claimed more than twenty million lives, and cost billions of dollars.

Timelines

One effective way to keep track of major events and developments is to create a timeline. A **timeline** can be used to organize information in chronological (time) order. The information shown in the cause-and-effect chart on the previous page, for example, can also be used to create a timeline, such as the one shown here:

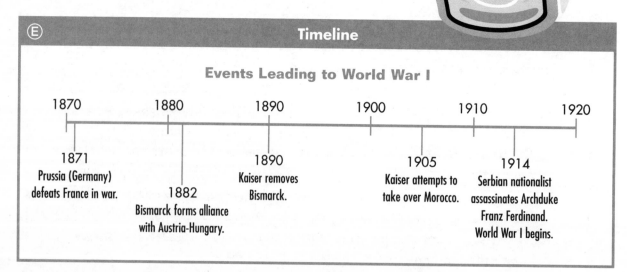

Timeline

Events Leading to World War I

1870	1880	1890	1900	1910	1920

1871
Prussia (Germany) defeats France in war.

1882
Bismarck forms alliance with Austria-Hungary.

1890
Kaiser removes Bismarck.

1905
Kaiser attempts to take over Morocco.

1914
Serbian nationalist assassinates Archduke Franz Ferdinand. World War I begins.

Sensory Detail Charts

Descriptive writing presents a picture in words. One way to gather information for descriptive writing is to use a **sensory detail chart.** Such a chart lists particular details that you perceive with each of your **senses**—sight, hearing, touch, smell, and taste. A sensory detail chart can help you to use all your senses to gather data about something so you can describe it thoroughly.

Here is an example of a sensory detail chart that contains descriptions of President Thomas Jefferson's favorite rooms at the White House. A short piece based on these descriptions follows the chart.

Meets
New York
Standards
1.A.1
1.A.3
1.A.4
1.A.6
1.B.3
1.B.4
1.B.5

(F) **Sensory Detail Chart**

President Thomas Jefferson's Favorite Rooms: His Office & the Dining Room

Sight	Sound	Touch	Smell	Taste
—desk in center of room	—caged songbird singing	—feeding the songbird	—roses and geraniums	—meals in dining room
—maps, globes, and books throughout the room	—sounds of the outdoors	—working with tools	—smell of food	
—flowers and plants in the windows	—conversation of guests	—writing or reading at desk		
—tools for carpentry and gardening in desk drawers				
—view from the window: White House grounds				

President Thomas Jefferson's favorite room was his office. A large desk filled the center of the room. Sometimes a visitor might catch a glimpse of Jefferson's gardening or carpentry tools. He usually kept them hidden in a drawer, but in his spare moments Jefferson enjoyed using them. Books, globes, charts, and maps were arranged around the room, showing Jefferson's love of knowledge and his curiosity about the world. Gazing through the office windows, Jefferson could see the White House grounds. On the windowsills stood various potted plants and flowers. Jefferson shared his office with a songbird that he kept in a cage near his roses and geraniums. He loved listening to the bird sing. Jefferson often let the bird out to eat from his hand or sit on his shoulder. Sometimes the bird sang to Jefferson when he took his afternoon nap.

Jefferson loved to entertain guests at meals, and so the White House dining room became another of his favorite places. Guests enjoyed specially prepared meals that were transported from the kitchen to the dining room by one of Jefferson's inventions—the dumbwaiter. To activate this, Jefferson pushed a button, and then a shelf that was built into the wall revolved from the dining room to the kitchen. This enabled White House servants to unload the used dishes and place the next course onto the shelf. Finally, the servants revolved the shelf with the full plates of food back into the dining room. This way, Jefferson and his guests could be served their meal while it was still piping hot.

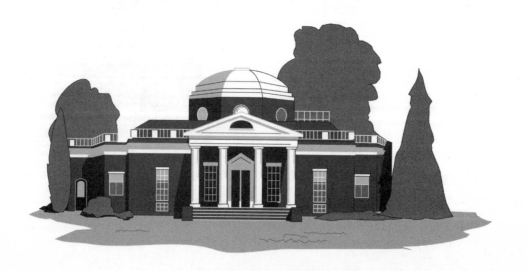

Character Analysis Chart

When reading a story, you might need to take note of the characters' thoughts, words, and actions, as well as statements made about them that reveal what they are like. A **character analysis chart,** such as the one shown below, is one way to list a character's traits.

Meets
New York
Standards
1.A.1
1.A.3
1.A.4
1.A.6
1.B.3
1.B.4
1.B.5

Ⓖ **Character Analysis Chart**

Character Analysis: President Thomas Jefferson

Character Trait	Evidence of the Trait in the Character
Intelligent	—Kept all kinds of books, maps, charts in office
	—Loved to learn
	—Liked to invent things
Friendly	—Liked to entertain guests
	—Enjoyed talking with people
Caring	—Took care of flowers and plants
	—Took care of a songbird

Notetaking and Graphic Organizers

Double-Ledger Chart

Another way of analyzing character traits is by using the **double-ledger chart.** Like other T-charts, this chart consists of two columns. Direct quotes from the passage are listed in one column, with the reader's thoughts and responses to each passage listed in the opposite column. These examples can then be used as supporting examples when analyzing a passage or a character. A double-ledger chart that contains information about Thomas Jefferson might look like this:

Double-Ledger Chart

Character Analysis: President Thomas Jefferson

Direct Quote	Response to Quote
"glimpse of gardening or carpentry tools"	Liked to work with his hands and to grow plants or make things
"Books, globes, charts, and maps were arranged around the room"	Was intelligent and liked to learn
"... a songbird that he kept in a cage ... He loved listening to the bird sing"	Loved animals; bird kept him company, even at work
"Jefferson loved to entertain guests"	Was friendly and enjoyed talking with people

Flow Chart

You can use a **flow chart** to organize the stages in a process or the steps necessary to complete an activity. In flow charts used by business people and computer scientists, an oval usually stands for start or stop, a diamond for a question or point of decision, and a rectangle for an action. The stages or steps are listed in order and are connected by arrows that show the direction of movement.

Study the flow chart and read the paragraph based on it.

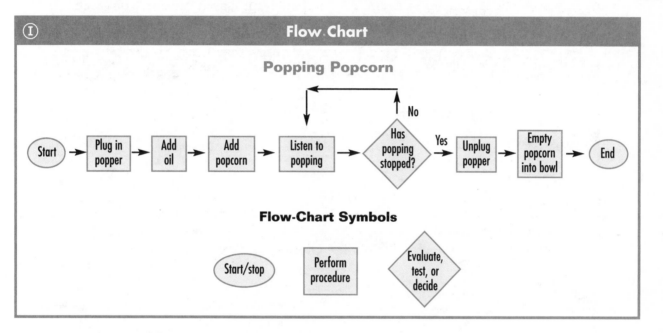

Making popcorn used to involve more than just putting a package in the microwave. If you want to make popcorn the "old-fashioned" way, you can use a popcorn popper, a machine specifically designed for the purpose. After plugging it in, you add the oil and then the popcorn. Next comes the hardest part: waiting. Once the oil heats up, the corn begins to pop. After a few minutes, you should check to see if it is done. If there are still popping sounds, you should wait a minute or two more, until the popping sound has completely stopped. Then you unplug your popper and empty the popcorn into a bowl. Now you are ready to eat.

Notetaking and Graphic Organizers

Word Webs or Cluster Charts

An excellent graphic organizer for generating ideas and showing how they are related to one another is the **word web,** or **cluster chart.** To create such a chart, write the subject you want to explore in the middle of the piece of paper and circle it. Outside the circle, write related main ideas, circle them, and connect them to the center circle with lines. Then, around each main idea, write related specific details, circle those, and connect them to the main idea with lines.

Look at the word web below. A paragraph based on this word web follows the chart.

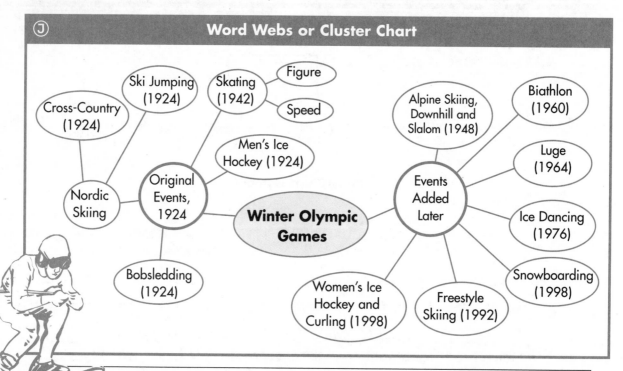

Word Webs or Cluster Chart

(J)

- Cross-Country (1924)
- Ski Jumping (1924)
- Skating (1942)
  - Figure
  - Speed
- Men's Ice Hockey (1924)
- Nordic Skiing
- Original Events, 1924
- Bobsledding (1924)
- **Winter Olympic Games**
- Events Added Later
  - Alpine Skiing, Downhill and Slalom (1948)
  - Biathlon (1960)
  - Luge (1964)
  - Ice Dancing (1976)
  - Snowboarding (1998)
  - Freestyle Skiing (1992)
  - Women's Ice Hockey and Curling (1998)

The Winter Olympic Games, which began in 1924, originally included Nordic skiing (cross-country and ski jumping), figure skating, speed skating, men's ice hockey, and bobsledding. Over the years, the International Olympic Committee added other events. Alpine skiing (downhill and slalom) started in 1948. The biathlon (cross-country skiing plus shooting) was introduced in 1960 and the luge (one- or two-person sledding) in 1964. Olympic ice dancing began in 1976 and freestyle skiing in 1992. Snowboarding and women's ice hockey made their Olympic debut in the 1998 Games in Nagano, Japan. Curling, a sport in which two teams of four persons slide granite stones across the ice toward a target circle, also became an Olympic sport for the first time in the 1998 Games.

How to Use Graphic Organizers

On a writing test, the **writing prompt** or question usually establishes the purpose of your response. Knowing the purpose of your response can help you to determine which type of graphic organizer might be the most useful. Look for key words such as *compare*, *explain*, or *persuade* in the prompt. These words are clues to the purpose of your writing. As shown in the chart below, these clues can also help you choose the best way to gather and organize the ideas for your response.

The standard graphic organizers, such as those illustrated in the chart below, are useful in many writing situations. If a prompt asks you to "*tell about* the events leading up to the Vietnam War," you might consider using a timeline or a cause-and-effect chart. Another prompt might require you to "*explain* steps necessary to build a rocket," in which case a flow chart would be a better choice. Once you understand the various types of graphic organizer available, you can select which ones work best for various types of writing and for your own style. Learning how to choose the best graphic organizer for the task at hand is a key strategy for good writing.

Meets New York Standards
1.A.1
1.A.3
1.A.4
1.A.6
1.B.3
1.B.4
1.B.5

Use this Graphic Organizer	when the key word in the prompt is
Venn Diagram	*compare, contrast, show similarities and/or differences, or illustrate.*
T-charts:	
Comparison-and-contrast chart	*compare, contrast, describe similarities and/or differences, or illustrate.*
Pro-and-con chart	*decide, persuade, review, express, criticize, or evaluate.*
Cause-and-effect chart	*evaluate, identify, explain, or describe.*
Double-ledger chart	*illustrate, argue, describe, or analyze.*
Rough outline	*summarize, list, paraphrase, describe, support, illustrate, show, explain, identify, or prove.*
Analysis chart	*analyze, interpret, judge, critique, assess, or evaluate.*
Sensory detail chart	*describe or illustrate.*
Timeline	*trace, list, or tell.*
Flow chart	*describe, review, explain, or illustrate.*
Word web	*identify, list, summarize, support, or illustrate.*

Meets
New York
Standards
1.A.1
1.A.3
1.A.4
1.A.6
1.B.3
1.B.4
1.B.5

Exercise   *Under each writing prompt below, list the type(s) of graphic organizer you might use to complete the assignment. You may list more than one, but list the best one first. (Note: Do NOT answer the prompt. You are simply being asked to choose the* **best** *type or types of graphic organizer to gather ideas for each topic.)*

1. Based on the information in this passage, explain how you would build a bluebird house.

    _____

    _____

    _____

2. Based on the information in this passage, identify the causes of acid rain.

    _____

    _____

    _____

3. Based on this passage from *Little Women*, analyze the character of Jo.

    _____

    _____

    _____

4. Write a report describing your trip to the Children's Museum.

    _____

    _____

    _____

Return to the exercises at the beginning of the chapter, revise your work as necessary, and submit the exercises to your teacher for grading.

Chapter 7

Listen Up!

Active Listening

Space Junk

by Wendy Howard

Ever since humankind began to explore space, layers of orbital debris have been forming around our planet. What makes up this orbiting junkyard? Mostly, it contains old satellites, pieces from rocket launchers, damaged parts of exploration equipment, chunks of trash, and millions of tiny objects such as bits of metal and paint chips.

A small object orbiting Earth can do incredible damage because it travels at a speed of several miles per second. Collisions between spacecraft and large objects are rare, but authorities agree that collisions with smaller debris pose serious threats. For example, a piece of orbital debris the size of a grain of rice can tear a hole in an astronaut's space suit. Collisions with small debris can also damage expensive space stations and communication and weather satellites.

For example, photographs of the Russian space station *Mir*, which orbited Earth for fifteen years between 1986 and 2001, show scars from such impacts. *Mir's* large solar panels were the most damaged because they had no protection from the debris.

The higher the altitude of a piece of space junk, the longer it stays in orbit. Objects floating within 373 miles of the Earth's surface usually fall back to Earth in a few years. Most of these objects burn up as they fall through the atmosphere. Objects orbiting 620 miles or higher above the Earth's surface can take centuries to fall back to Earth.

Experts at the National Air and Space Administration (NASA) recognize that space junk is an important problem that must be addressed. Researchers and engineers are improving radar and optical systems that can monitor existing space debris. Teams of scientists are developing new spacecraft and launching rockets that create less debris. Researchers know that space is a resource that needs to be respected and protected for future generations. ○

Image: JPL/NASA

Exercise A *Fill in the circle next to the correct answer to each multiple-choice question. You may refer to the notes you took while listening, but you may not look back at the article.*

1. What is the main idea of the article?
   - Ⓐ Scientists are developing new equipment that can monitor junk floating in space.
   - Ⓑ Debris orbiting in space severely damaged the Russian space station *Mir*.
   - Ⓒ Junk orbiting in space is a serious problem that needs to be addressed.
   - Ⓓ Congress should increase funds for space exploration.

2. According to the article, even a very small piece of debris in space can be dangerous, because
   - Ⓐ it is impossible for pilots to see debris in space.
   - Ⓑ debris travels at a speed of several miles per second.
   - Ⓒ spacecraft have no protection from flying debris.
   - Ⓓ the smaller debris is more likely to fall back to Earth.

3. What evidence is offered in the article to show that debris in space is a serious problem?
   - Ⓐ Several astronauts were badly wounded when they were hit by debris in space.
   - Ⓑ A space station was destroyed when it crashed into an old rocket launcher in space.
   - Ⓒ Debris has fallen from space, causing extensive damage to homes and businesses.
   - Ⓓ The Russian space station *Mir* was damaged by debris while orbiting the Earth.

4. Which of the following statements is true?
   - Ⓐ The higher the altitude of a piece of space junk, the longer it orbits the Earth.
   - Ⓑ Objects within 373 miles of Earth's surface will not burn as they fall back to Earth.
   - Ⓒ Objects orbiting 620 miles or higher will never fall back to Earth.
   - Ⓓ The larger the piece of debris, the more likely a spacecraft is to hit it.

Exercise B *Answer the following short-response questions. You may refer to the notes you took while listening, but you may not look back at the article.*

1. List three examples of debris that is currently floating around our planet:

1. _____

2. _____

3. _____

2. How are experts at NASA trying to address the problem of space junk?

_____

_____

_____

_____

_____

_____

Listen Up!

You have probably had this experience: For several days or weeks, you hear a song playing on the radio. Then, one day, you happen to listen closely to the lyrics. Suddenly, you have a whole new impression of the song. It may seem better, more interesting, or more real to you, or you may be shocked or offended. This experience shows that there is a big difference between just hearing and really listening. When you **listen,** you actively process what you hear. You think about it carefully. In this chapter, you will learn some techniques for improving your listening skills. These techniques will help you not only on the listening portions of state exams but also in important listening situations in your everyday life.

Listening in Everyday Life

Human beings are naturally social creatures. We often come together in groups, and we depend a great deal on our personal relationships with friends and family members. Almost all social situations involve listening skills. Here are some of the most common listening situations:

Common Listening Situations

- Personal interactions; conversations with friends and family
- Church, temple, or mosque
- Classroom demonstrations
- Classroom discussions
- Classroom lectures
- Pep rallies
- School assemblies
- Listening portions of state tests
- Meetings at school
- Meetings at work
- Meetings of civic organizations (such as the city council)
- Television, radio, movies, audiocassette tapes, CDs, MP3 files, other media

Because of all the listening that people do, learning to listen well can be really valuable!

Prelistening

In previous chapters, you have learned that before reading, you should do some prereading. **Prereading** is the process of looking over the selection and thinking about what you already know about the topic. Sometimes, before you begin listening, you can **prelisten,** or begin thinking about that topic. If you know what the topic is going to be, you can ask yourself questions like these:

- What do I already know about the topic?

- What do I expect to learn about the topic?

- What would I like to learn about the topic?

Also see if you can figure out, before you start listening, what kind of selection you are about to hear. Will it be a story? A drama? A comedy sketch? A political speech? A lecture? Figuring out the type of selection in advance can help you to figure out what to listen for.

Beginning to Listen

Often, the first few words that you hear will reveal the type of piece you are listening to and the topic. Suppose that a speaker begins like this:

> Once, long, long ago, there was a small farm in Greece, and on this farm lived a family of ducks, including a baby duck who loved looking at the stars at night.

The speaker has begun by introducing a setting and some characters, so you know that you are going to be listening to a story. You know that it will be a fictional story because it features a baby duck who likes looking at stars.

Suppose that the speaker begins like this instead:

> Only a few decades ago, the sport of snowboarding did not exist. Today, snowboarding is recognized as an official event in the Winter Olympics. How did this sport become popular so quickly?

From this brief opening, you can tell that you are going to hear a piece of informative nonfiction. The speaker is going to talk about how snowboarding developed and became popular.

Suppose that the speaker begins, instead, like this:

> Only last week, a child was attacked in our own Lynch Park by a dog that had been released by its owner and allowed to run free. This incident raises an important question: Should we have a leash law in the city of Smallville? I intend, today, to give you four good reasons why we should.

From this opening, you can tell that you are going to hear a piece of persuasion. In persuasive nonfiction, a person argues in favor of an opinion. This speaker's opinion is that Smallville should have a leash law. She is planning to provide four reasons to support that opinion.

Meets
New York
Standards
1.A.1
1.A.2
1.A.3
1.A.5
1.A.6

Active Listening 161

Using Selective Attention

Why is it important to figure out, early on, what kind of piece you are listening to? One reason is that it is not very useful to try to listen carefully to every single word. Listening well involves using **selective attention**—that is, paying closest attention to the most important parts of what you are hearing. To listen with selective attention, follow these guidelines:

Using the Strategy of Selective Attention

When listening to narratives (stories), pay attention to the following:

- The names and traits of **characters**
- The **motives** of characters (what makes them act and speak as they do)
- The **relationships** among characters
- **Conflicts,** or struggles
- The **setting** (the time and the place)
- The **mood,** or feeling, created by the setting
- **Events** and the order, or **sequence,** in which they occur, including any **foreshadowing** (hints about what is to come) or **flashbacks** (descriptions of events that took place before the current action)
- **Causes** and their **effects**
- The **inciting incident,** or event that introduces the conflict
- The **resolution,** or event that ends the conflict
- Any **motifs,** or elements that recur, or repeat
- The attitude, or **tone,** of the **narrator,** or voice telling the story
- General ideas, lessons, morals, or **themes**

More ▶

When listening to informative or persuasive material, look for these features:

- The **title** and **author** of the piece
- The **subject** of the piece (what it is about)
- The **purpose** of the piece (such as to inform, to persuade, or to entertain)
- The **thesis** (the main idea of the piece)
- **Names** of people and places
- Significant **facts** and **figures**
- Significant **events** and their **sequence,** including **dates**
- **Conflicts, questions, issues,** or **arguments pro and con**
- Similarities **(comparisons)** and differences **(contrasts)**
- **Causes** and **effects**
- **Questions** posed and **answers** given
- **Steps** in processes
- **Opinions** and **supporting evidence**
- **Definitions** and **key terms**

Listening Actively: Taking Notes and Responding

In many situations, it is important to take notes as you listen. Doing so is especially important when you are listening as part of a test. Notes will help you to remember what you have heard. The more complete your notes, the better off you will be. In fact, just by writing down main ideas and important details, you will find it easier to remember them, even if you never look back at your notes!

When you take notes, you can use rough outline form, as shown on the next page.

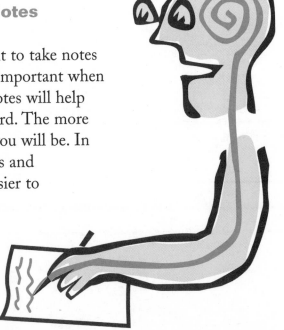

Here is an example of notes in rough outline form based on the opening selection:

One Student's Notes in Outline Form

Space Junk

Author—Wendy Howard

Main idea: Since man began to explore space, junk has been building up around Earth

Orbiting junkyard made up of
    —old satellites
    —pieces of rocket launchers
    —parts of explor. equipment
    —chunks of trash
    —mil. of bits of metal & paint chips

Even small objects can do incred. damage:
    —Debris travels @ speed of several miles per sec.
    —Collisions w/large objects rare but w/small objects more common
    —Rice-sized bits can tear holes in astronaut's suit
    —Small debris damaged solar panels on Mir

The higher the junk, the longer it stays in orbit
    —Objects within 373 mi. of Earth → a few years to fall back
    —Objects 620+ mi. above Earth → centuries to fall back

Experts at NASA recognize the problem / trying to address it
    —Improving systems (radar & optical) that keep track of space junk
    —Developing new spacecraft & launch rockets that create less debris

Meets
New York
Standards
1.A.1
1.A.3
1.A.4
1.A.5
1.A.6
2.A.1
2.A.2

Notice that when you take notes in rough outline form, you write the main ideas beginning at the left margin. Then you write subordinate or related ideas under the main ideas, using a dash (—) before each one. When taking notes using a rough outline form, use abbreviations and symbols to speed up your writing. See, for example, the following abbreviations and symbols in the notes about Space Junk: &, *mil.*, and →.

In some cases, you may want to take notes using a T-chart. Draw a line down the middle of your page, and label the two columns like this:

Record	Response

In the left-hand column, take notes on important parts of what you are hearing. In the right-hand column, respond to these points with your own questions, predictions, summaries, conclusions, and evaluations. You may not have time to write much in the right-hand column as you are listening. When the speaker is finished, you can go back and add more questions, predictions, and so on.

In some cases, you may want to include graphic organizers in your notes. For example, if a speaker describes a series of events, you might want to record these using a timeline. If a speaker gives pros and cons, you might want to use a pro-and-con chart. For more information on graphic organizers that you can use for taking notes, see Chapter 6, "Picture This! Notetaking and Graphic Organizers."

In some listening situations, such as in class, you may want to interact directly with the speaker by raising your hand and asking questions. Asking questions can help make clear what you do not understand. Do not be afraid to ask questions if possible. Bear in mind, however, that in test-taking situations, questions are usually not allowed.

After Listening

When you are done listening, glance quickly through your notes. Doing so will help you remember them. Make sure the notes are clear. Make any corrections that you need to make in them and fill in any gaps. Jot down your comments and reactions. Reading through your notes soon after taking them will make them easier to remember later.

Your Turn

Note to Teacher: The listening selections for the next two exercises follow on pages 169–70.

Exercise A *You will be listening to an article about some remarkable women. Your teacher will read the article aloud twice. The first time your teacher reads this article, listen carefully but do not take notes. The second time, take careful notes on your own paper, following the guidelines in this chapter. Then, using only your notes, answer each question below. Your notes will have to be thorough for you to answer the questions correctly.*

Note to Students: Here are the spellings of some names that you may need for your notes: Anne Frank, Hannah Senesh, Hungary, Yugoslavia, Yael Arad, Israel.

1. What war was going on when Anne Frank's family went into hiding?

   _____

2. How old was Anne when her family went into hiding?

   _____

3. How did Anne Frank tell about what she experienced during her two years in hiding?

   _____

4. How did Hannah Senesh get into Yugoslavia?

   _____

5. Besides being a freedom fighter, Hannah Senesh was also a writer. What did she write?

   _____

6. How old was Hannah Senesh when she died for her people?

   _____

7. Yael Arad was the first athlete from her country to win an Olympic medal. What country was she from?

   _____

8. In what sport did Yael Arad win a silver medal?

   _____

9. What city hosted the Olympics in which Yael Arad competed?

   _____

10. To whom did Yael Arad dedicate her medal?

   _____

Exercise B *You will be listening to a passage about ancient cave art. Your teacher will read the passage aloud twice. The first time your teacher reads the passage, listen carefully but do not take notes. The second time, take careful notes on your own paper, following the guidelines given in this chapter. Then, using only your notes, answer each of the following questions. Make sure that your notes are thorough.*

1. Which came first—houses, art, or writing?

   _____

2. How long ago did the earliest artists live?

   _____

3. Where are the cave paintings that the selection describes?

   _____

4. What did the artists have to figure out before they could create the paintings?

   _____

5. What are two of the animals that appear in the cave paintings?

   _____

6. During what age did the cave painters live? (Hint: How was the weather?)

   _____

More ▶

Meets
New York
Standards
1.A.1
1.A.3
1.A.4
1.A.6
1.B.1
1.B.4
2.A.1
2.A.2

7. It is possible that cave dwellers believed that their paintings had magic power to help them with certain activities. For which of the following activities might they have been seeking help?

_____

_____

_____

8. Which of the following is a true statement?

   Ⓐ Cave painters had magic powers that could be passed to people who touched them.

   Ⓑ Cave people had a lot of free time to make art because they had an easy life.

   Ⓒ Studying the art of ancient people like the cave dwellers can teach us about how they lived.

   Ⓓ The caves were like art museums where people paid money to come and see the paintings.

9. Which of the following statements is NOT true?

   Ⓐ Only modern civilizations have produced works of art.

   Ⓑ People were making art before they organized into towns.

   Ⓒ Cave people made paints that have lasted for many centuries.

   Ⓓ Woolly elephants, or mammoths, are now extinct.

10. The writer of this selection would PROBABLY agree with which of the following statements?

    Ⓐ Cave people were not very smart because they did not know how to write.

    Ⓑ Ancient artists have nothing in common with modern artists.

    Ⓒ The cave paintings are very simple, so they were probably made by children.

    Ⓓ Although they lived a long time ago and had primitive tools, cave painters made beautiful works of art.

Three Heroines
by Jill Wiseman

In the middle of World War II, a thirteen-year-old Jewish girl and her family went into hiding to escape from the Nazis, who were trying to exterminate her people. For two years, the girl and her family lived in some hidden rooms in an office building. During that time Anne Frank wrote her diary, which is now famous all over the world. In it we learn of some of the hardships the Jewish people faced during World War II. We also learn much about human courage and spirit.

Anne Frank is just one of many Jewish women who have given something special to the world. Another young woman who showed great bravery in World War II was Hannah Senesh. She wanted to help her people, so she joined the British army and trained for a daring mission to rescue Jews in Hungary. She parachuted into Yugoslavia and sneaked across the border into Hungary, only to be captured, imprisoned, tortured, and then killed at the age of twenty-three. In her short life, she managed to write beautiful poetry that has stood the test of time.

More recently, Yael Arad honored her people in another way. She represented Israel in athletic competitions all over the world. Yael became the first athlete from Israel ever to win an Olympic medal. At the 1992 Olympics in Barcelona, Spain, Yael won a silver medal in judo. She dedicated her medal to the eleven Israeli athletes who had been killed at the Olympics twenty years earlier in Munich, Germany. She helped the whole world remember her people, and she made Jews and Israelis everywhere proud. ○

Listening Selection #2

Ancient Artists
by Henry Aberle

People in every culture in every age have expressed themselves through art. Art existed long before writing appeared or villages were built. The earliest artists we know of lived in caves more than 20,000 years ago. They made beautiful paintings, mostly of people and animals, on the walls of caves in regions that are now France and Spain. The cave artists were very skillful at drawing. They also figured out how to make bright-colored paints, as well as the tools needed for painting.

We don't know for sure why these cave dwellers made their paintings. Maybe they thought that the paintings had magic power to help them hunt. In any case, the paintings teach us a lot about the way people lived during the Ice Age. The animals they hunted included some that are now extinct, such as cave bears, woolly rhinoceroses, and woolly elephants called mammoths. There were also animals living then that still exist, such as reindeer. The people who created these ancient paintings faced a constant struggle just to stay alive, but they managed to create works of art that have survived until today. ○

Return to the exercises at the beginning of the chapter, revise your work as necessary, and submit the exercises to your teacher for grading.

Chapter 8

Step by Step

The Writing Process for Examinations

Below is a writing prompt for a test. Do NOT write a response to the prompt. Instead, simply read the prompt. Then try your hand at the exercise that follows it. You will not be graded on the exercise at this time. At the end of the chapter, you will be directed to return to this exercise to revise and correct your work.

What subject do you like most in school? Imagine that you are helping to create a handbook for students coming into your grade. You have been asked to choose one subject that you really like and to write a paragraph about it. The paragraph will be included in the student handbook. The purpose of the paragraph will be to encourage students to take an interest in the subject. Show why students should be interested in this subject. Make sure that you describe three interesting activities or topics related to the subject as it is taught at your school.

Sample Writing Prompt from a Test

Your Turn

Exercise *Answer each question in complete sentences.*

Meets
New York
Standards
1.A.1
1.A.5
1.A.6
1.B.1
1.B.4
1.B.5
3.A.1

1. What is the topic of the piece of writing described in the prompt?

    _____

    _____

2. How long should the piece of writing be?

    _____

    _____

3. What purpose should the piece of writing serve?

    _____

    _____

4. Who is the intended audience for this piece of writing?

    _____

    _____

5. What specific information does the prompt say to include in the piece of writing?

    _____

    _____

6. What would be a good topic sentence for this piece of writing?

    _____

    _____

Step by Step

When people go on vacation, they usually do not simply jump into a car or an airplane and take off. First, they plan their trip. They answer questions like these:

- Where are we going?
- How will we get there?
- Where will we stay?
- What will we do there?
- How long will we stay?
- What do we need to bring?

Next, they make arrangements to be away from work or school. They make reservations, and, when the time comes, they pack. Then comes the actual travel and the trip. While on vacation, they might make changes to their scheduled activities. For example, they might decide to rent a car and visit the sights on their own instead of taking a guided tour. While driving, they might see a monument or spectacular view and make an unexpected stop there. After the trip, they might get together with family members or friends to tell them about the vacation. Taking a vacation is a process that involves several different parts, or stages. Writing is also a process. In this chapter, you will learn about the stages in the process of writing. You will also learn how to adapt what you do during each stage when writing for a test, such as the ELA exam.

Stages in the Process of Writing

The writing process has five stages, as follows:

Meets
New York
Standards
1.A.1
1.A.3
1.B.1
1.B.3
1.B.4
1.B.5
1.B.6
3.A.1
3.A.2
3.A.4
3.B.3
3.B.4

1 Prewriting

In this stage, you choose a subject to write about. You also choose the genre, or type, of writing that you want to do and the purpose that you want to achieve. You narrow your subject, if necessary. Then you come up with a main idea, which is expressed in your thesis statement or topic sentence. Finally, you gather ideas to use in your writing and organize these ideas in a reasonable way.

2 Drafting

In this stage, you put your ideas down on paper. At this point, you do not worry much about spelling, grammar, usage, and mechanics. When drafting, you think mostly about what you want to say, not about how you are saying it. The first version of your piece of writing is called the **rough draft.**

3 Evaluation and Revision

In this stage, you look over your rough draft. You try to find ways to make it better. You try to improve its content, focus, organization, and style. You make corrections or changes. You add, cut, move, or change material as needed. The purpose of evaluation and revision is to create a **final draft.**

4 Proofreading

In this stage, you make a clean copy and proofread it. When you **proofread,** you check your final draft for errors in grammar, usage, mechanics (including punctuation and capitalization), spelling, and manuscript form. Another name for proofreading is **copyediting.**

5 Publishing

In this stage, you share your writing with an audience.

On the next two pages, you will find a flow chart that shows the stages in the writing process in more detail.

The Writing Process

 Prewriting

Choose subject, genre, purpose, audience

Narrow/focus topic
   Use graphic organizer

Write thesis statement

Gather ideas
Brainstorm	Observe
Discuss	Recall
Freewrite	Research
Interview	Use graphic organizer

Organize ideas/plan the piece

   Use rough outline
      or
   Use graphic organizer

Graphic Organizers*

Analysis chart

Cause-and-effect chart

Comparison-and-contrast chart

Cycle chart

Double-entry ledger (T-chart)

Flow chart

Paragraph-planning chart

Pro-and-con chart

Reporter's questions chart

Sensory detail chart

Step-and-landing chart

Timeline

Tree diagram

Venn diagram

Word web/cluster chart

*For examples of these graphic organizers, see Chapter 6, "Picture This! Notetaking and Graphic Organizers."

 Drafting

Get it all down roughly

      or

Get main ideas down and fill in supporting details and examples later

      or

Create a careful, complete draft, revising as you go

"Don't think of a draft as a finished sculpture. Think of it as raw clay—the material you will shape into the finished piece."

Revision

Evaluate and revise...
    for audience.
    for purpose.
    for focus and elaboration.
    for structure and organization.
    for style and voice.
       for word choice.
       for sentence variety.
       for sound and for figurative language.

"Good writing is rewriting."

Meets
New York
Standards
1.A.1
1.A.3
1.B.1
1.B.3
1.B.4
1.B.5
1.B.6
3.A.1
3.A.2
3.A.4
3.B.3
3.B.4

 ## Proofreading

Proof...
    for manuscript form.
    for grammar and usage.
    for mechanics.
       for capitalization.
       for punctuation.
    for spelling.

 ## Publishing

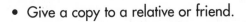

- Give a copy to a relative or friend.

- Read it aloud.

- Bind it into a book.

- Put it on a bulletin board.

- Send it to the school or local paper.

- Put it in your portfolio.

- Enter a writing contest.

- Post it online.

- Record or perform it.

The Writing Process

Prewriting

In the prewriting stage, you have to make a lot of decisions about your piece of writing. Follow these steps, though not necessarily in this order:

1. **Choose a subject and focus it.** Choose a subject and, if necessary, narrow or focus it to make it less broad. Here are some examples of general subjects that have been narrowed to create specific topics for writing:

GENERAL SUBJECT: Crafts

↓

NARROWED SUBJECT: Pottery

↓

MORE FOCUSED TOPIC: How to use a kiln to fire a pot

GENERAL SUBJECT: Holidays

↓

NARROWED SUBJECT: St. Patrick's Day

↓

MORE FOCUSED TOPIC: Who was St. Patrick?

2. **Choose a genre, or type of writing.** There are many genres, or types of writing. Here is a list of some of the genres: a short story, a poem, a letter, a memo, a paragraph, an essay, a news story, or a scene for a play.

When you are doing a writing assignment for class or taking a writing exam, the type of writing that you will do will usually be specified by the writing prompt.

3. **Choose a purpose for writing.** Your **purpose** is what you want the writing to accomplish. The following are some common purposes for writing:

- to describe
- to inform
- to persuade
- to tell a story

Often a piece of writing serves more than one of these purposes. For example, a biographical essay might tell a story and also inform.

4. **Choose an audience.** Again, your audience is usually determined by the assignment or writing prompt. Keeping your audience in mind will help you throughout the writing process. It can help you to decide, for example, whether the writing should be formal or informal. It can help you to decide whether to use simple or complex language. It can also help you decide how much background information to include. For example, if you are writing about contemporary popular music for an audience of parents, you might have to include a lot of details that an audience of kids would already know!

5. **Write a statement of your main idea.** For most kinds of writing, it is a good idea to begin by coming up with a sentence that states the main idea of your piece. This will help you to keep your writing focused and on track. When you are writing a single paragraph, you should state your main idea in the **topic sentence.** For an essay with more than one paragraph, the main or central idea should be expressed in the **thesis statement.**

6. **Gather details.** Once you have a statement of your main idea, you can start gathering details to use in your writing. To gather ideas for a piece of writing, you can try one or more of these techniques:

- **Brainstorming** is working with one or more partners to come up with as many ideas as you can, as quickly as you can, without stopping to judge the ideas.

- **Discussion** is talking about a subject with others.

- **Freewriting** is writing down whatever comes to mind about a subject without stopping to think about grammar, usage, mechanics, or spelling.

- **Interviewing** is questioning someone who is knowledgeable about a topic.

- **Recalling** is thinking about your own past experiences.

- **Research** is gathering information using print and electronic resources, such as reference works and the World Wide Web.

- **Reflection** is simply thinking about a topic on your own.

As you gather information, use a rough outline or a graphic organizer to record it. See Chapter 6, "Picture This! Notetaking and Graphic Organizers," for more suggestions.

7. Organize your ideas. Before you begin writing, it is a good idea to put the ideas that you have gathered into a sensible order. The following chart describes some of the most common ways to organize ideas:

Common Ways to Organize Ideas

Chronological order. Events are presented in the order in which they happened.

Spatial order. Details are presented in order of their position in space. For example, they might be presented from top to bottom, bottom to top, left to right, right to left, front to back, back to front, or in order of impression. When details are presented in **order of impression,** the first thing to grab the viewer's attention is presented first; the second, second; and so on.

Degree order. Ideas are presented from less to more or from more to less with regard to some quality. For example, a writer might present less familiar or important ideas first and more familiar or important ones later (or vice versa). Ideas organized by degree might be presented in order of familiarity, importance, value, interest, urgency, and so on.

Part-by-part order. Ideas organized in this way follow no overall organizational pattern. However, each idea should be logically connected to the one before it and to the one that follows it.

Problem-solution order. First, you present a problem. Then you present a solution to the problem.

Cause-and-effect order. First, you present one or more causes. Then you present one or more effects that result from the cause or causes. Another approach is to give the effect or effects first, followed by the cause or causes.

Comparison-contrast order. Comparison-contrast writing shows how two or more subjects are similar and how they are different. One way to organize comparison-contrast writing is first to describe the similarities and then to describe the differences. Another way is to describe one subject completely and then to describe how the other is similar and different.

One Student's Process: Prewriting

Shaundra read the writing prompt at the beginning of this chapter. Then she made the following decisions based on the prompt:

> Topic: Favorite subject at school
> Genre: Persuasive writing
> Purpose: To persuade other kids that the subject is interesting
> Audience: Students who will be in my grade next year
> Length: A paragraph—about five sentences

Shaundra decided that her focused topic would be science, since that was her favorite subject. Then she wrote the following statement of her main idea:

> One of the most interesting classes that you will take this year is science.

Shaundra used recalling and reflecting to come up with ideas about her topic. She created the following word web based on her recollections and reflections:

Then she organized her ideas into a rough outline. In the rough outline, she put her main ideas in degree order, ending with the part she liked best.

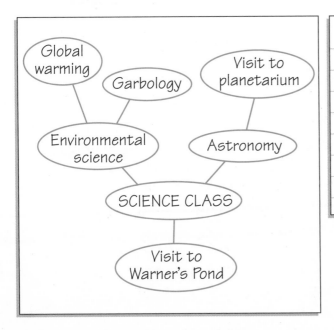

Your Turn

Exercise A *Read the following writing prompt and answer the questions about it, using complete sentences. Do NOT write a response to the prompt.*

WRITING PROMPT: Many people want to have pets but do not realize the responsibilities that come with pet ownership. Choose a type of pet you know well (a cat, dog, hamster, gerbil, or tropical fish, for example). Then write a brochure to be given out by veterinarians explaining what a responsible owner of that type of pet needs to do.

1. What is the writing topic?

    _____

2. Who is the audience?

    _____

3. What is the purpose?

    _____

4. What form of writing would you create in response to this prompt?

    _____

Exercise B *For each of the following general subjects, choose a narrower topic that is related. Then focus on a more specific aspect of that topic that could serve as a good topic for writing. An example has been done for you. Save your focused topics for the next exercise.*

GENERAL SUBJECT: Movies
↓
NARROW TOPIC: Special effects in movies
↓
NARROWER, MORE FOCUSED TOPIC: Special effects in the movie <u>Star Wars,</u>
<u>Episode II: Attack of the Clones</u>

1. GENERAL SUBJECT: Pets
    ↓
    NARROW TOPIC: _____
    ↓
    NARROWER, MORE FOCUSED TOPIC: _____

2. GENERAL SUBJECT: *Popular music*

   ↓

   NARROW TOPIC: _____

   ↓

   NARROWER, MORE FOCUSED TOPIC: _____

Meets
New York
Standards
1.A.1
1.A.3
1.A.6
1.B.1
1.B.2
1.B.5

3. GENERAL SUBJECT: *Extracurricular activities*

   ↓

   NARROW TOPIC: _____

   ↓

   NARROWER, MORE FOCUSED TOPIC: _____

4. GENERAL SUBJECT: *Games*

   ↓

   NARROW TOPIC: _____

   ↓

   NARROWER, MORE FOCUSED TOPIC: _____

Exercise C *Choose two of your focused topics from Exercise B. Imagine that you are going to write essays based on these topics. Write a thesis statement, or statement of your main idea, for each essay. (Do NOT write the essays. You are simply being asked to create two thesis statements.) Save your thesis statements for the exercises on page 186.*

1. TOPIC: _____

   THESIS: _____

   _____

2. TOPIC: _____

   THESIS: _____

   _____

Exercise D Yolanda created a word web to gather ideas for an essay on "Three Things That I Want to Accomplish in My Lifetime." Her word web appears below. Now she needs to organize her ideas before she can draft her essay. On your own paper, make a rough outline for Yolanda's essay based on the ideas in her word web.

Med school · Residency · My own practice

College

Study, get an M.D., & practice as a medical doctor

Meet husband · Marry

Date · Raise a family · Have kids

Three things I want to accomplish in my lifetime

Go to Central & South America

Go to Asia

See the world

Go to Europe

Go to Africa

The Writing Process

Drafting

The second stage in the writing process is drafting. **Drafting** is simply the process of getting your ideas down on paper. People draft in different ways. Some people draft very quickly. They just try to get their ideas on paper. They don't worry about cleaning up their writing until they go back later. Other people draft very slowly and carefully, correcting their work as they go. You should choose the drafting method that is comfortable for you. Sometimes you might change your drafting method depending on the situation. For example, when you are writing for a test, you should draft carefully because you will not have a lot of time to revise.

One Student's Process: Drafting

Shaundra was writing for a test, so she decided to draft slowly and carefully, following her rough outline. Here is the draft that she created:

Meets
New York
Standards
1.A.1
1.A.3
1.A.6
1.B.1
1.B.2
1.B.3
1.B.4
1.B.5
3.B.1
3.B.2

One Student's Rough Draft

One of the most interesting classes that you will take this year is science. One really interesting part of science is the enviromental science unit this unit has lessons on topics from global warming to garbology. In this unit, students can learn how they can help protect the enviroment wear they live. Another interesting science unit is the one on astronomy. And the visit to Warner's Pond. Thats really great because of learning about all the animals that live their. Like turtles and fish and insects and microscopic things. And how the animals depend on one another. Garbology by the way is the study of garbarge—how it is produced, whats in it and how to get rid of it.

topic sentence

Even though Shaundra was trying to draft carefully, she still needs to revise and proofread her writing to fix errors in spelling and grammar and to organize her ideas. For now, however, she has succeeded in getting her main idea and some supporting details down on paper.

Your Turn

Exercise A When you freewrite, you simply start writing whatever comes into your mind about a subject, without stopping to worry about whether you are making sense. You do not worry about organization, or about grammar, usage, mechanics, and spelling. Freewriting is an excellent way to gather ideas for writing.

On the lines below, try your hand at freewriting. Choose one of the topics from Exercise C on page 183. Then, just start writing about it. If you find your mind wandering away from the topic a little, try to come back to it again, but do not worry too much about what you are saying or how you are saying it. Simply write whatever comes into your head about the subject.

_____

_____

_____

_____

_____

_____

_____

_____

_____

_____

_____

_____

_____

Exercise B Use ideas from your freewriting to draft a paragraph on your own paper. Draft your paragraph slowly and carefully. Make sure that the paragraph begins with a topic sentence that states a main idea. Also make sure that the ideas in the body of the paragraph are organized and that they support the main idea. Save your response for use later in this chapter.

Evaluation and Revision

The third stage of the writing process is evaluation and revision. **Evaluation** is the process of looking over your writing to see how its organization and content can be improved. **Revision** is the process of making changes in your writing to improve it. When you revise, you can do any of the following.

You can **add** material
                                          secret
                                    a ^ notebook

You can **replace** material
                                    ~~some things~~ I need to do
                                    homework

You can **cut,** or **delete,** material
                                    a ~~really, really, very~~ long time

You can **move** material.
                                    to (boldly) go   or   to boldly (go)

When you evaluate your work, you can use the following checklist:

Meets
New York
Standards
1.A.3
1.A.4
1.B.1
1.B.3
1.B.4
1.B.5
3.A.1
3.A.2
3.A.4
3.B.3

Evaluation and Revision Checklist

Questions to Ask about Any Piece of Writing

✔ **Audience:**

❑ Is the piece appropriate to its audience?

❑ Is the writing as formal or informal as it should be?

❑ How much do readers know about this subject?

❑ Has the necessary background information been included?

✔ **Purpose:**

❑ Does the piece meet the purpose for which it was written?

❑ (For writing done for tests) Does the piece answer the test prompt completely?

More ▶

The Writing Process

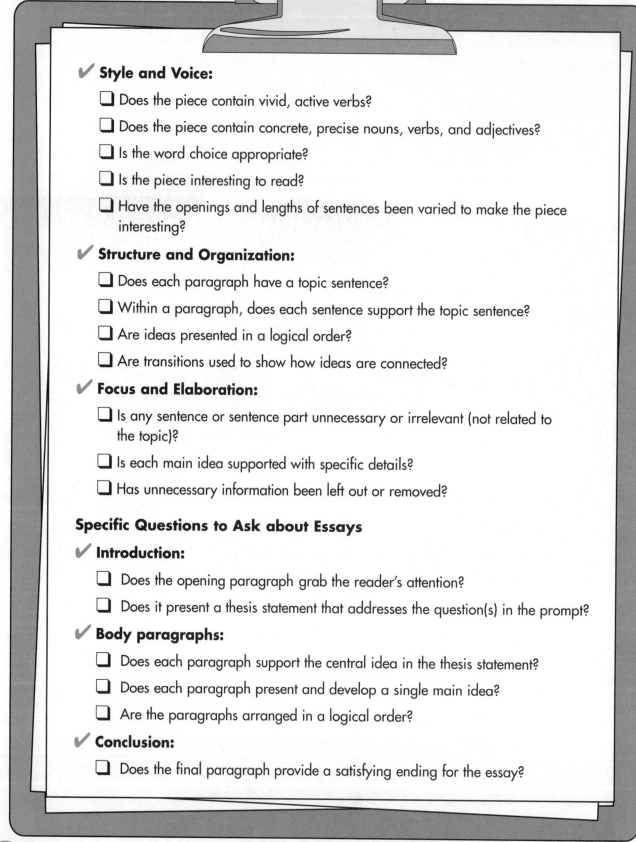

✔ **Style and Voice:**

❑ Does the piece contain vivid, active verbs?

❑ Does the piece contain concrete, precise nouns, verbs, and adjectives?

❑ Is the word choice appropriate?

❑ Is the piece interesting to read?

❑ Have the openings and lengths of sentences been varied to make the piece interesting?

✔ **Structure and Organization:**

❑ Does each paragraph have a topic sentence?

❑ Within a paragraph, does each sentence support the topic sentence?

❑ Are ideas presented in a logical order?

❑ Are transitions used to show how ideas are connected?

✔ **Focus and Elaboration:**

❑ Is any sentence or sentence part unnecessary or irrelevant (not related to the topic)?

❑ Is each main idea supported with specific details?

❑ Has unnecessary information been left out or removed?

Specific Questions to Ask about Essays

✔ **Introduction:**

❑ Does the opening paragraph grab the reader's attention?

❑ Does it present a thesis statement that addresses the question(s) in the prompt?

✔ **Body paragraphs:**

❑ Does each paragraph support the central idea in the thesis statement?

❑ Does each paragraph present and develop a single main idea?

❑ Are the paragraphs arranged in a logical order?

✔ **Conclusion:**

❑ Does the final paragraph provide a satisfying ending for the essay?

One Student's Process: Revision

As Shaundra looked over her draft (see page 185), she thought about how she could improve its organization and content. She realized that her original last sentence was out of place, so she moved it. She decided that her second point, about the astronomy unit, needed more details to back it up, so she added a sentence. In several places, she replaced vague words or phrases with ones that were more specific and concrete. Study the revisions that she made and see if you can tell why she made each one.

Notice that Shaundra added the phrase "the best of all, though" as a transition to show how her third example was related to the rest of the ideas in the paragraph. At the end of her piece, Shaundra also added a final clincher sentence to sum up her paragraph. Shaundra's changes improved her content and her organization, but she wasn't through yet.

One Student's Revised Draft

One of the most interesting classes that you will take this year

is science. One ~~really~~ interesting part of science is the enviromental
                   ^ especially

science unit this unit ~~has~~ lessons on topics from global warming
                       ^ includes

to garbology. In this unit, ~~students can~~ learn how ~~they~~ can help
                            ^ you will   ^   ^ you

to protect the enviroment wear ~~they~~ live. Another interesting
                          ^ you

During this unit ^ you will take a trip to the Planetarium at the Science Museum o
science unit is the one on astronomy. ~~And~~ the visit to Warner's

is the best of all ^ though o It's   you get to learn
Pond. ~~Thats~~ really great because ~~of learning~~ about all the animals
      ^   ^

                 painted   catfish   dragonflies   tadpoels o
that live their. Like turtles and ~~fish~~ and ~~insects~~ and ~~microscopic~~
                                  ^   ^   ^

          You will also learn   in the pond
~~things. And~~ how the animals depend on one another. Garbology
        ^

                g
~~by the way~~ is the study of garbarge—how it is produced, whats
        ^

           it is disposed of and recycled o
in it and how ~~to get rid of it.~~ All these interesting activities make
              ^

science at St. Elmo's a blast!

The Writing Process

Proofreading

The fourth stage in the writing process is proofreading. In this stage, you read over your work carefully to correct errors in grammar and usage. You also correct problems in punctuation and capitalization. At this stage, you may also want to correct errors in manuscript form, such as paragraphs that are not indented or improper margins. When you proofread your work, you can use the following checklist:

Proofreading Checklist

✔ **Manuscript Form**

- ❑ Every paragraph is indented.
- ❑ Ample margins have been left on either side.
- ❑ The writing is legible.

✔ **Grammar and Usage**

- ❑ Each verb agrees with its subject.
- ❑ Each pronoun has a clear noun to which it refers.
- ❑ Commonly confused pronouns, such as *I/me* and *who/whom,* are used correctly.
- ❑ Commonly confused words, such as *to/too/two, there/their/they're,* and *effect/affect,* are used correctly.
- ❑ There are no sentence fragments or run-ons.
- ❑ There are no double negatives.

✔ **Spelling**

- ❑ All words, including names, are spelled correctly.

✔ **Capitalization and Punctuation**

- ❑ Every sentence begins with a capital letter.
- ❑ All proper nouns and proper adjectives, including the names of people and places, begin with a capital letter.
- ❑ Every sentence contains an end mark—a period (.), exclamation mark (!), or question mark (?).
- ❑ Commas and other punctuation marks are used correctly.
- ❑ All direct quotations are enclosed in quotation marks.

One Student's Process: Proofreading

Shaundra made corrections in her grammar, usage, mechanics (capitalization and punctuation), spelling, and manuscript form. The following is her proofread paragraph. Her proofreading corrections are shown in blue.

Meets
New York
Standards
1.B.5
1.B.6
2.B.3
3.B.3
3.B.4

One Student's Proofreading Corrections

One of the most interesting classes that you will take this year is science. One especially interesting part of science is the enviromental science unit. this unit includes lessons on topics from global warming to garbology. Garbology is the study of garbage—how it is produced, whats in it and how it is disposed of and recycled. In this unit, you will learn how you can help to protect the enviroment wear you live. Another interesting science unit is the one on astronomy. During this unit, you will take a trip to the Planetarium at the Science Museum. The visit to Warner's Pond is the best of all, though. It's really great because you get to learn about all the animals that live their. Like painted turtles and catfish and dragonflies and tadpoels. You will also learn how the animals in the pond depend on one another. All these interesting activities make science at St. Elmo's a blast!

Notice that Shaundra made a number of important corrections. She added missing commas and apostrophes. She corrected misspelled words. She corrected a run-on sentence and a sentence fragment.

Using Revision and Proofreading Symbols

When you revise and proofread your writing, you should make changes as neatly as possible. When you want to cut or replace some material, simply draw a line through it or use a deletion mark:

deleted   deleted

Do not scratch through the material like this:

deleted

Using the standard revision and proofreading symbols will help you and others who read your writing to see your corrections clearly.

The Writing Process

The following chart shows some of the standard revision and proofreading symbols and how they are used:

Revision and Proofreading Symbols

Symbol and Example	Meaning of the Symbol
∧ bicycle built *for* two	Insert (add) something that is missing.
ℓ Paris in the ~~the~~ spring	Delete (cut) these letters or words.
/ e/treme skiing (*x*)	Replace this letter.
⎯ Say it ~~ain't~~ so. (*isn't*)	Replace this word.
∽ the glass delicate slippers	Transpose (switch) the order.
↶ give to the needy (gifts)	Move this word (or group of words)
◡ chair person	Close up this space.
ȣ tru ℓy	Delete (omit) this letter and close up the space.
≡ five portuguese sailors	Capitalize this letter.
(lc) / a lantern and a ʃleeping bag	Lowercase this letter.
¶ waves. "Help me," she cried.	Begin a new paragraph here.
⊙ All's well that ends well⊙	Put a period here.
∧ parrots˄ macaws, and toucans	Put a comma here.
˅ children˅s toys	Put an apostrophe here.
⊙ There are three good reasons⊙	Put a colon here.
# the grand#opening	Put a space here.

Publishing

The fifth and final stage in the writing process is publishing. In this stage, you share your writing with other people. Not all writing reaches this stage. For example, you might keep a diary or a journal that is meant just for you. In most cases, however, you will want other people to enjoy or benefit from what you have written.

There are many ways to publish. You can give a copy of your work to a relative or friend. You can read your work aloud to friends or classmates. You can post your work on a bulletin board or online. You can put it into a scrapbook that your teacher and/or family can look over later on. You can enter your work in a writing contest. You can record it or perform it for others.

Your Turn

Exercise A *Use revision and proofreading symbols to make the corrections described below. A sample correction has been made for you.*

EXAMPLE: Capitalize the proper nouns and adjectives in the following sentence, and add commas as necessary.

In the myths of ancient mexico belize and guatemala the jaguar

is often identified with the sun.

1. A **run-on sentence** is created when two separate sentences are written as though they were one. Correct the following run-on sentence by turning it into two sentences.

   Jaguars are endangered animals they are found in the rain forests,

   swampy grasslands, and mountains of Central and South America.

2. Move the phrase *in California* so that it follows the word *jaguar.*

   In 1860 the last wild jaguar was killed by hunters in California.

3. A **sentence fragment** is a group of words that does not express a complete idea. Correct the sentence fragment.

   One big cat that is very similar to the jaguar is the leopard.

   Which is found in the Old World.

4. Add commas to show items in a series. Capitalize the first letter of the first word of the sentence, and add a period at the end of the sentence.

   jaguars eat fish turtles caimans snakes deer sloths capybaras

   monkeys armadillos and many other creatures

5. Add apostrophes where needed in the words *jaguars* and *leopards,* and add a comma before the word *however.*

   A jaguars spots are different from a leopards however.

More ▶

Meets
New York
Standards
1.B.5
1.B.6
2.B.3
3.B.3
3.B.4

6. Make the first letter of the word *jaguar* lower case. Close the space between *spot* and *s*. Add a space between *small* and *spots*.

A Jaguar's spot s contain one or two smallspots inside a

rosette, or rose-shaped blotch.

7. Change the phrase *the same* to the word *similar*. Change the word *beefier* to the phrase *more stocky*.

A jaguar is the same in size to a leopard, but it is beefier.

8. Correct the spelling of *leopards*.

Some jaguars, like some leoperds, are black.

9. Add a comma after the phrase *Like some leopards*. Also add a period at the end of the sentence.

Like some leopards some jaguars are black

10. Combine the two groups of words to make one sentence by changing the first period to a comma and making *Whereas* lowercase. Capitalize the first letter in British, and correct the spelling of the word *syllables*.

Americans pronounce the word *jaguar* as two sylables.

Whereas the british pronounce it as three sylables.

Exercise B Use the Revision Checklist on pages 187–88 and the Proofreading Checklist on page 190 to revise and proofread the paragraph you wrote for Exercise B on page 186. Use the proofreading symbols to make corrections to your paragraph.

Return to the exercises at the beginning of the chapter, revise your work as necessary, and submit the exercises to your teacher for grading.

Chapter 9

Sentence Sense

Constructing and Editing Sentences

Read this passage about a famous landmark. The passage contains a number of errors. Then try your hand at the exercises that follow the passage. You will not be graded on the exercises at this time. At the end of the chapter, you will be directed to return to these exercises to revise and correct your work.

The Coliseum of Ancient Rome

by Anupam Chopra

[1] Imagine sitting in a large, outdoor arena and watching a sports event. [2] The day is warm and sunny the athletes look determined the crowd is filled with excitement. [3] Thousands of spectators cheer loudly for the athletes they admire. [4] On one side of the arena, the emperor addresses the noisy crowd. [5] Regally looks down to the arena floor. [6] Imagine you are sitting in the awesome Coliseum of ancient Rome. [7] This amazing place was both similar to and it differed from today's sports arenas.

[8] The emperor Vespasian began building the arena. [9] His son Titus, the next emperor, finished the construction. [10] Titus opened the arena in A.D. 80. [11] Since the emperors were from the Flavius family, the building was called the Flavian Amphitheater. [12] It got the name *Coliseum* because it stood near a colossal, or large, statue of the emperor Nero.

[13] The Coliseum was spacious; four levels of seats held more than 50,000 spectators. [14] People could go in and out quickly through the Coliseum's eighty

entrances. ¹⁵A system of corridors and stairways. ¹⁶People could move about easily. ¹⁷A large cloth could be stretched overhead to provide shade.

¹⁸The ancient Romans loved sports, and they especially enjoyed violent fights, and the Coliseum offered many bloody sports. ¹⁹In the mornings, events involving animals usually could be seen. ²⁰Sometimes humans hunted the animals, and other times, the animals fought each other or fought criminals. ²¹In the afternoon came the gladiators. ²²These men were slaves or criminals who received training. ²³Occasionally, women gladiators fought, as did men who volunteered in hope of becoming famous. ²⁴Armed in various ways, these gladiators knew danger was on the line. ○

Constructing and Editing Sentences (**197**)

Your Turn

Exercise A *Fill in the circle next to the correct answer to each multiple-choice question.*

1. What change, if any, should be made in sentence 2?
   - Ⓐ Add a comma after *sunny*.
   - Ⓑ Add the word *and* before *the athletes*.
   - Ⓒ Place a comma after *warm*.
   - Ⓓ Make three separate sentences.

2. The best way to improve sentences 4 and 5 is to
   - Ⓐ replace the period after *crowd* with a semicolon.
   - Ⓑ replace the word *noisy* with *loudly*.
   - Ⓒ make *Regally* lowercase and add *He* before it.
   - Ⓓ make no change.

3. What is the best way to improve sentence 7?
   - Ⓐ Place a comma after *to*.
   - Ⓑ Change *it differed* to *different*.
   - Ⓒ Make two separate sentences.
   - Ⓓ Make no change.

4. What is the best way to combine sentences 9 and 10?
   - Ⓐ His son Titus, the next emperor, finishing construction. He opened the arena in A.D. 80.
   - Ⓑ His son Titus the next emperor finished the construction he opened the arena in A.D. 80.
   - Ⓒ His son Titus, the next emperor, finished the construction and opened the arena in A.D. 80.
   - Ⓓ His son Titus finished construction, he opened the arena in A.D. 80.

5. What is the best way to correct sentences 15 and 16?
   - Ⓐ A system of corridors and stairways. Allowed people to move around the arena easily.
   - Ⓑ Moving about easily, a system of corridors and stairways was allowed.
   - Ⓒ There was a system of corridors and stairways, it allowed people to move around easily.
   - Ⓓ A system of corridors and stairways allowed people to move around the arena easily.

6. What is the best way to revise sentence 17 to call attention to the purpose of the cover?

   Ⓐ A large cloth could, to provide shade, be stretched overhead.

   Ⓑ A cloth could provide large shade overhead.

   Ⓒ Overhead, a large cloth could be stretched to provide shade.

   Ⓓ To provide shade, a large cloth could be stretched overhead.

7. How could you improve sentence 18?

   Ⓐ Split it into two or three separate sentences.

   Ⓑ Remove the comma after *fights.*

   Ⓒ Take out the word *especially.*

   Ⓓ Make no change.

8. What is the best way to revise sentence 19? (Hint: Make it active voice.)

   Ⓐ Events involving animals in the mornings usually could be seen.

   Ⓑ In the mornings, events involving animals could usually be seen by spectators.

   Ⓒ In the mornings, spectators usually could see events involving animals.

   Ⓓ In the mornings, animals could usually see events involving spectators.

9. What change would make sentence 22 more informative and specific?

   Ⓐ These men were slaves or criminals who received training and were taught.

   Ⓑ These men often were slaves or criminals who received training as professional fighters.

   Ⓒ Criminals, these men received training as slaves.

   Ⓓ These people trained in the Coliseum.

10. What is the best way to revise sentence 24?

   Ⓐ Take out the comma after *ways.*

   Ⓑ Split it into two sentences.

   Ⓒ Replace the word *various* with *different.*

   Ⓓ Change *danger was* to *their lives were.*

Exercise B *Some modern sporting events are played before small crowds. Others attract large crowds or no spectators at all. Think of a game you have watched in person or on television, and write a paragraph in which you describe the crowd. Explain whether the crowd's behavior had an effect on the players. Follow the guidelines shown below as you write your paragraph on your own paper.*

1. Include a topic sentence.

2. Write several sentences that are related to your topic sentence.

3. Use at least three of the four following sentence types: statements, questions, commands, and exclamations.

4. Vary the length, beginnings, and structure of your sentences.

5. Avoid sentence fragments and run-on sentences.

6. Use sentences in the active voice, not the passive voice.

Use the graphic organizer below to plan your paragraph. Write a rough draft on your own paper.

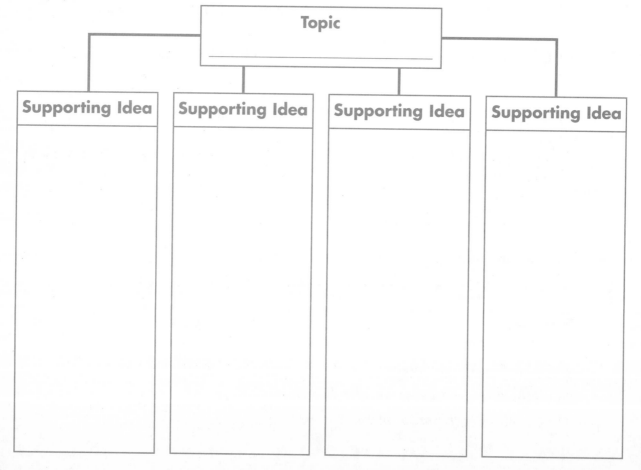

Topic

_____

| Supporting Idea | Supporting Idea | Supporting Idea | Supporting Idea |

Sentence Sense

Great chefs often do their own grocery shopping. Many shop every day, going to markets to buy fresh vegetables, fruits, fish, and so on. That's because one secret to making a great meal is having good ingredients.

Good ingredients play a key role in writing, too. One secret to good writing is creating a variety of well-crafted sentences. In this chapter, you will learn how to create well-crafted sentences. In the two chapters that follow, you will learn how to use sentences as ingredients in longer pieces of writing.

Sentence Types

When you write, you should use a variety of sentence types. You can divide sentences into different types based on their **functions,** or what they do. Sentences can perform four different functions.

Sentence Functions

A **declarative sentence** makes a statement. This type of sentence ends with a period.

EXAMPLES:

The Mound Builders were an ancient people.
They lived in what is now the eastern United States.

An **imperative sentence** gives a command or makes a request. This type of sentence usually ends with a period.

A strong or urgent command, however, may end with an exclamation point.

EXAMPLES:

Read this article about mounds.
Don't turn the page yet!

An **interrogative sentence** asks a question. This type of sentence ends with a question mark.

EXAMPLES:

What happened to the Mound Builders?
Do their descendants live today?

An **exclamatory sentence** expresses strong feeling. This type of sentence ends with an exclamation point.

EXAMPLES:

What an interesting culture they had!
It must have been difficult to build such large mounds with so few tools!

Read the following paragraph:

The Mound Builders lived along rivers in what is now the eastern United States. These ancient people built mounds of earth for various purposes. Important people were buried in some mounds. Sacred temples stood on the tops of others. The largest known mound is almost 100 feet tall and 975 feet long. The Mound Builders' only tools were their hands, digging sticks, and baskets to carry dirt. Building these mounds must have taken a lot of work.

Meets New York Standards
1.A.1
1.A.3
1.B.1
1.B.3
1.B.4
1.B.5
1.B.6
3.B.1
3.B.2
3.B.3
3.B.4

Constructing and Editing Sentences

The paragraph on the previous page contains only declarative sentences. Now read the revised version below. By using sentences of different types, the writer has made the paragraph more lively and interesting.

The Mound Builders lived along rivers in what is now the eastern United States. Why are these ancient people called "Mound Builders"? They built mounds of earth for various purposes. Important people were buried in some mounds, while sacred temples stood on the tops of others. The largest known mound is almost 100 feet tall and 975 feet long. Imagine using only your hands, digging sticks, and baskets to build such large mounds. Constructing these mounds must have taken a lot of work!

Sentence Structure

Sentences can also be classified by their **structure,** or how they are put together. A **simple sentence** contains one subject and one main verb, and it expresses a complete thought. Here are some ways a single subject and a single verb can be combined to make simple sentences:

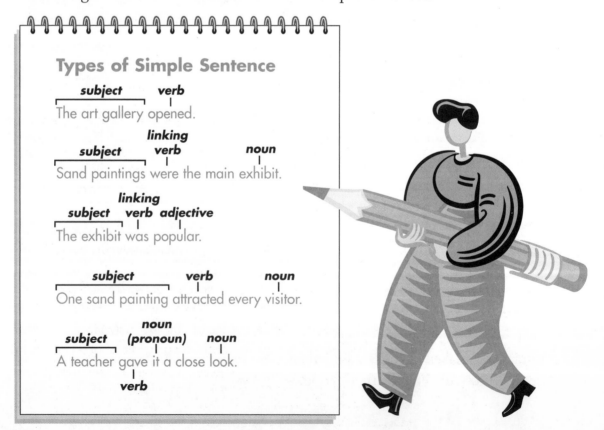

Types of Simple Sentence

subject	*verb*	
The art gallery opened.		

	linking	
subject	*verb*	*noun*
Sand paintings were the main exhibit.		

	linking	
subject	*verb*	*adjective*
The exhibit was popular.		

| *subject* | *verb* | *noun* |
| One sand painting attracted every visitor. | | |

	noun	
subject	*(pronoun)*	*noun*
A teacher gave it a close look.		
	verb	

Combining and Expanding Sentences

Simple sentences can be combined. They can also be expanded by adding new parts:

COMBINING: A teacher gave it a close look, and she called the work a masterpiece.

EXPANDING: Beautiful sand paintings by Navajo artists were the main exhibit last month.

By starting with a simple sentence and combining or expanding, you can build sentences that are quite interesting and complex.

Within a sentence, a **clause** is a group of words that has a subject and a verb. An **independent clause** is a complete thought that can stand alone as a simple sentence. It is sometimes called a **main clause.** A **dependent clause** expresses only part of a thought. It cannot stand alone as a sentence. A dependent clause is sometimes called a **subordinate clause.**

EXAMPLES:

INDEPENDENT CLAUSE: No one knows.

DEPENDENT CLAUSE: when the first sand painting was created

A **compound sentence** contains at least two independent clauses but no dependent clauses. To create a compound sentence, place a comma and a conjunction—*and, but, or, nor, for, so,* or *yet*—between the independent clauses.

INDEPENDENT CLAUSE (IC) + COMMA AND CONJUNCTION + INDEPENDENT CLAUSE

┌────── IC ──────┐   ┌───── IC ─────┐
The sand paintings are gorgeous, **but** they are not for sale.

┌────── IC ──────┐   ┌───── IC ─────┐
Sand paintings are beautiful, **and** they also serve a purpose.

Constructing and Editing Sentences

A **complex sentence** contains one independent clause and at least one dependent clause. Notice the way commas are used to set off clauses within complex sentences.

DEPENDENT CLAUSE (DC)   +   INDEPENDENT CLAUSE (IC)

┌──────*DC*──────┐ ┌──────────*IC*──────────┐
If you study Navajo culture, you will learn about sand painting.

INDEPENDENT CLAUSE   +   DEPENDENT CLAUSE

┌──────────*IC*──────────┐ ┌──────────*DC*──────────┐
Many Navajo know about sand painting because it is an ancient tradition.

DEPENDENT CLAUSE THAT INTERRUPTS AN INDEPENDENT CLAUSE:

┌──────────────────────*IC*──────────────────────┐
      ┌──────────*DC*──────────┐
Sand painting, which the Navajo call *iikaah*, is a traditional way of treating illness.

A sentence that contains two or more independent clauses and at least one dependent clause is called a **compound-complex sentence.** Notice where the commas appear in these compound-complex sentences.

DEPENDENT CLAUSE + INDEPENDENT CLAUSE + INDEPENDENT CLAUSE:

┌──────────*DC*──────────┐
Although some sand paintings are small,

┌──────*IC*──────┐
others are quite large,

┌──────────*IC*──────────┐
and several people work on them at once.

TWO INDEPENDENT CLAUSES WITH A DEPENDENT CLAUSE INTERRUPTING THE FIRST:

┌──────────────────────*IC*──────────────────────┐
      ┌──────────*DC*──────────┐
A director, who stands in the center of the work area, takes charge,

┌──────────*IC*──────────┐
and the other workers listen to him.

Read the following paragraph:

Meets
New York
Standards
1.B.5
1.B.6
2.B.3
2.B.4
3.A.1
3.A.2
3.A.4
3.B.3
3.B.4

One part of traditional Navajo belief is *hozho*. *Hozho* means "balance." Sometimes a person's *hozho* is upset. Then the person becomes ill. So the Navajo believe. Balance, therefore, must be restored. Then the person can get better. Sand paintings are a part of the traditional healing ceremony. A healer examines the sick person. He figures out the cause of the illness. Then he figures out what kind of sand painting the sick person needs. The colors and designs have religious importance. They are chosen carefully. The colors and designs have healing powers. The patient sits in the center of the sand painting for the last part of the healing ceremony. After that, the sand painting is destroyed.

The paragraph contains only simple sentences. When you read it aloud, it sounds a bit choppy. Compare it to the following revised paragraph. See how the paragraph flows more smoothly and becomes more interesting when its sentences have a variety of structures.

One part of traditional Navajo belief is *hozho,* which means "balance." The Navajo believe that when a person's *hozho* is upset, the person becomes ill. Balance, therefore, must be restored before the person can get better. Sand paintings are a part of the traditional healing ceremony. A healer examines the sick person and figures out the cause of the illness. Then he chooses colors and designs for their religious importance as well as their healing powers. For the last part of the healing ceremony, the patient sits in the center of the sand painting. Finally, the sand painting is destroyed.

Your Turn

Exercise A In the space provided, write the letter of the item in Column B that correctly identifies the type of sentence listed in Column A.

Column A	Column B
_____ 1. Healers play an important part in Navajo culture.	**a.** declarative sentence
_____ 2. I can't wait to learn more about sand paintings!	**b.** interrogative sentence
_____ 3. Where can I learn more about Navajo healers?	**c.** imperative sentence
_____ 4. Go to the library and check out a book on Navajo culture.	**d.** exclamatory sentence

Exercise B On the lines provided below, write a sentence in each of the forms described. An example of each type of sentence is provided for you.

1. Simple sentence: Subject + linking verb + adjective

   EXAMPLE: _Juan is twelve._ _____

   _____

   _____

2. Simple sentence: Subject + action verb + noun

   EXAMPLE: _Juan loves video games._ _____

   _____

   _____

3. Simple sentence: Subject + action verb + noun (pronoun) + noun

   EXAMPLE: _Juan loaned me a video game._ _____

   _____

   _____

4. Compound sentence: Independent clause + conjunction + independent clause

EXAMPLE: <u>I went to Juan's house, and we played video games.</u>

_____

_____

5. Complex sentence: Dependent clause + independent clause (in either order)

EXAMPLE: <u>When we were done playing, I walked home.</u>

_____

_____

6. Compound-complex sentence: Two independent clauses + dependent clause(s)

EXAMPLE: <u>My cousin Max, who lives in Ohio, is coming to visit next week, and he likes</u>

<u>video games, too.</u>

_____

_____

Constructing and Editing Sentences

Expanding and Combining Sentences

When you write, you should try to use a variety of sentence types. Using a wide variety of sentence types will make your writing more interesting. Two ways to introduce sentence variety into your writing are sentence expanding and sentence combining. **Sentence expanding** is simply the process of adding material to existing sentences. **Sentence combining** is the process of putting sentences or parts of sentences together to create compound, complex, and compound-complex sentences.

SENTENCE EXPANDING:

ORIGINAL: The Cherokee lived in a village.

EXPANDED: The Cherokee lived in an enormous village called Tenasi.

EXPANDED: The Cherokee lived in an enormous village called Tenasi, from which we get the name Tennessee.

SENTENCE COMBINING:

SEPARATE: Many Cherokee lived in the eastern part of the continent.
 +
SEPARATE: They were forcibly moved to the western part of the continent.
 +
SEPARATE: They were forcibly moved by the U.S. Army.

COMBINED: Many Cherokee who lived on the eastern part of the continent were forcibly moved to the western part of the continent by the U.S. Army.

Expanding Sentences

You can add words, phrases, and clauses to a sentence to make it clearer, more descriptive, or more informative.

Ways to Expand Sentences

✔ Add **modifiers,** or words that describe other words and make their meaning more specific.

ORIGINAL: That twig is an insect.

EXPANDED: That brown, swaying twig is actually an unusual insect.

✔ Add **prepositional phrases,** or groups of words beginning with a preposition and ending with a noun or pronoun. Prepositional phrases can act as modifiers.

ORIGINAL: The stick insect is a master of disguise.

EXPANDED: With its plantlike shape, the stick insect is a master of disguise.

✔ Add **appositive phrases,** or groups of words consisting of an appositive and its modifiers. An **appositive** is a noun or pronoun placed next to another noun or pronoun to identify or explain it.

ORIGINAL: The inchworm can look like a twig, too.

EXPANDED: The inchworm, a type of caterpillar, can look like a twig, too.

✔ Add **predicates,** or verb phrases, to give more information.

ORIGINAL: Some butterflies resemble leaves.

EXPANDED: Some butterflies resemble leaves and blend in with their surroundings.

✔ Add **dependent clauses,** or groups of words containing a subject and a verb, to give more information.

ORIGINAL: The dead leaf mantis can easily hide on a forest floor.

EXPANDED: Because it is shaped like a dried-up leaf, the dead leaf mantis can easily hide on a forest floor.

✔ Add **verb phrases,** including **participial phrases** and **infinitive phrases,** to describe and give information. A **participle** is a verb form that ends in *–ing, –ed, –d, –en,* or *–t.* Participles often function as adjectives. An **infinitive,** the most basic form of a verb, often follows the word *to* and can act as an adjective or adverb.

ORIGINAL: A thorn bug looks dangerous.

EXPANDED: Resting on a branch, a thorn bug looks dangerous.
     (participial phrase added)

ORIGINAL: You must look closely.

EXPANDED: To tell a thorn bug from a real thorn, you must look closely.
     (infinitive phrase added)

Meets New York Standards
1.B.5
1.B.6
2.B.3
2.B.4
3.B.3
3.B.4

Constructing and Editing Sentences

Read the following paragraph:

The peppered moth is a fascinating insect. Its original coloring helped it blend in with various background items until its environment changed. Soot filled the air. Birds could then find the peppered moths. Peppered moths with dark wings could survive better. Darker moths had more offspring. The moth population changed.

Here is a revised version of the paragraph. Notice how expanding the sentences makes the writing more informative and more interesting.

The peppered moth of England is a fascinating insect. Its original coloring, white with small black spots, helped it blend in with various background items until its environment changed. As more and more factories were built, soot from chimneys filled the air and covered everything. Birds could then find the peppered moths because their pale wings stood out against the dark soot. Peppered moths with dark wings were able to survive better than their lighter cousins could. Darker moths had more offspring, and their numbers grew. The moth population changed dramatically in a short period of time.

Combining Sentences

Take a look at your favorite book or short story. How does the author construct the sentences? Do they all have the same structure? Are they all the same length? Most likely, the author uses a variety of sentence structures and a combination of short and long sentences. An important element of writing is sentence variety. A piece of writing that contains sentences that vary in length and structure is more engaging for the reader.

One way to vary sentences in your writing is to combine short sentences to make longer ones. The chart below shows some ways to combine sentences:

Meets
New York
Standards
1.B.5
1.B.6
2.B.3
2.B.4
3.B.3
3.B.4

Ways to Combine Sentences

✔ **Move individual words.**

SEPARATE: The Venus flytrap is a plant. It is carnivorous.

COMBINED: The Venus flytrap is a carnivorous plant.

✔ **Turn a sentence or sentence parts into a phrase; then move the phrase.**

- **Use a participial phrase.**

    SEPARATE: It is often grown as a houseplant. It has leaves with spines along the edge.

    COMBINED: Often grown as a houseplant, it has leaves with spines along the edge.

- **Use an appositive phrase.**

    SEPARATE: Insects are attracted to the plant's nectar. Nectar is a sweet-smelling substance that some insects can't resist.

    COMBINED: Insects are attracted to this plant's nectar, a sweet-smelling substance that some insects can't resist.

- **Use a prepositional phrase.**

    SEPARATE: When the insect lands on a leaf, the plant reacts. The insect's presence causes the reaction.

    COMBINED: When the insect lands on a leaf, the plant reacts to the insect's presence.

✔ **Move clauses.**

- **Use a clause to form a compound sentence.**

    SEPARATE: The leaf snaps shut. Digestive juices begin their work.

    COMBINED: The leaf snaps shut, and digestive juices begin their work.

- **Use a clause to form a complex sentence.**

    SEPARATE: Soon digestion is complete. The leaf opens again.

    COMBINED: When digestion is complete, the leaf opens again.

Read the following paragraph. Notice how the use of too many short sentences makes the writing sound choppy.

> The sundew is a carnivorous plant. It is like the Venus flytrap. The sundew has tentacles. Those tentacles are sticky. They are used to catch prey. An insect lands. It immediately becomes stuck. The plant closes around the insect. The insect is doomed. It may struggle. It cannot escape. The sundew releases digestive juices. It begins to feed on its prey.

Here is a revision of the paragraph. Notice how the writer has improved the flow of the paragraph by combining sentences.

> Like the Venus flytrap, the sundew is a carnivorous plant. The sundew has sticky tentacles, which the plant uses to catch prey. When an insect lands, it immediately becomes stuck. Then, the plant begins to close around the insect. The doomed insect may struggle, but it cannot escape. Releasing digestive juices, the sundew begins to feed on its prey.

Your Turn

Exercise A *Many children's poems, like "The House That Jack Built" and "There Was an Old Woman Who Swallowed a Spider," are created by expanding the first line. The poet takes a line and builds on it by adding phrases or clauses. Try creating your own bit of silly writing by expanding a sentence. Follow this example:*

1. This is the pen.

2. This is the pen that wrote the poem.

3. This is the pen that wrote the poem that made Molly laugh.

4. This is the pen that wrote the poem that made Molly laugh so hard that she didn't see the car.

5. This is the pen that wrote the poem that made Molly laugh so hard that she didn't see the car that ran over her foot.

6. This is the pen that wrote the poem that made Molly laugh so hard that she didn't see the car that ran over her foot that swelled up so big.

7. This is the pen that wrote the poem that made Molly laugh so hard that she didn't see the car that ran over her foot that swelled up so big that she had to wear a clown's shoe.

Create your poem on the lines below by expanding the following sentence. Add at least five phrases or clauses to the opening sentence.

SENTENCE TO EXPAND: This is the dog.

1. This is the dog that _____.

2. _____
   _____

3. _____
   _____

4. _____
   _____

5. _____
   _____

Exercise B *Follow the directions in italics to combine the sentences below.*

1. *Combine this pair of simple sentences into a compound sentence.*
    (Use the word *but* between the two sentences.)

    Some sand painting artists buy colored sand.
    Others make their own.

    _____

    _____

2. *Combine this pair of simple sentences into a complex sentence.*
    (Use the word *Because* at the beginning of the first sentence.)

    The sand painters respect their art.
    They work with care.

    _____

    _____

3. *Combine these three simple sentences into a compound-complex sentence.*
    (Use the word *If* at the beginning of the first sentence and the word
    and between the second and the third sentences.)

    The sand is not spread correctly.
    It will look too weak or too lumpy.
    The sand painting will be ruined.

    _____

    _____

    _____

Exercise C *Read the following paragraph. Then, on the lines below, revise the paragraph. Follow the instructions for combining the numbered pairs of sentences.*

¹Pitcher plants are rare carnivorous plants. ²Their bodies are shaped like pitchers. They hold digestive juices. ³The plant produces nectar. It attracts insects. ⁴Insects slip on the leaves and fall inside the pitcher. ⁵Then digestive juices go to work. These are chemicals that dissolve and consume the prey. ⁶Most of the plants' meals are insects. Frogs and small birds have also been found inside pitcher plants.

1. Combine the pair of sentences labeled (2) to form a complex sentence. (Add the word *which* after *bodies,* replace the period after *pitchers* with a comma, and remove the word *They.*)

    _____

    _____

2. Combine the pair of sentences labeled (3) to form a complex sentence. (Remove the period after *nectar,* and replace the word *It* with *that.*)

    _____

    _____

3. Use an appositive phrase to combine the pair of sentences labeled (5). (Take the words highlighted in blue from the second sentence in that pair, and add them to the first sentence after the word *juices.* Use commas to separate that phrase from the rest of the sentence.)

    _____

    _____

4. Combine the sentences labeled (6) to form a complex sentence. (Add the word *Though* to the beginning of the first sentence, and replace the period after *insects* with a comma.)

    _____

    _____

Your Turn

Exercise D *Read the following paragraph. Then, on the lines below, revise the paragraph. Follow the instructions for expanding and combining some of the numbered sentences.*

¹Some insects protect themselves. ²They do this by imitating other insects. ³The viceroy butterfly resembles the monarch butterfly. ⁴The resemblance is in wing shape, coloring, and markings. ⁵Most birds do not like the taste of monarch butterflies. ⁶They prefer to look for a better meal. ⁷The predators are fooled by the viceroy butterfly's appearance. ⁸They leave the viceroy butterfly alone. ⁹The viceroy butterfly has adapted well to its environment. ¹⁰It is just one of thousands of insect species that use mimicry.

1. Use a prepositional phrase to expand sentence 1. Take the words highlighted in blue from sentence 2 to create the phrase.

    _____

    _____

2. Use a prepositional phrase to expand sentence 3. Take the words highlighted in blue from sentence 4 to create the phrase.

    _____

    _____

    _____

3. Combine sentences 7 and 8 using a comma and the word *and*.

    _____

    _____

    _____

4. Use an appositive phrase to expand sentence 9. Take the words highlighted in blue from sentence 10 to create the appositive.

    _____

    _____

Constructing and Editing Sentences

Editing Your Sentences

No two professional writers sound exactly alike. There is a big difference, for example, between the sound of a book by J. K. Rowling, author of the Harry Potter series, and one by J. R. R. Tolkien, author of *The Lord of the Rings*. The unique sound of a particular person's writing is called his or her **voice.** The characteristics of a piece of writing that give it a particular sound make up a writer's **style.** In this section of the chapter, you will learn how to edit, or change, your sentences to vary your style. This will help you to create your own voice.

Creating Sentences with Style

- **Vary your sentence openings.**

  BEGIN WITH A MODIFIER: Excitedly, the chimpanzee called to its group.

  BEGIN WITH A PREPOSITIONAL PHRASE: In a few moments, the other chimpanzees arrived.

  BEGIN WITH A DEPENDENT CLAUSE: After the chimpanzees had eaten, they rested.

- **Vary your sentence length.**

  USE A MIX OF SHORT AND LONG SENTENCES: There are five known kinds of apes: bonobos, chimpanzees, gibbons, gorillas, and orangutans. Bonobos were the last ape species to be identified. They live in the Congo River Basin. Bonobos, also known as pygmy chimpanzees, are known for their peacefulness, their close social bonds, and their equal treatment of males and females of their species.

- **Vary your sentence structure.**

  ORIGINAL: Bonobos live in only one place. They live in the Democratic Republic of Congo, or DRC. The DRC used to be called Zaire.

  REVISED: Bonobos live in only one place. Formerly known as Zaire, their home is now called the Democratic Republic of Congo, or DRC.

- **Change sentences with passive voice to the active voice.**

  ORIGINAL: The left bank of the Congo River is inhabited by bonobos.

  REVISED: Bonobos live on the left bank of the Congo River.

- **Correct sentence structure to make it parallel.**

  ORIGINAL: Bonobos have long arms, broad feet, and their toes are fairly short.

  REVISED: Bonobos have long arms, broad feet, and fairly short toes.

- **Emphasize particular ideas by changing the order of the words.**

  ORIGINAL: Read on to learn more about chimpanzees.

  REVISED: To learn more about chimpanzees, read on.

Constructing and Editing Sentences

Correcting Mistakes

After you have created a piece of writing, you should look it over to find ways to improve it. Follow the guidelines below to correct common errors in sentences:

Correcting Mistakes

- **Avoid wordiness.**

  ORIGINAL: At the present time, chimpanzees face considerable danger in the form of hazards introduced into their world by the presence of humans.

  REVISED: Today, chimpanzees face danger from humans.

- **Correct sentence fragments.**

  ORIGINAL: Cutting down large parts of Africa's forests.

  REVISED: Humans are cutting down large parts of Africa's forests.

- **Correct run-on sentences.**

  ORIGINAL: People want the land to plant crops and to build houses, that is why they clear the land.

  REVISED: People clear the land because they want to plant crops and build houses.

- **Revise stringy sentences.**

  ORIGINAL: Land developers are moving farther into undeveloped areas, and bringing in food becomes more expensive, and hunting game animals remains inexpensive and convenient, and that is why some chimpanzees are hunted for food.

  REVISED: As land developers move farther into undeveloped areas, bringing in food becomes more expensive. However, hunting game animals remains inexpensive and more convenient. For this reason, some chimpanzees are hunted for food.

- **Correct dangling modifiers (words that describe a noun or pronoun which is not in the sentence).** (Hint: Who is hoping to become rich?)

  ORIGINAL: Hoping to become rich, young chimpanzees are caught and sold as pets.

  REVISED: Hoping to become rich, poachers trap and sell young chimpanzees as pets.

- **Correct misplaced modifiers (words that describe the wrong word in a sentence).** (Hint: Where are the politicians working?)

  ORIGINAL: Some politicians are working in the wild to protect chimps.

  REVISED: Some politicians are working to protect chimps in the wild.

Your Turn

Exercise A *Each sentence below is an example of a type of sentence error. Rewrite the sentences correctly on the lines provided.*

Meets
New York
Standards
1.B.5
1.B.6
2.B.3
2.B.4
3.A.1
3.A.2
3.A.4
3.B.3
3.B.4

1. RUN-ON: Typically, chimpanzees live in a group with a few dozen members, smaller bands within the group also exist.

    _____

    _____

2. SENTENCE IN PASSIVE VOICE: Within the group, hunting and protection duties are taken care of by the males.

    _____

    _____

3. STRINGY SENTENCE: Most of the time, related female chimpanzees stay together, but sometimes females from one small band may move to another small band, and occasionally they will join a different large group.

    _____

    _____

    _____

    _____

4. WORDY SENTENCE: When traveling about, young chimps of an early age ride on their mothers' backs for the purpose of transportation.

    _____

    _____

5. FAULTY PARALLELISM: The study of chimpanzee behavior is both fascinating and there are rewards to be had, too.

    _____

    _____

More ▶

Your Turn

6. **RUN-ON:** Chimpanzees patrol their territories, they chase away members of rival troops who cross their borders.

_____

_____

7. **MISPLACED MODIFIER:** Some chimpanzees hold their hands during grooming above their heads.

_____

_____

8. **DANGLING MODIFIER:** Keeping their arms down, grooming is carried out differently in other groups.

_____

_____

9. **FRAGMENT WITH FAULTY PARALLELISM:** Often show anger by hooting and screech when they are afraid.

_____

_____

10. **MISPLACED MODIFIER (PARTICIPIAL PHRASE):** Moving about in tops of trees, visitors to the Gombe Game Reserve often see foraging chimpanzees.

_____

_____

Meets
New York
Standards
1.B.5
1.B.6
2.B.3
2.B.4
3.A.1
3.A.2
3.A.4
3.B.3
3.B.4

Jane Goodall's Chimpanzee Discoveries

[1]We can thank Jane Goodall for much of what we know about chimpanzees. [2]She started observing wild chimpanzees in 1960. [3]At that time, members of the scientific community believed that only humans used tools. Boy, were they wrong. [4]According to Goodall, a twig was stripped of its leaves by a chimpanzee and then was used to pull tasty termites out of a nest. [5]Goodall also observed that chimpanzees exhibit such "human" emotions as happiness, sorrow, and are compassionate. [6]Jane Goodall also learned that chimpanzees are not strict vegetarians. [7]Sometimes they hunt. Sometimes they kill animals. Then they eat the meat. [8]Another observation, chimpanzees have been known to stare at waterfalls for many minutes, perhaps they share our appreciation and wonder at the beauty of nature.

1. What is the best way to improve the pair of sentences labeled 3?
   - Ⓐ At that time, science members believed that only humans incorrectly used tools.
   - Ⓑ At that time, scientists mistakenly believed that only humans used tools.
   - Ⓒ At that time, chimpanzees believed that only humans used tools.
   - Ⓓ Make no change.

2. What is the best way to revise sentence 4?
   - Ⓐ A chimpanzee stripped a twig of its leaves and then was used to pull tasty termites out of a nest, according to Goodall.
   - Ⓑ According to Goodall, a twig was stripped of its leaves by a chimpanzee and then using it to pull tasty termites out of a nest.
   - Ⓒ According to Goodall, a chimpanzee stripped a twig of its leaves and then used the twig to pull tasty termites out of a nest.
   - Ⓓ Make no change.

More ▶

3. What is the best way to improve sentence 5?

Ⓐ Change *are compassionate* to *compassion.*

Ⓑ Take out the commas after *happiness* and *sorrow.*

Ⓒ Take out *Goodall also observed.*

Ⓓ Make no change.

4. What is the best way to combine the three sentences labeled 7 into one sentence?

Ⓐ They hunt, and they kill animals, and they eat meat. Sometimes.

Ⓑ They eat meat at the times they hunt, and sometimes they kill animals.

Ⓒ They eat meat at times, and sometimes they kill animals. When they hunt.

Ⓓ Sometimes they hunt and kill animals and then eat the meat.

5. What is the best way to improve sentence 8?

Ⓐ Chimpanzees have also been known to stare at waterfalls for many minutes. Perhaps they share our wonder at the beauty of nature.

Ⓑ Another observation is chimpanzees stare at waterfalls for many minutes. Appreciating the beauty of nature.

Ⓒ Staring at waterfalls, nature seems very beautiful to the chimpanzees who observe it.

Ⓓ Make no change.

Return to the exercises at the beginning of the chapter, revise your work as necessary, and submit the exercises to your teacher for grading.

Chapter 10

Perfect Paragraphs

Main Ideas and Supporting Details

223

Read this informative essay about the theater. Then try your hand at the exercises that follow the essay. You will not be graded on the exercises at this time. At the end of the chapter, you will be directed to return to these exercises to revise and correct your work.

Behind the Scenes

by Rick Poulos

Most theatergoers think of actors as the stars of a play. Behind the scenes, though, there are many people who make important contributions to every theatrical performance. Among the most important behind-the-scenes members of a theatrical team are the director, the set and lighting designers, and the costume manager.

Although others play key roles on and off the stage, in many ways, the director is the team leader for a play. The director of a play is much like the coach of a sports team. He or she studies the play carefully and decides on the best approach. The director then  chooses the actors who will make up the cast. Another duty of the director is to supervise practice—all the rehearsals. At rehearsal, the director helps the actors perform at their best. In each scene of the play, he or she coaches the actors as they deliver their lines. The director also suggests gestures and movements that will be effective on stage.

Two other important members of a theater team are the set and lighting designers. The set designer is responsible for the physical "look" of a production. The set designer must keep in mind all the changes in location and mood that may occur during the play. A set may be as simple as a chair and table

Costumes can make characters in a play seem more or less believable. They add to the illusion created on the stage by the actors and set and lighting designers.

The performers, of course, are a key element in the success of any dramatic production. No production would be possible, however, without the contributions of the director, the set and lighting designers, and the costume manager. It takes teamwork among many people, offstage and on, to put on a successful play. ○

on stage, or it may be more elaborate. The lighting designer for a play usually works very closely with the set designer. For example, the set designer might want one part of the stage to be brightly lit in one scene and full of shadows in the next. Together, sets and lighting can have a powerful impact on the emotions of the audience.

Finally, every theater production team needs a costume manager. This person must work closely with the director. For example, if the director decides to modernize a play, the costume manager must design modern costumes instead of historical ones. The costume manager must also work closely with the performers. He or she is responsible for seeing that every costume fits and that each one is stored properly. As with set and lighting design, the costumes contribute to the overall mood or atmosphere created in the play.

Your Turn

Exercise A The essay you have just read is five paragraphs long. It follows a standard format, starting with an introductory paragraph and ending with a concluding paragraph. In between are three body paragraphs. Look back at the paragraph about the costume manager (the third body paragraph). On the first two lines below, write the topic sentence of that paragraph. Then list two more examples the writer uses to make his point. Next, list a transitional word or group of words that the writer uses to connect the ideas in one sentence to the next. Some examples are provided to help you get started.

TOPIC SENTENCE: _____

_____

SUPPORTING IDEAS (EXAMPLES):

1. The costume manager must make sure the costumes fit. _____

2. _____

3. _____

WORDS OR PHRASES (GROUPS OF WORDS) THAT CONNECT IDEAS:

1. For example _____

2. _____

Exercise B Imagine that your class is putting on a play. Your teacher has asked every student to help out in some way. Which theater "job" would you like to do most? What experience or talents do you have that you think make you well suited for this job? On your own paper, write a paragraph-length response. Use information from the essay as well as any additional knowledge that you have of theater productions. Your paragraph should include the following:

• A clear topic sentence

• At least three supporting sentences that develop and support the main idea

• At least one quotation from the passage

Perfect Paragraphs

A fine painting is made up of many elements, including shape and color. Depending on their purpose, some painters keep their work very simple. They may use only one or two colors and only a few bold shapes or strokes on the canvas. Other painters create elaborate murals. They may use a complicated pattern of shapes, colors, and details to express their ideas.

If you read different types of writing, you will notice that paragraphs also come in different shapes and sizes. Some paragraphs are short and simple. Others are longer and more elaborate. As in painting, the writer usually starts with an idea and then fills in some details. The main idea (or, in a longer piece, a series of ideas) provides the basic form of the piece. The details the writer chooses to illustrate each main idea are important; they help the rest of the piece of writing take shape. By choosing the right details and examples, you can add color and depth to your own writing. In this chapter, you will learn how to use details to support your ideas and create well-written paragraphs.

What Is a Paragraph?

A **paragraph** is a unit of writing that communicates a main idea. Most paragraphs are a group of sentences that are all about one idea or one aspect of a topic. You can recognize a paragraph because the first line is indented. The first sentence in a paragraph usually introduces the topic, or main idea, of the paragraph. Then the sentences in the rest of the paragraph develop that idea. Many paragraphs, however, do not follow this model.

A newspaper writer, for example, often writes in short paragraphs that are only one sentence long. The first paragraph of a news story is often a colorful "lead" that is designed to catch your eye. In the lead sentence, the writer usually tells you the answers to the "reporter's questions": *who, what, where,* and *when.* If you want to know more about the topic, such as *how* or *why,* you have to read more paragraphs.

Main Ideas and Supporting Details

Here is the first paragraph of a review of a play that was a success on opening night. The review appeared in a newspaper. Notice that the first paragraph is only one sentence long.

> When the curtain came down on last night's long-awaited revival of Shakespeare's *Macbeth* at the Lyceum, there was little doubt that the audience had witnessed a memorable evening in the theater.

Paragraph (Review of a Play)
from a Newspaper

The type of writing usually influences the shape and structure of the writer's paragraphs. Writers use different paragraphs for different purposes. A writer uses one kind of paragraph to explain the steps in a process. He or she uses another kind to compare two things, two places, or two people. When a writer is telling a story, he or she will use another type of paragraph: The writer will often just describe a series of events, one after another. In the introductory paragraph of a narrative, the writer usually "sets the scene" for the rest of the action, as shown in the following example.

> It was only three days till opening night. The previous rehearsals had gone well, but the dress rehearsal was a complete flop. I tried to console myself with the old saying that a poor dress rehearsal means a winner of an opening night.

Paragraph from a Short Story

Sometimes a writer lets a story unfold by letting the characters tell it in dialogue form. Each time a new person begins speaking, the writer must begin a new paragraph.

> "I'm having some problems memorizing my part for the school play," Nan told Robert.
> Robert answered, "What I always do is break a scene down into small sections, and then I work on each section separately."

Dialogue Paragraphs from a Story

Writing a Paragraph in Standard Form

As you can see, paragraphs take many shapes and forms, depending on the writers' purposes. In most of the writing you do for school, however, your purpose will be to persuade or to inform. When you are doing this type of writing, your paragraphs should be in standard form. **The paragraphs that you write in response to ELA reading questions should be in standard form as well.** A **paragraph in standard form** focuses on a single main idea. It begins with a **topic sentence** that introduces this main idea. It continues with at least two or three sentences that are related to that idea. In those sentences, you should provide **supporting details** or examples that illustrate or explain your main idea. At the end of the paragraph, you may wish to sum up your main point in a **concluding sentence.** This type of sentence is also called a **clincher sentence** because it reinforces your main idea.

Topic Sentences

Whenever you are writing to explain or inform, your main idea should stand out clearly in a topic sentence. In the following paragraph, the topic sentence appears at the beginning.

> In the preparation of a play for performance, there are three types of rehearsal. In scene rehearsals, the actors work with the director on the interpretation of each scene, in any order. In a second type of rehearsal, called a technical rehearsal, the entire play is performed in proper sequence to make sure that all the lighting, props, and sets are ready. Finally, in a dress rehearsal shortly before the play's opening, the director supervises a last run-through. This time, however, all the actors are in full costume. They perform the play as if they are in front of an audience.

Paragraph with Opening Topic Sentence

Now look at another paragraph that opens in a different way. The writer is using a question as an interesting lead to capture the reader's attention. The topic sentence is the second sentence, not the first. In this case, the topic sentence is **embedded** in the middle of the paragraph.

> In the theater, who manages the finances? The producer is in charge of raising and spending money for a play's production. A play on Broadway in New York City, for example, may have a budget that runs into millions of dollars! The producer must rent a theater for the performance. He or she also must make sure that all the actors, staff, and suppliers get paid. Finally, the producer supervises ticket sales and keeps track of income and expenses for the production as a whole.

Paragraph with Embedded Topic Sentence

Meets
New York
Standards
1.B.1
1.B.2
1.B.3
1.B.4
2.A.1
2.A.2
2.B.3
3.B.1
3.B.3

Main Ideas and Supporting Details

Sometimes the topic sentence appears at the end of the paragraph instead of at the beginning. The following paragraph is not just about Greek tragedies and comedies, so the first sentence is not broad enough to cover the main idea of the paragraph. The main idea is expressed in the *last* sentence of this paragraph.

> In the fifth century B.C., the ancient Greeks developed two types of play: tragedies and comedies. According to legend, the first tragedies were created by a man named Thespis. His name is the origin of our word *thespian*, which means "actor." The plays Thespis wrote were designed to be performed by a single actor. A chorus recited or sang lines that helped the audience understand what was happening on stage. Eventually, more characters (and thus more actors) were added on stage, and the chorus was dropped. Some Greek playwrights, such as Sophocles and Euripedes, wrote plays that are still performed today. The Greek dramas addressed themes such as jealousy, love and hate, and pride—themes that are still the focus of modern drama. Although theater has changed drastically over the centuries, the ancient Greek playwrights were the inventors of Western theater.

Paragraph with Closing Topic Sentence

At other times, even though an entire paragraph focuses on a single idea, the main idea is not stated directly anywhere in the paragraph. A paragraph of this type is said to have an **implied topic sentence.**

> Unlike a short story or a poem, a play is incomplete on the printed page. Many directors and actors consider the script merely a blueprint. Only in a play's performance does it come fully alive. The ancient Greek word for *theater* (*theatron*) means "watching place." This word origin highlights the fact that dramas are meant to be performed before an audience of spectators. The interaction between performers and spectators is an important part of dramatic theater.

Paragraph with Implied Topic Sentence

In this paragraph, the topic sentence is implied. It might be stated as follows: A drama needs to be performed in order to achieve its full effect.

Although there are times that you might want to use an implied topic sentence in your own writing, do not use this technique on a test. On tests and in most writing assignments for class, your teacher will want to see how clearly you can state or explain the main idea of each paragraph in a topic sentence. You will also be scored on how well your examples and details support that main idea.

Your Turn

Exercise *Circle the topic sentence of each of the following paragraphs. If the paragraph does NOT have a topic sentence, write a topic sentence for the paragraph on the lines provided below.*

Meets New York Standards
1.A.1
1.A.3
1.A.4
1.A.6
1.B.1
1.B.2
1.B.3
1.B.4
2.A.1
2.A.2

1.   The set designer's task involves a series of steps. First, he or she must study the script as a whole. If the play is set in historical times, the set designer may do extensive research on the furniture, costumes, architecture, and customs of the period. Next, the set designer must work with the director to decide what kind of sets to build and how they should be arranged on stage. After this preliminary planning, the designer usually makes rough sketches of the setting for each scene. These sketches are called *set renderings*.

_____

_____

2.   The producer provides money to cover the expenses of the production. He or she may also be involved in making key decisions, such as hiring the director. The director oversees the entire creative staff, casts the show, and rehearses the actors. The actors, of course, portray characters on stage. The stage manager makes up schedules and takes notes during rehearsals. He or she may also serve as prompter, feeding lines to the actors. The lighting designer plans the lighting for the play. The set designer plans the stage set and may oversee its construction and installation. The properties manager gathers and oversees placement of small, moveable objects, or properties, used onstage by the actors. The costume designer plans the costumes and oversees the people who make them. The makeup designer plans the makeup for the actors. The house manager oversees the selling and collection of tickets, the opening and closing of the theater, and the activities of the ushers. The ushers escort people to their seats. The grips do the physical work involved in changing the set between scenes. A theatrical production is always a group effort, involving numerous people carrying out important, interconnected roles.

_____

_____

More ▶

3.　　A spotlight lights up a small part of the stage with a very bright beam. A spotlight is only one type of illumination available to theater lighting designers. A striplight, for example, is a narrow, rectangular fixture usually containing a row of bulbs. Striplights are often hung above the stage to cast light on the set. They may also be placed on the ground to light a *cyclorama,* a painted screen that is placed at the back of the stage. In some theaters, lighting designers have special instruments for creating effects such as clouds passing overhead or dappled sunlight peeking through treetops.

_____

_____

4.　　The costumes in a play help to set the mood of a drama. More importantly, the costumes help the audience to understand the characters and the setting. For example, the costumes help the audience to recognize the period and region in which the action takes place. Costumes can show the social and economic background of the characters in a play. Along with makeup, costumes can also make an actor look much older or younger than he or she really is. This is important when a character is supposed to age during a play.

_____

_____

Main Ideas and Supporting Details

Elaboration, or the Art of Building Paragraphs

When you are writing for a test, each paragraph you write should contain a topic sentence. Each paragraph should also include at least two—and usually three or more—sentences that support or relate to the main idea in the topic sentence. The **supporting sentences** in a paragraph are like the evidence presented in a trial or the information gathered by a scientist to support a hypothesis. The supporting sentences should provide specific details to back up or develop the main idea in the topic sentence. The process of supporting a topic sentence is called **elaboration.** As you write, you can use some or all of the types of elaboration listed below to build your paragraphs.

Meets New York Standards
1.A.1
1.A.3
1.A.4
1.A.6
1.B.1
1.B.2
1.B.4
3.B.1
3.B.2

Types of Elaboration

Analogies	Extended comparisons, generally of things that share some traits but not others
Causes	Statements that tell why something has happened, or why it exists now, or why it will happen
Effects	Statements that tell what happened, is happening, or will happen as a result of something else
Events	Statements describing what has happened, is happening, or will happen
Facts	Statements that can be proved to be true
Figures of Speech	Descriptive statements that are not literal, including metaphors, similes, and personifications
Illustrations and Examples	Statements that give examples of things
Negations	Statements that contradict other statements
Opinions	Statements of obligation, belief, judgment, or value
Paraphrases	An idea from another person, put in your own words
Qualifications	Statements that limit the range, scope, or intensity of something; often these statements use a word such as *but* or *however*
Quotations	The words of another person, repeated exactly and placed in quotation marks
Reasons	Statements that explain why
Sensory Details/ Description	Sentences or details that tell how things look, taste, smell, sound, or feel
Statistics	Statements that present information in numerical form
Summaries	Brief retellings (in fewer words) of information that someone else has written

Your Turn

Exercise A *Read the two paragraphs below. In each paragraph, circle the topic sentence. Then identify the type or types of elaboration used in each paragraph.*

1. There are four basic types of stage in the theater today. The most common type is the proscenium stage. This stage is like a picture frame through which the audience views the actors and scenery. In the open stage, seats for the spectators are set up around three sides of a raised platform. In a third kind of stage, called theater-in-the-round, the audience sits on all sides of the stage. Finally, in an arrangement called flexible stage space, the director can change the stage's location in relation to the audience to suit the nature of the production.

   TYPES OF ELABORATION: _____

   _____

2. What will you find behind the scenes in a fully equipped theater? The behind-the-scenes spaces will almost surely include rehearsal and dressing rooms. In addition, there may be workshops for making scenery and costumes; office space for staff; storage space for costumes, props, and scenery; and a lounge where performers can relax. This area is called the "green room." Above or behind the audience are the lighting and sound booths.

   TYPES OF ELABORATION: _____

   _____

Exercise B *Have you ever been in a play or concert? Have you been in the audience of a play or concert? Was it a success or a less-than-perfect performance? On your own paper, write a paragraph describing why the play or concert was a success, a flop, or something in between. Before you draft your paragraph, think about the kinds of details you should use to support your answer. Use a graphic organizer to gather and organize your ideas. Then write your draft. Save it for use later in this chapter.*

Main Ideas and Supporting Details

Organizing Ideas in a Paragraph

Meets
New York
Standards
1.A.1
1.A.3
1.A.6
1.B.1
1.B.2
1.B.3
1.B.4
1.B.5
2.A.1
2.A.2
2.B.3

Read the following paragraph:

> In Shakespeare's day, the female roles were performed by boys. It was only in the second part of the seventeenth century in England that female actors began to perform in public. The tradition of the all-male cast grew out of the performance customs of medieval times. These young people, aged twelve to eighteen, were trained in special schools. In the Middle Ages, all the roles in plays were performed by male officials of the church.

This paragraph is confusing to read because the order of events is mixed up. Now read another version of the paragraph:

> In Shakespeare's day, female roles in plays were performed by boys. These young actors, aged twelve to eighteen, were trained in special schools. The tradition of the all-male cast grew out of the performance customs of medieval times. In the Middle Ages, all the roles in plays were performed by male officials of the church. It was only in the second part of the seventeenth century in England that female actors began to perform before the public.

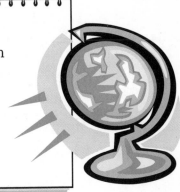

When you write a paragraph, you need to organize your ideas in a clear and sensible way. Sometimes a good way to order the details in a paragraph is obvious. For example, in a narrative paragraph, you might simply put the supporting sentences in **chronological (time) order.** This means that you describe the events in the order that they happened.

In a descriptive paragraph, you might place the supporting sentences in **spatial order,** from left to right, top to bottom, front to back, back to front, near to far, and so on. The following paragraph is organized in spatial order:

> The stage was set for the first act. A four-poster bed stood upstage right. The fireplace, with its fake fire blazing, sat center stage, flanked by two armchairs. Upstage left was a dimly lit kitchen furnished with a small round table and four chairs. Downstage right was the front porch with two rocking chairs, where most of the action would take place.

Main Ideas and Supporting Details

In informative or persuasive paragraphs, writers often place supporting sentences in **degree order.** This means that they describe the most important characteristic or detail first and then work their way "down" to the least important one, or vice versa. The following paragraph is organized in degree order:

> When you attend a play, there are certain rules of etiquette, or behavior, that you should follow. First of all, it is very important not to talk while the actors are performing. Talking during a performance is not only distracting to those around you but could even disturb the performers. Generally, during a play, audience members are discouraged from getting up and leaving the auditorium. In an emergency, of course, you should leave quickly but quietly. Finally, to show your appreciation for their efforts, you should clap for the actors when the performance is over.

When people are doing persuasive or informative writing in the real world, they usually use **part-by-part order.** Although details are connected, they are not presented according to one overall pattern of organization. Instead, each sentence is logically connected in some way to the sentence that came before it and to the sentence that follows it. For example, a writer might begin with a topic sentence like this:

> An actor needs many different talents.

The writer of this topic sentence can use a series of examples as elaboration to develop this point. In part-by-part order, the next sentence in the paragraph should be logically connected to the topic sentence:

> For example, performers need to be able to use their bodies to express a broad range of roles, reactions, emotions, and attitudes.

In the next sentence, the writer gives two more examples of useful talents for performers:

> In today's professional theater, it is especially useful for a performer to be able to dance and to fence.

In the next sentence, the writer lists another skill that makes performers successful:

> In order to play a role successfully, an actor must also be very familiar with human emotions and motivations.

The next sentence expands on this point:

> Therefore, good performers observe the behavior of other people closely.

The writer wraps up the paragraph with another example of the skills and talents a good performer needs:

> Finally, good actors need the ability to focus intensely on an imagined situation. Their goal is to create a convincing illusion that they are playing characters different from their real-life selves.

As you can see, there is no overall pattern of organization in the paragraph. Instead, each idea is logically connected to the next, and all the ideas support the main idea. For more information about ways to organize ideas, see page 180.

Using Transitions to Make Your Organization Clear

One way to help readers follow the connections between ideas in a paragraph is to use transitional words and phrases, or transitions. A **transition** is a word or phrase that shows how ideas are connected to one another. For example, if you want to show an effect or result of a certain cause, you may start a sentence with the phrase *as a result* or with the word *consequently*. If you want to describe a series of events in time order, you might begin your sentences with words such as *first, then, next, after,* and *finally*. The chart below shows some useful transitions.

Meets
New York
Standards
1.B.1
1.B.3
1.B.4
2.B.3
3.B.1
3.B.3

Transitional Words and Phrases

Transitions to Show Time/Narration

after	eventually	next
at last	finally	then
at once	first	thereafter
before	meanwhile	when

Transitions to Show Place/Description

above	beyond	into
across	down	next to
around	here	over
before	in	there
behind	inside	under

Transitions to Show Importance/Evaluation

first	mainly	then
last	more important	to begin with

Transitions to Show Cause and Effect

as a result	for	so that
because	since	therefore
consequently	so	

More ▶

Transitional Words and Phrases, contd.

Transitions to Compare Ideas

also	as well	moreover
and	like	similarly
another	likewise	too

Transitions to Contrast Ideas

although	in spite of	on the other hand
but	instead	still
however	nevertheless	yet

Transitions for Classification

another group	one kind	other sorts
the first type	other kinds	other types

Transitions to Introduce Examples

for example	one example	one sort of
for instance	one kind	another

Transitions to Introduce a Contradiction

however	instead	on the contrary
in spite of this	nonetheless	otherwise

Transitions to Introduce a Conclusion, Summary, or Generalization

as a result	in general	therefore
in conclusion	in summary	thus

Your Turn

Exercise A *Read the two paragraphs below. Circle the transitional words and phrases used in the paragraphs.*

Meets
New York
Standards
1.B.1
1.B.3
1.B.4
1.B.5
3.A.1
3.A.4
3.B.3

1. For an actor, creating a role in a play is a complex activity. First, performers must study the entire script carefully. Then, each actor analyzes his or her own part. For example, each actor must think about the character's age and physical appearance, occupation, attitudes, and overall personality. The next step for an actor is to consider the goals and conflicts that may be involved in playing the role, as well as the motivations that drive his or her character.

2. Since drama is a spoken art, an actor's voice is a very powerful tool. When an actor studies a role, he or she has to decide how each line of the part should be spoken. At times, for example, the character may need to sound sharp and abrupt. At other times, the same character may need to speak softly and gently. Thus, it is not unusual for an actor to experiment with many different tones of voice for the delivery of a single line in the script. Nevertheless, the voice an actor uses has to be consistent with the overall personality of the character.

Exercise B *Reread the rough draft of the paragraph you created for Exercise B on page 234. Revise the paragraph, as necessary, to improve the organization. Use transitional words and phrases to connect your ideas. Then write the final copy of your paragraph on your own paper.*

Return to the exercises at the beginning of the chapter, revise your work as necessary, and submit the exercises to your teacher for grading.

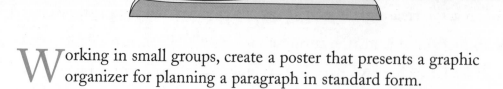

Meets
New York
Standards
1.A.3
1.A.6
1.B.1
1.B.3
2.A.2

Working in small groups, create a poster that presents a graphic organizer for planning a paragraph in standard form.

✔ The poster should contain a model paragraph in standard form, guidelines for constructing such a paragraph, and a graphic organizer for paragraphs.

✔ The graphic organizer should show the topic sentence, supporting sentences, and the concluding or clincher sentence, and the model paragraph should contain all of these elements as well.

A possible graphic organizer for use in your poster is shown below.

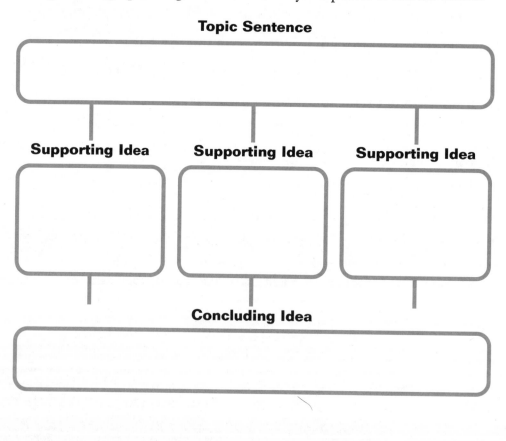

Topic Sentence

Supporting Idea   **Supporting Idea**   **Supporting Idea**

Concluding Idea

Chapter 11
Excellent Essays

Introduction, Body, and Conclusion

Read the writing prompt and the essay written in response to that prompt. Then try your hand at the exercises that follow the prompt and the student essay. You will not be graded on the exercises at this time. At the end of the chapter, you will be directed to return to these exercises to revise and correct your work.

Jeff Villanueva read the following prompt on a writing test:

Writing Prompt

Long ago, a Greek philosopher said, "You can't step in the same river twice." What he meant is that life is always changing. Write about a change that happened in your life and explain three ways in which it affected you.

In your answer, be sure to
• tell about a change in your life
• explain three ways that you were affected by the change
• include details to make your writing more interesting

Jeff thought about times in his life when he experienced change. There was the time when his family moved and he went to a new school. There was the time when his baby sister was born. There was the time when his mother quit her job to go to school. There was also the time when the family got a new dog.

Jeff decided to write about getting the dog. The next thing he did was to make a list of ways in which getting the dog affected his life. Here is Jeff's list:

One Student's List
—Lots of affection/companionship from the dog
—More responsibility
  —Walking dog
  —Feeding dog
  —Training dog
  —Giving dog bath
  —Giving dog medicines
—Learned important lessons
  —Everything in life a trade-off
  —Need to work for what you get
  —Love & discipline can go together

Here is the final version of Jeff's essay:

One Student's Essay

The Beagle Who Trained Me

by Jeff Villanueva

I admit it. Before Beauregarde came, I was a spoiled brat. Basically, I went to school, and that was about it. I didn't do a thing around the house. My room was always a mess, and I never did any housework or chores. Then, after months of begging my parents to get me a dog, I finally wore them down, and Beauregarde the Beagle entered my life. From that point on, Beauregarde started training me, and my life hasn't been the same since.

The first big change that Beauregarde made in my life was to teach me what complete, absolute, unconditional love means. Sure, my parents love me, and (though she wouldn't admit it) so does my sister, but Beauregarde is in a league of his own. When I come home from school in the evening, he is always bouncing in the doorway with excitement. My mom says that he hears the school bus when it is still three blocks away, jumps off the sofa, and runs to the door. Immediately, when I open the door, he can't help jumping on me. He barks and wags his tail. From that point on, he doesn't leave my side. He sits next to me while I do my homework, while I eat, and while I talk to my friends on the telephone. When I go to bed, he sleeps on the floor nearby. My mother has even started making fun of us, singing some song from back in the seventies when she sees us: "Just like me, he wants to be . . . close to you."

Of course, the dog has also brought a lot of new chores into my life. Before we

More ▶

Introduction, Body, and Conclusion 243

got him, my parents made me promise that I would take care of him, and they have insisted that I keep my part of that bargain. In the morning, I walk Beauregarde around the neighborhood and, yes, I pick up his messes. Then I feed him. I also have to brush him, give him baths every couple of weeks, and feed him his monthly heartworm medicine. I also have to help Mom when she takes him to the groomer or the vet. I also had to train him to be a well-behaved dog. So, the coming of Beauregarde has meant a lot of extra work for me.

The biggest change of all, however, is in me. I've learned a lot because of the dog coming into my life, and I've changed in many ways. I've learned that life involves trade-offs. For example, a dog gives you affection and companionship, but in exchange, you have to do more work. I've also learned that you need to work for what you get, and this has affected my attitudes about schoolwork. I take school more seriously now. I've even started picking up my room and helping with the dishes sometimes. I've also learned that love and discipline go together. I love Beauregarde, and one of the ways that I show this love is to teach him what's right and wrong. As a result of all that I've learned, I've changed my own behavior quite a bit. I try to be more helpful around the house and to work harder in school.

Back when I first mentioned wanting to have a dog, my dad said, "Well, you know that you're going to have to train him. A dog requires a lot of training." Having had Beauregarde for two years now, I guess

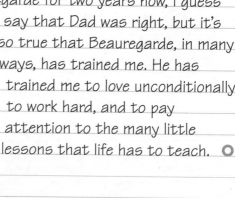 I can say that Dad was right, but it's also true that Beauregarde, in many ways, has trained me. He has trained me to love unconditionally, to work hard, and to pay attention to the many little lessons that life has to teach. ○

Your Turn

Exercise *On the lines below, answer the following questions about the essay you have just read.*

Meets New York Standards
1.A.1
1.A.3
1.A.4
1.A.6
1.B.3
1.B.4
3.A.1

1. Where in the opening paragraph does the writer's thesis statement appear? What is this statement?

   _____

   _____

2. In the first body paragraph, what is the topic sentence? What are two details that help to support the topic sentence in this paragraph?

   MAIN IDEA (TOPIC): _____

   _____

   SUPPORTING DETAILS:

   1. _____

   2. _____

3. In the second body paragraph, what is the topic sentence? What are two details that help to support the topic sentence in this paragraph?

   MAIN IDEA (TOPIC): _____

   _____

   SUPPORTING DETAILS:

   1. _____

   2. _____

More ▶

Meets
New York
Standards
1.A.1
1.A.3
1.A.4
1.A.6
1.B.3
1.B.4
3.A.1

4. What is the topic sentence of the third body paragraph? What are two details that support the topic sentence?

MAIN IDEA (TOPIC): _____

_____

SUPPORTING DETAILS:

1. _____

2. _____

5. In the third body paragraph, what are three transitions that the writer uses to make the flow of ideas in the paragraph clear and easy to follow?

1. _____

2. _____

3. _____

6. What sentence in the conclusion of the essay restates the three main ideas from the body paragraphs of the essay?

_____

_____

_____

Excellent Essays

You are standing in line at the supermarket. While you wait, you glance at the magazines on display. One of the titles on the cover attracts your attention. You pick up the magazine. You find the article and start to read. Suddenly, it is your turn to check out. What made the waiting time fly by? You were caught up in reading an interesting essay!

What Is an Essay?

An **essay** is a short piece of nonfiction writing that focuses on part of a larger subject. An essay is not an extended book-length discussion of a subject, like Ingrid Wickelgren's 144-page *Rambling Robots: Building a Breed of Mechanical Beasts*. Instead, it discusses a small part of the subject, as Isaac Asimov does in "The Robot as Enemy," which discusses the possible dangers from robots.

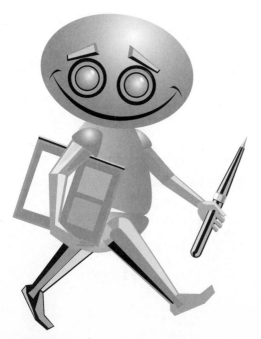

The word *essay* comes from the French word *essais*, which means "attempts." Today, the term "essay" is used to describe any brief piece of nonfiction (more than one paragraph long) that focuses on part of a subject. A good essay should get your attention quickly and be readable in a fairly short period of time.

The idea of focus is central to the essay. A piece of writing is **focused** if it does not wander off onto unrelated topics. A good essay presents a main idea and then supports that idea with related facts, details, and other types of elaboration. In other words, it sticks to the topic.

You have learned that paragraphs come in many different sizes and shapes. Likewise, there are many different types of essay and many ways to put them together. Magazines, for example, are full of essays on every possible topic, from astronomy to zebras.

Introduction, Body, and Conclusion

In this chapter, you will learn how to write one kind of essay, the standard classroom theme. As you grow as a writer, you will start to move beyond this simple kind of essay. Even in the more complicated essays that you write in the future, however, you will still focus on a single overall idea, or **thesis.**

Learning to write essays is an important skill. On the ELA exam, you will be asked to write an essay in response to an independent writing prompt. You will have to draw on your own ideas, knowledge, and experience to write the essay.

Some of the essays you may be asked to write in classes, in school, or on exams will fall into the categories listed below:

- **Narrative essays** based on real-life events

- **Personal essays** about experiences you have had

- **Persuasive essays** that attempt to convince others to take a certain action or to adopt a certain point of view

- **Informative** or **expository essays** that define, analyze, compare and contrast, classify, or describe

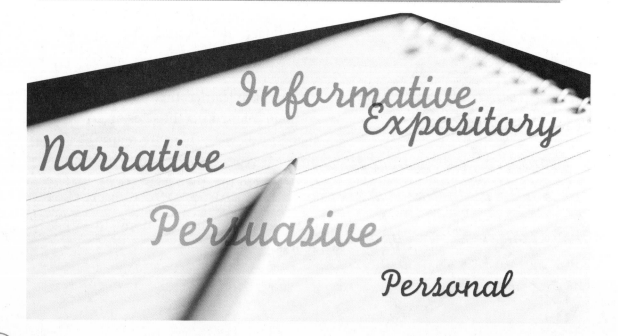

Whatever type of essay you are asked to write, you will generally do well if you construct your essay in the format of the **standard classroom theme.** This type of essay has the following features:

Essay Model: The Standard Classroom Theme

Characteristics

1. It is at least four or five paragraphs long.

2. It presents and develops a central idea, or **thesis.**

3. It contains a clear beginning (introduction), middle (body), and end (conclusion).

Structure

Introduction (Paragraph 1)

The **introduction** has two purposes or goals:

- to grab the reader's attention

- to state the essay's main idea, or thesis

Body Paragraphs (Paragraphs 2, 3, and 4, if present)

Each **body paragraph** presents a major idea in support of the thesis statement. The main idea of each body paragraph is presented in a topic sentence. The topic sentence is supported by sentences that present additional information and details. The topic sentence can appear at the beginning, at the end, or somewhere in the middle of a body paragraph. Sometimes, the topic sentence can be implied.

Conclusion (Paragraph 4 or 5)

The **conclusion** should give the reader the sense of an ending. Often the conclusion sums up the main ideas in the essay or restates the thesis. There are many ways to write a conclusion. These will be discussed later in this chapter.

Introduction, Body, and Conclusion

The graphic organizer below shows how you can organize the parts of a standard classroom theme, or essay. It is a helpful tool for planning an essay for a school assignment or for the ELA test.

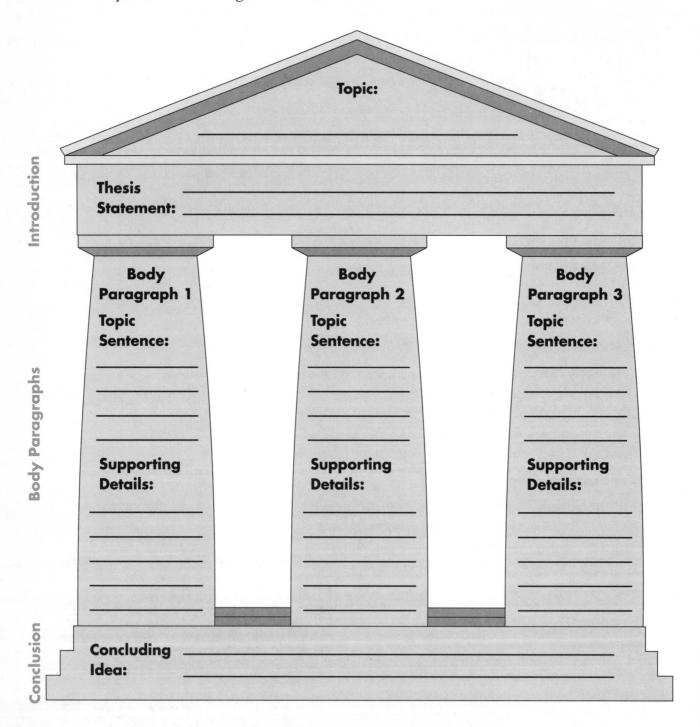

Topic: _____

Introduction

Thesis Statement: _____

Body Paragraphs

Body Paragraph 1
Topic Sentence:
_____
_____
_____

Supporting Details:
_____
_____
_____
_____

Body Paragraph 2
Topic Sentence:
_____
_____
_____

Supporting Details:
_____
_____
_____
_____

Body Paragraph 3
Topic Sentence:
_____
_____
_____

Supporting Details:
_____
_____
_____
_____

Conclusion

Concluding Idea: _____

Prewriting: Planning an Essay

The prewriting process includes all the thinking and planning you do before you write an essay. On an exam, your first task is to analyze the writing prompt. Study the prompt to make sure you understand the following parts of the writing assignment:

Meets
New York
Standards
1.B.1
1.B.2
1.B.3
1.B.4
1.B.5
2.B.3
3.B.1
3.B.2

- **The topic.** What you are supposed to write about

- **The audience.** The person or persons for whom you are supposed to write

- **The purpose.** What the writing is supposed to achieve (for example, to inform, to explain, or to persuade)

- **Specific details.** Any particular details that the piece of writing must contain, according to the directions

Your second job in prewriting is to create a thesis statement for your essay. The thesis statement should be the main idea that your essay will present. It should also be a one- or two-sentence general answer to the writing prompt.

After you have written a thesis statement, gather information related to that statement. Use one or more of the standard brainstorming or notetaking methods you have learned (See Chapter 6, "Picture This! Notetaking and Graphic Organizers"). Once you have generated some ideas, look for two or three main ideas related to the thesis statement. These ideas will become the topic sentences of the body paragraphs in your essay. Now you are ready to make a rough outline. Organize the ideas in the rough outline in a logical order. For example, you might put them in

chronological order or in order of importance. Make sure that your rough outline contains information for three main body paragraphs.

The chart below summarizes the steps for essay writing that we have covered so far.

Prewriting Steps for Writing Essays in Response to Test Prompts

1. Think about the prompt carefully to find out what it is asking you to do.

2. Write a one- or two-sentence answer to the prompt. This will serve as the thesis statement for your essay.

3. Gather ideas for the essay.

4. Organize your ideas into a rough outline.

Here is a rough outline that Jeff created before he wrote about the changes that occurred in his life after he got a dog:

One Student's Rough Outline

Thesis: Life hasn't been the same since Beauregarde the Beagle entered my life.

Body ¶1: Beau taught me abt. unconditional love
— Meets me at doorway, bouncing & wagging
— Listens for my school bus
— Sits with me/next to me all the time
— Sleeps next to my bed
— Mom's "Close to you" song

Body ¶2: Lots of new chores
— Agreemt w/parents to take care of dog
— Walk him
— Clean up "messes"
— Brush him
— Bathe him
— Give him heartworm medicine
— Help take him to vet/groomer
— Train him

Body ¶3: Dog has taught me a lot
— Life involves trade-offs
— Need to work for what you get
— Love + discipline go together
— Being responsible for him → changes in my behavior

Exercise *Follow the directions given below.*

1. Choose a subject and circle it, or come up with a subject of your own and write it on the line provided.

   nature   friendships   games   books

   sports   amusement parks   school   the future

   animals   movies

   OTHER SUBJECT: _____

2. Narrow your subject to come up with a more specific topic for an essay. Follow the model provided.

   GENERAL SUBJECT: Nature

   NARROWED SUBJECT: National parks

   MORE FOCUSED TOPIC: My visit to Yellowstone National Park

   GENERAL SUBJECT: _____

   NARROWED SUBJECT: _____

   MORE FOCUSED TOPIC: _____

3. Plan an essay on your topic by filling in the chart below. Save your essay plan for use in exercises later in this chapter.

   ## My Essay Plan

   FOCUSED TOPIC: _____

   AUDIENCE: _____

   PURPOSE: _____

   THESIS STATEMENT: _____

   _____

   _____

More ▶

4. In the space below, make a word web to gather information or ideas for your essay.

5. In the space below, make a rough outline of your essay. Use the information that you gathered in your word web. Follow the plan you made on the previous page. Use the outline format shown on page 252. Save your outline for use in exercises later in this chapter.

Meets
New York
Standards
1.B.1
1.B.3
1.B.4
1.B.5
3.B.2

Introduction, Body, and Conclusion

Drafting: Writing the Introduction

Writing is a process. It nearly always involves shifts and turns and changes. The unexpected often happens. New thoughts and ideas pop into a writer's mind all the time. Therefore, the exact sequence of steps in the writing process depends on the individual writer.

Some writers begin drafting an essay by writing an introduction. Other writers, however, prefer to write the introduction last. That way, they can have a clearer idea of the main points they want to make. You can choose either method. However, when you are writing an essay in response to a prompt on a test, you may find it easier simply to begin with the introduction.

The introduction should grab the readers' attention. It should also present the thesis statement, or central idea of the essay. There are many ways you can capture your readers' attention. Study the examples given below:

Ways to Begin an Introduction

Below are some common types of introduction. These are all introductions for an informative essay about communication in honeybees, dolphins, and elephants.

- **Begin with an interesting fact.**

  A well-trained elephant can understand more than fifty different commands. Ants lay down a chemical trail to help them stay together as they march from their nest to a food source and back. Some chimpanzees and apes have learned to communicate using simplified versions of sign language. These are just three of the surprising facts that scientists have discovered about animal communication. Three animals that have particularly interesting forms of communication are honeybees, songbirds, and elephants.

- **Begin with a quotation or proverb.**

  "Birds of a feather flock together," as the proverb goes, but how does the flock stay together? The answer may lay partly in how birds communicate with one other. Communication among birds is but one example of animal communication. Other animals with fascinating forms of communication include honeybees and elephants.

  More ▶

Ways to Begin an Introduction, contd.

- **Begin with an anecdote, or very brief story.**

  One day I watched a column of ants travel in a straight line for over two hundred yards. They marched from their nest to a food source. They looked like soldiers in a formation. I wondered how these tiny insects could all stay together. I did some research on the Internet. I found out that many ant species lay down a chemical "scent trail." This is only one of the many fascinating ways in which animals communicate with one another. Other animals that communicate in especially interesting ways include honeybees, songbirds, and elephants.

- **Begin with an analogy to something else.** (An **analogy** is a comparison of unlike things, usually presented to make a point.)

  Years ago, people left a "calling card" on the hall table of a home when they visited. Today, scientists say that animals have left their "calling card" when the animals have left their scent to mark an area. Anyone who has ever walked a dog is familiar with scent marking. By this means, dogs communicate to one another what territory they have claimed as their own. What are some of the other ways animals communicate? Three animals with interesting forms of communication are honeybees, songbirds, and elephants.

- **Begin with a question.**

  What is my dog (or cat) trying to tell me? This is a question that pet owners often ask themselves. While much of animal communication remains a mystery, scientists are learning a great deal about how our fellow creatures on the planet communicate with one another. Three animals with especially interesting forms of communication are honeybees, songbirds, and elephants.

Meets
New York
Standards
1.B.1
1.B.2
1.B.3
1.B.5
2.B.3
3.B.4

Exercise On the lines below, write a rough draft of an introduction for the essay that you started in the exercises on pages 253–55. Somewhere in your introduction, use the thesis statement you wrote on page 253.

_____

_____

_____

_____

_____

_____

_____

_____

_____

_____

_____

_____

_____

_____

_____

_____

_____

Introduction, Body, and Conclusion

Drafting: Writing the Body Paragraphs

Look back at the graphic organizer on page 250. You can see that developing an essay is rather like constructing a temple. The thesis statement is like the pediment, or top. The thesis is held up or supported by the columns, the body paragraphs. The body paragraphs must provide strong support, or the thesis will not be convincing or persuasive. It may come crashing down!

Each body paragraph in an essay should contain the following parts:

- A **main idea** in the form of a topic sentence

- At least two or three **sentences that support the main idea**

- **Transitional words and phrases** that connect ideas

The main headings in your rough outline state the ideas that will become topic sentences in the body paragraphs of the essay. In each body paragraph, the topic sentence should directly support the thesis statement, or overall focus of the essay. The topic sentence of a body paragraph may appear at the beginning of the paragraph, at the end, or somewhere in the middle.

One good way to plan a body paragraph is to create a paragraph-planning chart. Here is a paragraph-planning chart for a body paragraph in an essay about animal communication.

Meets New York Standards
1.B.1
1.B.2
1.B.3
1.B.4
1.B.5
2.B.3
3.B.1
3.B.2
3.B.3
3.B.4

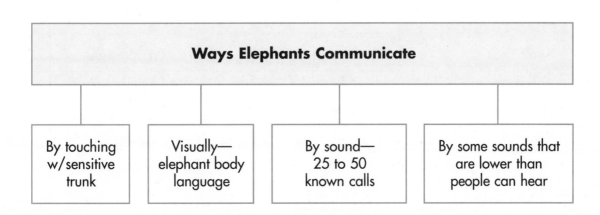

Ways Elephants Communicate

| By touching w/sensitive trunk | Visually— elephant body language | By sound— 25 to 50 known calls | By some sounds that are lower than people can hear |

Introduction, Body, and Conclusion

Organizing Body Paragraphs and Using Transitions

The ideas in a body paragraph of an essay should be presented in a logical order. In addition, the paragraphs themselves should be presented in an order that makes sense. The following are some common methods of organization:

Methods of Organization

- Chronological order
- Spatial order
- Degree order (order of familiarity, value, importance, etc.)
- Part-by-part order
- Problem-solution order
- Cause-and-effect order

The topic
The audience
The purpose

As you write, you should use transitional words and phrases to connect ideas. For a list of transitions, see pages 237–38.

Using Supporting Ideas in Body Paragraphs

Within each body paragraph of an essay, there are many ways in which you can develop the main idea of the paragraph. The list below shows some of these ways.

Types of Elaboration

- Analogies
- Anecdotes
- Causes
- Comparisons/contrasts
- Descriptions/sensory details
- Effects
- Events
- Facts
- Figures of speech
- Illustrations/examples
- Negations
- Opinions
- Paraphrases
- Qualifications
- Reasons
- Statistics
- Summaries

For a detailed explanation of each of these types of elaboration, see page 233.

If you are writing an essay based on a reading passage that has been provided on a test, then the body paragraphs of your writing must contain evidence (details and examples) from the passage. This evidence can take the form of direct quotations, paraphrases, or summaries. **Quotations** are exact words taken from the passage. They should be placed in quotation marks. When you **paraphrase,** you restate an idea or a passage in your own words. When you **summarize,** you restate the main points of a passage using fewer words than the writer.

For example, a body paragraph in an essay about animal communication might quote evidence from other sources. It might also paraphrase and summarize the evidence.

Here is an example of a body paragraph that summarizes and quotes evidence from a book:

Meets
New York
Standards
1.B.1
1.B.2
1.B.3
1.B.4
2.B.3
3.B.1
3.B.2
3.B.3

Professor Donald R. Griffin is a world-famous scientist. He played a key role in discovering how bats use echolocation to navigate in the dark. In his book *Animal Minds,* Griffin discusses various methods of animal communication. Griffin is interested in making a link between animal communication and intelligence. As Griffin states, "One of the clearest examples of natural animal communication that suggests conscious thinking stems from studies of alarm calls of vervet monkeys" (page 156).

summary

quotation

Notice how the writer mentions the name of the book from which the evidence was taken and gives the page number where the information can be found. He also uses quotation marks at the beginning and end of the direct quotation from the book. If you are quoting from a reading passage on a test, you will not have to tell which part of the passage the quote came from, but you will need to place it in quotation marks.

Your Turn

Exercise   On the lines below, begin drafting the body paragraphs for your essay. (If you run out of room, you may continue on your own paper.) For each body paragraph, be sure to include a topic sentence and details that develop one of the main ideas in the outline you created on page 255. Keep your audience and purpose in mind as you draft these paragraphs.

_____

_____

_____

_____

_____

_____

_____

_____

_____

_____

_____

_____

_____

_____

_____

_____

_____

_____

_____

Introduction, Body, and Conclusion

Drafting: Writing the Conclusion

There are many ways of concluding an essay. In a conclusion, your goal is to give the reader a satisfying sense of an ending. The chart below shows some strategies for concluding an essay.

Meets
New York
Standards
1.B.1
1.B.2
1.B.3
1.B.4
1.B.5
2.B.3
3.B.1
3.B.2
3.B.3

Strategies for Concluding an Essay

1. Restate the thesis in different words. Summarize the main ideas presented in the essay to support the thesis.

2. Restate the thesis. Call attention to its importance or interest.

3. Relate the thesis to the reader's life or to some broader context.

4. Call on the reader to adopt some belief or to take some action related to the thesis.

5. Tie together any loose ends.

6. Briefly touch on the consequences of what was discussed in the essay.

Sometimes writers end an essay with their last point. Sometimes they end with the final event they want to describe. This kind of "ending without a formal conclusion" is especially common in a newspaper story. When you write for an examination, do not end this way. The person who scores your writing will be looking for a formal conclusion.

A conclusion often begins with a transitional phrase, such as *In conclusion, In summary, As the preceding paragraphs show, Finally, Thus,* or *As we have seen.* The transition signals that the essay is about to end.

Introduction, Body, and Conclusion (**263**)

Introduction, Body, and Conclusion

Read the following examples of conclusions:

1. Here is an example of a concluding paragraph from an informative essay about making a scrapbook. The rest of the essay (not shown here) has dealt with how to gather materials for a scrapbook and how to create one that looks nice and represents a certain activity, holiday, or vacation. In this concluding paragraph, the author shifts the focus to the reader.

> As the preceding paragraphs show, making a scrapbook can be fun, and you can definitely do great work on a budget! Creating a scrapbook of a recent trip you have taken or of a holiday that you have spent with your family allows you to preserve your memories in a creative and unique way. Why not try making a scrapbook yourself the next time your family takes a vacation? Show your friends your crafts skills and what a great time you had!

2. This concluding paragraph comes from an essay that compares and contrasts. In this essay, the author has written about the advantages of DVDs over videotape. In this conclusion, the author summarizes those advantages and makes a prediction about the future of these two technologies:

> In conclusion, although DVDs and videotapes both provide consumers with an easy way to watch their favorite recorded movies or documentaries, DVDs are clearly superior. First, DVDs are smaller and more easily stored. Second, they do not become tangled or crimped, as tape does. Third, DVDs provide superior sound and picture quality. Fourth, they allow additional materials, such as behind-the-scenes footage, to be stored and accessed via a menu. Despite these many advantages, however, we can expect that videotapes will not disappear entirely. Just as CDs never entirely replaced cassette tapes, and e-mail never entirely replaced the handwritten letter, the chances are slim that DVDs will completely replace videotapes any time soon!

Exercise A On the lines below, write a draft of a concluding paragraph for the essay you have been creating throughout this chapter. Underline the transitional phrase you use to let readers know that this paragraph is a conclusion to your essay.

Meets
New York
Standards
1.B.1
1.B.2
1.B.3
1.B.4
1.B.5
2.B.3
3.B.1
3.B.2
3.B.3

Exercise B *Use the checklists on pages 187–88 and 190 to revise and proofread your introduction, body paragraphs, and conclusion. Then, on the lines provided, write a clean final copy of your essay.*

_____

_____

_____

_____

_____

_____

_____

_____

_____

_____

_____

_____

_____

_____

_____

_____

_____

_____

More ▶

Your Turn

Return to the exercises at the beginning of the chapter, revise your work as necessary, and submit the exercises to your teacher for grading.

Posttest
English Language Arts

Session 1

This session contains two parts. In Part 1, you will read passages and answer multiple-choice questions about them. You may look back at passages as often as you like. In Part 2, you will listen to a passage and then write about it. You will hear the listening passage twice.

Session 1
Part 1: Reading

Directions *Read the following article about coral reefs. Then answer questions 1 through 5.*

Saving Our Coral Reefs
by Robin Lamb

Have you ever visited southern Florida, Puerto Rico, or Hawaii? These are just a few of the fabulous places that millions of tourists flock to each year to visit spectacular coral reefs. Coral reefs are made up of the skeletons of tiny sea creatures called corals. These reefs provide a good place for small fishes, crabs, and other sea creatures to hide from larger predators. In fact, coral reefs are home to such an abundance of wildlife that they are often called the "rain forests of the sea." Unfortunately, coral reefs are endangered and need our help. Our federal government should act immediately to protect coral reefs before they are lost forever.

Why are coral reefs important? First, millions of tourists visit places with clear ocean water and coral reefs offshore.

Some people see the reefs through glass-bottomed boats. Others dive right in and visit the reefs with snorkel or SCUBA gear. In 2001, more than 3.6 million people participated in reef-related activities in the Florida Keys alone. Tourists who come to Florida to see the reefs spend more than $1 billion a year on hotels, restaurants, rental cars, sportfishing, and other vacation services. This creates jobs for other people and is very important to Florida's economy. Second, coral reefs are important to the fishing industry. Coral reefs are places where many baby fish hatch. The fish hide in the reefs until they are big enough to survive in more open water. More than 50 percent of the species of fish that people eat depend upon coral reefs during some part of their life cycle. Third, coral reefs help to protect coastal areas by absorbing powerful waves that might otherwise destroy shorelines. Most important

Photo: Florida Keys National Marine Sanctuary

GO ON

of all, coral reefs are fascinating underwater communities where a variety of fishes, sponges, sea anemones, crabs, and other species live. It is estimated that there are up to 8 million species in the coral reefs of the world that haven't even been discovered yet!

In recent years, coral reefs have been devastated. In 2000, scientists estimated that 27 percent of the world's coral reefs had already been destroyed and that 58 percent might be lost by the year 2030. The causes of destruction of coral reefs include pollution, overfishing, harmful fishing practices such as using poison or dynamite, trawling (dragging fish nets along the bottom of the ocean), and dredging (or scooping out) sand and coral for the building industry. Divers can also damage reefs by breaking off pieces of coral, either accidentally or on purpose. Since corals are living creatures, they can

be affected by disease outbreaks, which can damage reefs. Reefs can also be damaged by boats that run aground or anchor on them and by changes in ocean temperature associated with global warming.

We need to understand and reduce the threats to coral reefs, so we can help the reefs and the creatures that live there survive. Laws that already protect coral reefs should be strictly enforced. The fishing industry should avoid using methods that in the long run could wipe out the very fish they are trying to catch. People who damage reefs by anchoring their boats there or by breaking off pieces of coral as souvenirs should pay stiff fines. Our government should also support research into ways to prevent diseases of coral reefs and to reduce global warming. We need to act now to preserve coral reefs and the creatures that depend on them for food or homes. The longer we wait, the graver the danger to our reefs—those sources of recreation, food, tourist and fishing income, beauty, and wonder. ⭕

Note: The facts in this essay were taken from a National Oceanic and Atmospheric Administration (NOAA) report, *A National Coral Reef Action Strategy,* 2002. The opinions expressed here are those of the author.

1. What is the main purpose of the article?

   Ⓐ to describe a visit that the author made to a coral reef off the Florida coast

   Ⓑ to persuade readers to join the Coral Reef Protection Society

   Ⓒ to persuade readers that coral reefs are important and need to be protected

   Ⓓ to inform readers about the fish that can be found near coral reefs

2. Which of the following is NOT one of the reasons that coral reefs are important, according to the article?

   Ⓐ Coral reefs create jobs in the tourist industry.

   Ⓑ Coral reefs are the best places for anchoring boats.

   Ⓒ Coral reefs are important to the fishing industry.

   Ⓓ Coral reefs protect coastlines from powerful waves.

3. If the destruction of coral reefs continues at its present rate, how much of the world's coral reefs will have been destroyed by 2030?

   Ⓐ 20 percent   Ⓑ 27 percent   Ⓒ 32 percent   Ⓓ 58 percent

4. The following word web lists some of the threats to coral reefs. From the answer choices below, choose the one that belongs in the blank circle.

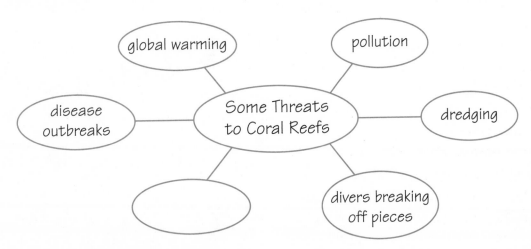

   Ⓐ harmful fishing practices

   Ⓑ not enough sunlight

   Ⓒ too many fish eggs

   Ⓓ build-up of coral skeletons

5. Which of the following statements is an opinion of the author?

Ⓐ "Divers can also damage reefs by breaking off pieces of coral, either accidentally or on purpose."

Ⓑ "Coral reefs are home to such an abundance of wildlife that they are often called the 'rain forests of the sea.'"

Ⓒ "Our government should also support research into ways to prevent diseases of coral reefs and to reduce global warming."

Ⓓ "In 2001, more than 3.6 million people participated in reef-related activities in the Florida Keys alone."

Directions *Read the following story based on a Greek myth. Then answer questions 6 through 10.*

Eos and Tithonus: A Greek myth
retold by Marie Germain

The sky was inky black when lovely Eos, the dawn, awoke. Slowly rising from her pink pillows, she yawned and stretched. She arose from bed ever so gently and tiptoed out of the room, careful not to disturb her husband, Tithonus. She was forever worrying about him when he was awake, so the longer he slept, the better.

Eos's long, glowing tresses[1] lit her way through the dim palace to the kitchen. She poured cool water into a crystal bowl and carried it to an open window. Dipping her rosy fingers into the water, Eos leaned over the sill and delicately sprinkled dewdrops over the world. It made her happy to imagine all the thirsty plants, drinking in her gift.

Then Eos ambled down the path to open the palace gates for her brother Helios, the sun. As his golden chariot approached from the stables, Eos pulled a pair of shaded spectacles from her pocket: Her brother was far too brilliant to gaze upon with unprotected eyes. When he reached the gates, Helios reined in his four prancing stallions and halted beside his sister. Impatient to be off, the four steeds shook their fiery manes and stamped their golden hooves on the paving stones.

"Good morning, Eos," said Helios. "I've been meaning to talk to you," Helios hesitated, "about...old Tithy."

"His name is Tithonus." Eos scowled at her brother. "What about him?"

"I paid him a little visit last night, you know. He does *not* look well. He's so shriveled that I almost sat on him, and I couldn't make out a word he said."

"What do you expect, Helios? He's 450 years old."

"Eos, this is your husband we're talking about! I would be ashamed to be married to that...that..."

---

[1]**tresses.** Ringlets of hair

"Well, you don't have to worry about it, do you?" said Eos defensively. "Shouldn't you be going? The mortals below will be wondering what's happened to you. Pretty soon they'll be thinking it's the end of the world or something."

"Yes, I suppose you're right. Why don't you talk to our dear sister, Selene? Didn't she have a similar problem with What's His Name?"

"Endymion. Selene never has any practical advice, but I'll talk to her. Now go!"

Helios's four flaming stallions lunged skyward, and his shining chariot climbed slowly into the heavens, transforming dawn to day.

Eos latched the gates and strolled back to the kitchen where Selene was eating breakfast—or dinner, in her case. As the moon, Selene's job was the opposite of her brother's: Each night, she watched over the world with her shimmering silver gaze. She, too, drove a chariot, but hers was gleaming silver and her horses were pale gray.

"How was your night?" Eos began.

"Fine, I suppose," said Selene. "*You* know. I'm waxing right now, so I feel a little bloated, but that'll be over soon, thank goodness. I'll be full in a couple of days; then I can start shedding this extra weight."

"So—how's your husband?" Eos inquired. Selene visited her husband, Endymion, every night on some mountaintop in Asia Minor.

"Oh, handsomer than ever," Selene said, yawning, "but rather boring company, considering he sleeps all the time."

"He never wakes up at *all?*" Eos gasped. "Have you consulted Zeus?"

"Zeus?" Selene waved her hand dismissively. "He just says, 'I told you so!' But the thing is, he *didn't* tell me so. When I married Endymion, I was so in love that I went to Zeus and said, 'Please make my husband young and handsome forever.' And Zeus said, 'How do you suggest I do that, Selene? Mortals always shrivel up and die, sooner or later.' So *I* said (just throwing out an idea, mind you): 'How about putting him to sleep for eternity?' And Zeus just went ahead and did it. No advice. No warning. Nothing!"

Eos sighed. "I was in such a hurry to get immortality for *my* husband that I forgot to ask Zeus to grant Tithonus eternal youth, too. Instead of warning me, Zeus just said, 'Immortality? Fine!' and *poof! Now* look what's happened!"

"If only we could combine Tithonus and Endymion," said Selene dreamily. "Then at least one of us would have a young, handsome, immortal husband who could stay awake once in awhile!"

Typical, Eos thought bitterly. Another one of Selene's impractical solutions.

Disappointed, she headed back down the hallway to her bedchamber. It just wasn't fair. Zeus had tricked her and now her husband was a… a…well, he was hardly a man anymore. Each night she worried that she would roll over and crush him, and each day she worried that someone might step on him. From her bedchamber came the sound of a tiny cough; Tithonus must be awake. Eos hurried down the hallway.

When she got to her room, Tithonus was nowhere to be seen. After a frantic search, she found him crouched in a corner, a tiny, shriveled creature, hunched over with age. In fact, Eos almost squashed him; he looked so much like a grasshopper. His unintelligible chirping sounded a lot like a grasshopper, too.

Suddenly, Eos had an inspiration: Tithonus looked so much like a grasshopper, why not make a little cage for him and place him on the windowsill. So, she did, and there he sat for eternity, turning a little greener each day, and lulling Eos to sleep each night with his lyrical chirping. ○

GO ON

6. What is Eos's main problem in this myth?
   Ⓐ She does not get along well with her sister and brother.
   Ⓑ She is tired of doing the same old chores every day.
   Ⓒ She is worried about Selene and Endymion's marital troubles.
   Ⓓ Her husband is immortal, but he does not have eternal youth.

7. Which of the following is one of the natural events explained by the myth?
   Ⓐ how mountains are formed
   Ⓑ why there are oceans
   Ⓒ where morning dew comes from
   Ⓓ how lightning is formed

8. Read these sentences from the story:

   "I'm waxing right now, so I feel a little bloated, but that'll be over soon, thank goodness. I'll be full in a couple of days; then I can start shedding this extra weight."

   What does *waxing* mean?
   Ⓐ shining brightly
   Ⓑ getting larger
   Ⓒ becoming ill
   Ⓓ getting smaller

9. How is Eos's situation different from Selene's situation?
   Ⓐ Selene's husband is immortal and youthful, but he is always asleep. Eos's husband is immortal and wakes up each day, but he continues to grow older.
   Ⓑ Selene forgot to ask Zeus to make her husband immortal, and Eos forgot to ask Zeus to keep her husband youthful.
   Ⓒ Selene is married to a god, and Eos is married to a human being.
   Ⓓ Selene is always sleepy, and she drives a silver chariot. Eos is always wide-awake, and she drives a golden chariot.

10. What lesson does this myth teach?
    Ⓐ Listen to the advice of those who are more experienced.
    Ⓑ Do not take your loved ones for granted.
    Ⓒ Be careful what you wish for.
    Ⓓ Do not quarrel with family members.

Directions *Read the following article about citizenship. Then answer questions 11 through 15.*

Becoming a Citizen
by Lina Scott

E ach year, hundreds of thousands of people flock to the United States from countries all over the world. Some come to visit; others come to stay. Those who are given "green cards" are allowed to settle here as legal residents. Legal residents enjoy many, but not all, of the rights and privileges granted to citizens of the United States. Those who want all the rights and privileges of U.S. citizenship must go through a process called **naturalization.**

It is not easy to become a naturalized citizen. Imagine that you moved here from another country and you wanted to become a citizen. First you would have

to apply for citizenship. (By the way, you cannot apply unless you have lived in the United States for five years.[1]) Once you completed the application, the Federal Bureau of Investigation (FBI) and the Central Intelligence Agency (CIA) would do a series of background checks to verify that you are "of good moral character." This means that you have no connections to any known criminals, you have not committed any major crimes while living in the United States, and you have been a responsible, productive member of society. After being cleared by the security agencies, you would have to take some tests to show that you have a basic understanding of English and of U.S. government and history.

The following are some questions that have been asked on the citizenship test. How many of these questions can you answer?

- What do the stars on our flag mean?
- How many branches are there in our government?
- Who makes the laws in the United States?
- What is the basic belief of the Declaration of Independence?
- What is the Bill of Rights?

---

[1]A foreigner who is married to a U.S. citizen may apply for citizenship after three years of residence in the country.

The final step in the naturalization process is to take the Oath of Allegiance. The oath requires applicants to promise to

- give up any allegiance to other countries,
- support and defend the Constitution and the laws of the United States,
- swear allegiance to the United States, and
- serve the country when needed.

It often takes a year or more to complete the naturalization process. You may wonder why so many immigrants work hard to earn citizenship. After all, they can receive many of the rights guaranteed in the Constitution just by being legal residents. For example, all legal residents of the United States have the right to a trial by jury if accused of a crime, the right to freedom of speech, and the right to privacy. So what does it mean to be a United States citizen?

Being a U.S. citizen brings with it many privileges. In addition to the rights enjoyed by all legal residents of the United States, a citizen has the right to get a passport. With a U.S. passport, you can travel freely throughout most of the world. Citizens also have the right to protection and assistance from the U.S. government when they are traveling in other countries. Even within the United States, citizens are often eligible for more assistance from the government than legal residents are. For example, some of the government programs designed to help the needy are not available to non-citizens. The greatest right that

American citizens have, however—the "badge of citizenship," as it is often called—is the right to vote. It is this right that makes our country a free and democratic nation.

Sadly, many American citizens do not take advantage of this precious right. Only 51 percent of eligible voters in America voted in the 2000 presidential election.[2] Many brave people throughout history have fought and died for the right to vote; the least that the citizens of this country can do is take advantage of that right. One of the great American presidents, Theodore Roosevelt said, "…if the right of self-government is a valuable right, then [it] must be retained exactly as our forefathers acquired [it], by labor." In other words, the citizens of a democracy must work hard to preserve the freedoms they enjoy. But it is easy to take for granted what you have always had.

Perhaps those who are born U.S. citizens should have to take the citizenship test and the Oath of Allegiance as well. Having to take the citizenship test would help to ensure that all Americans understand the Constitution. This document is the foundation upon which our country was built. Having to take the oath would remind all Americans that it is our duty to support and defend the ideals set forth in the Constitution. All people, either naturalized or native-born, who receive the privileges of U.S. citizenship must live up to the responsibilities that come with that honor. O

---

[2]Statistic from the U.S. Census Bureau's *Statistical Abstract of the United States*

11. The following chart lists the steps in the process of naturalization. One of the steps is missing. From the answer choices below, choose the step that belongs in the blank space in the chart.

Steps to Becoming a Naturalized Citizen
1. Apply for citizenship
2. Go through background checks
3.
4. Take the Oath of Allegiance

Ⓐ Destroy passport from previous country of residence

Ⓑ Marry a person who is already a U.S. citizen

Ⓒ Take tests in English and U.S. government and history

Ⓓ Register to vote with the local election board

12. All citizens of the United States are expected to support and defend what?

Ⓐ the country where they were born

Ⓑ the president of the United States

Ⓒ the right to vote in elections

Ⓓ the Constitution of the United States

13. Which of the following statements made by the author is an opinion?

Ⓐ "Legal residents enjoy many, but not all, of the rights and privileges granted to citizens of the United States."

Ⓑ "Having to take the citizenship test would help to ensure that all Americans understand the Constitution."

Ⓒ "Even within the United States, citizens are often eligible for more assistance from the government than legal residents are."

Ⓓ "Only 51 percent of registered voters in America voted in the 2000 presidential election."

GO ON

14. Read this sentence from the article:

> Within the United States, citizens are usually eligible for more assistance from the government than legal residents are.

What does *eligible* mean in this sentence?

Ⓐ allowed to compete

Ⓑ readable; easy to read

Ⓒ responsible for

Ⓓ qualified for; entitled to

15. With which of the following statements would the author of the article MOST LIKELY agree?

Ⓐ All Americans who value democracy should pay attention to politics and vote in elections.

Ⓑ Legal residents should not receive the right to a trial by jury until they have earned citizenship.

Ⓒ Theodore Roosevelt was the greatest president in U.S. history.

Ⓓ Any American who does not vote should lose his or her citizenship and have to leave the country.

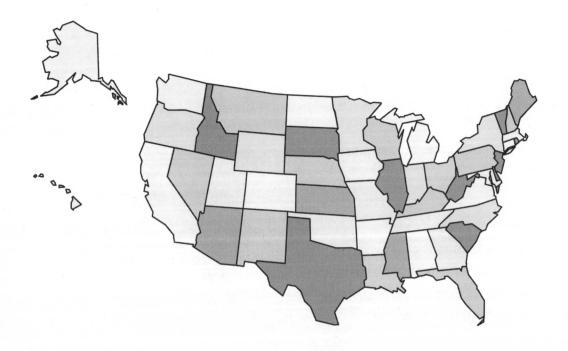

Directions *Read the following page from a travel guidebook. Then answer questions 16 through 19.*

Travel Guide to North Dakota

Big Things to See in North Dakota

While traveling across North Dakota, you will appreciate the state's unique natural landscape and encounter warm people and quaint towns. North Dakota, however, does have some strange attractions. Take a look at some of the oddest:

- Wee'l, which some claim holds the title of world's largest turtle, is made from more than two thousand steel wheel rims all welded together. You can see Wee'l in Dunseith, North Dakota.

- Some claim that Salem Sue is the world's largest dairy cow. Sue is almost forty feet tall. She can be seen from five miles away. She stands just outside New Salem, ND. Take Exit 127 off of Highway 94 to get a closer look.

- Og, a two-and-half-ton gorilla, is a big attraction. (There is no cause for alarm. Og is not really a gorilla. He is just a model made of steel, chicken wire, and papier mâché.) You will find Og on Highway 52, in Harvey, ND.

- What many people believe to be the world's largest buffalo is so big that you could hold a picnic under his legs. You can see this sixty-ton, concrete mammoth where Interstate 94 and Highway 281 meet, in Jamestown, ND.

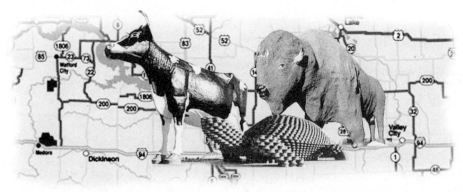

24

GO ON

16. What is the purpose of the selection?
    Ⓐ to describe some of the strangest attractions in the United States
    Ⓑ to inform travelers about interesting food they can eat in North Dakota
    Ⓒ to persuade travelers to spend their next vacation in North Dakota
    Ⓓ to describe some of the strangest attractions in North Dakota

17. According to the selection, what is Og?
    Ⓐ a two-and-a-half ton gorilla
    Ⓑ the world's largest cow
    Ⓒ a city in North Dakota
    Ⓓ a gigantic buffalo

18. Where would you go to see a turtle made of tire rims?
    Ⓐ New Salem
    Ⓑ Dunseith
    Ⓒ Harvey
    Ⓓ Jamestown

19. What do all of these attractions have in common?
    Ⓐ They are all located off of Highway 94.
    Ⓑ They are all made out of tire rims.
    Ⓒ They are all extremely large.
    Ⓓ They all have restaurants next to them.

Directions *Read the following article about an ancient city. Then answer questions 20 through 25.*

The Aztec Capital
by Rena Korb

This map shows the three major causeways leading to the Aztec capital, Tenochtitlán.

Why would a group of people choose to put their capital on an island in the middle of a swampy lake? As strange as that might seem, the ancient Mexica (meh-SHEE-kah) tribe, one of the most powerful tribes in the Aztec empire, did just that.

In the early 1300s, the Mexica arrived at the swampy shores of Lake Texcoco, in what is now Mexico. According to legend, as the Mexica wandered the swamps around Lake Texcoco, one of their priests had a vision: An Aztec god told the priest that his people would find their homeland where an eagle lived atop a cactus. When the Mexica saw an eagle and a cactus on an island in the middle of Lake Texcoco, they knew they had found their home. There on the island, they built a religious shrine. They named it Tenochtitlán (tay-noach-teet-LAHN).

Years later, when the Mexica had become the most powerful tribe in the Aztec empire, this island is where they decided to locate their capital.

The Mexica designed Tenochtitlán very carefully, drawing upon the best features of two ancient capitals that their ancestors had occupied. The city was planned along a grid: The streets and canals intersected at regular intervals, creating neat squares of buildings in between. At the center of the city stood an enormous plaza, or public square, filled with temples and pyramids and lined by palaces with beautiful gardens. More than a thousand workers cleaned the plaza and streets of Tenochtitlán each day, so that they were clean enough to walk in bare feet. At night, pine torches lit the streets. To get around, people who lived in Tenochtitlán mainly used the vast canal system. Numerous waterways criss-crossed the five square miles of the city. People and goods traveled easily and quickly by canoe.

The Aztec capital was filled with marvels of technology. Stone causeways—raised roads that run across bodies of water—linked the city to the mainland. The longest causeway stretched almost five miles. The widest one was broad enough to let up to ten people ride side by side on horseback. Drawbridges were placed at intervals along each of the causeways that led into the city. The bridges were raised to let boats pass.

More importantly, the bridges could be lifted to seal off the city in case of an enemy attack.

With a population that eventually reached 200,000 people at its peak, Tenochtitlán was bigger than the largest European cities of the time. However, farmland on the island was scarce. To provide enough food for the city's people, the Mexica created raised fields called *chinampas*. First, they wove raftlike bases from reeds, rushes, and other plants that grew around the island. Then they dug canals, or ditches, around the edge of the island. The dirt, weeds, and mud that they dug up were piled onto the bases, forming small islands in the canals. At the corners of each *chinampa*, the Mexica drove stakes into the lake bottom to hold the plot in place. These "floating gardens" made very productive fields. One plot could grow enough food for a whole family.

Lake Texcoco and the lakes to its north were salty. Lake Texcoco was connected to two more lakes to the south, which had fresh water, instead of salt water. To hold back the salt water of Lake Texcoco and the lakes to the north, the Mexica built a ten-mile-long dike—a damlike structure. The dike helped to keep out the salt water. In time, the water around the island became fresher, like the water in the lakes to the south. The Mexica knew it was important to keep the water in their irrigation canals as fresh as possible, because crops cannot grow in salty water. The dike also had gates built into it. The Mexica could close these gates during rainy seasons to keep excess water from flooding the city.

To maintain a constant supply of fresh water for drinking, the Mexica built an aqueduct: a pipe that brought fresh water to the city from springs on the mainland three miles away. The aqueduct led to the plaza, where the water flowed into the fountains of the biggest palaces. The aqueduct also had openings at many of the bridges that it crossed as it passed through the city. Ordinary citizens could gather water at these openings. Some water was used for drinking, while some was channeled through canals to irrigate the *chinampas*.

With much resourcefulness and hard work, the Mexica transformed a swampy island into a thriving city. By the 1400s, the mighty Aztec empire stretched throughout what is now Mexico. Tenochtitlán became the capital of the Aztec empire in 1428. The city was one of the largest and grandest in the world. Visitors who entered it were simply amazed. By the time the Spanish explorer Cortés arrived, around 1520, Tenochtitlán was the crown jewel of the vast Aztec empire. Even the Spanish soldiers who had visited the great cities of Europe were amazed by the technological innovations and the beauty of the Aztec capital.

Unfortunately, their admiration for Tenochtitlán did not keep the Spanish from attacking it. The entire city was destroyed and the citizens fled. Eventually the lakes dried up. The current capital of Mexico, Mexico City, was built over Tenochtitlán's remains, in the dry valley that formed where the salty lakes had been. Little is left of the ancient Aztec capital, but the world still remembers Tenochtitlán as one of the largest and most impressive cities of its time. ○

20. Which statement BEST describes the main idea of this article?

    Ⓐ Tenochtitlán was a great city with many technological achievements.

    Ⓑ The people of Tenochtitlán were very proud of their city.

    Ⓒ The Mexica created farming systems to provide food for 200,000 people.

    Ⓓ Tenochtitlán was destroyed by Spanish explorers in the early 1500s.

21. According to the map, how many causeways led into the city?

    Ⓐ one

    Ⓑ two

    Ⓒ three

    Ⓓ five

22. How were the lakes to the south of Lake Texcoco different from the lakes to the north?

    Ⓐ The lakes to the south were salty.

    Ⓑ The lakes to the south had fresh water.

    Ⓒ The lakes to the south were swampy.

    Ⓓ The lakes to the south were shallower.

23. Which of the following events would have caused the Mexica to lift their drawbridges?

    Ⓐ a terrible rainstorm

    Ⓑ the arrival of a merchant

    Ⓒ a threat of attack

    Ⓓ regular street cleaning

GO ON

24. The following word web lists some of the "marvels of technology" that made it possible for Tenochtitlán to grow and prosper on an island in the middle of a lake. From the answer choices below, choose the missing "marvel of technology" that belongs in the blank circle.

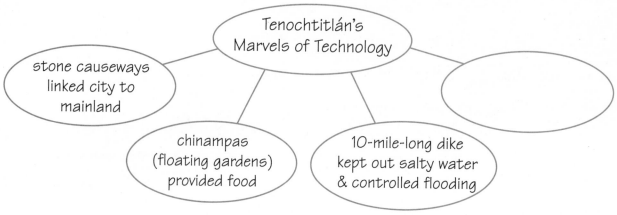

Ⓐ pine torches lit streets at night

Ⓑ gardens made plaza beautiful

Ⓒ canoes carried people around city

Ⓓ an aqueduct brought fresh water to city

25. The author of the article would MOST LIKELY agree with which of the following?

Ⓐ The Aztec capital was not as well planned as most European cities of the day.

Ⓑ The Mexica should have chosen a different place to build the Aztec capital.

Ⓒ The Mexica were very resourceful and creative when it came to problem solving.

Ⓓ The Aztec capital did not show the glory and wealth of the Aztec empire.

Stop! End of Session 1, Part 1

A note about the rest of the test:

This part of the test asks you to write about what you have listened to or read. Your writing will NOT be scored on your personal opinions. It WILL be scored on

- how clearly you organize and express your ideas
- how accurately and completely you answer the questions
- how well you support your ideas with examples
- how interesting and enjoyable your writing is
- how correctly you use grammar, spelling, punctuation, and paragraphs

 Whenever you see this symbol, be sure to plan and check your writing.

GO ON

Session 1
Part 2: Listening

Directions *In this part of the test, you will listen to an article called "Koko Can!" by Gina Bernard. Then you will answer some questions to show how well you understood what was read. You will listen to the article twice. As you listen carefully, you may take notes on the article anytime you wish. You may use these notes to answer the questions that follow. Use the space below and on the next page for your notes.*

This article is about some research that was done to find out whether humans could "talk" to another species.

Here are the spellings and pronunciations of some words from the article that may not be familiar to you:

Koko

Ndume (en • DOO • may)

Dr. Penny Patterson

ASL (American Sign Language)

conservation The preservation, protection, or restoration of wildlife or natural resources

Notes

Note to Teachers: The listening selection appears in the Teacher's Guide for AIM Higher! New York ELA Review.

Notes

GO ON

26. What three examples in the article show that Koko is creative?

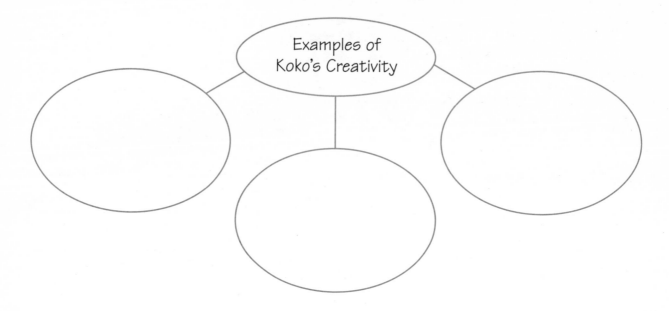

Examples of
Koko's Creativity

27. Explain at least two ways that Koko's caretakers know that she feels emotions such as love and grief.

_____

_____

_____

_____

_____

_____

28. What do Koko's caretakers think is the reason that she has not had a baby? Why do they think she is more likely to have a baby if she moves to the new site in Hawaii?

_____

_____

_____

_____

_____

_____

_____

GO ON

Planning Page

You may PLAN your writing for question 29 here if you wish, but do NOT write your final answer on this page. Your writing on this Planning Page will NOT count toward your final score. Write your final answer on the next two pages.

Notes

29. What was the original purpose of Dr. Patterson's research and how has the purpose of her project changed? What has her research taught us about gorillas? How might this new information about gorillas affect efforts to preserve and protect gorillas?

In your answer, be sure to include

- a description of Dr. Patterson's purpose and how it has changed over the years

- an explanation of what her research has taught us about gorillas

- your ideas about how this information might affect gorilla conservation efforts

 Check your writing for correct spelling, grammar, and punctuation.

_____

_____

_____

_____

_____

_____

_____

_____

_____

_____

_____

_____

_____

GO ON

_____

_____

_____

_____

_____

_____

_____

_____

_____

_____

_____

_____

_____

_____

_____

_____

_____

 **Stop! End of Session 1,
Part 2**

Session 2

This session contains two parts. In Part 1, you will read two passages and write about them. In Part 2, you will write an essay.

Session 2
Part 1: Reading

Directions In this part of the test, you are going to read a poem called "The Blind Men and the Elephant," by John Godfrey Saxe. You will also read a story called "Leading the Way," by Victoria Fortune. You will answer questions and write about what you have read. You may look back at the poem and the story as often as you like.

GO ON

The Blind Men and the Elephant: A Hindu Tale
retold by John Godfrey Saxe

There is an old Hindu parable about six blind men who try to discover what an elephant is like. Various versions of the story also appear in many other cultures. This version is told in verse:

It was six men of Indostan
To learning much inclined,
Who went to see the Elephant
(Though all of them were blind.)
That each by observation
Might satisfy his mind.

The first approached the Elephant
And happening to fall
Against his broad and sturdy side
At once began to bawl,
"God bless me, but the Elephant
Is very like a wall!"

The second, feeling of the tusk,
Cried, "Ho! What have we here
So very round and smooth and sharp?
To me 'tis mighty clear
This wonder of an Elephant
Is very like a spear."

The third approached the animal,
And happening to take
The squirming trunk within his hands,
Thus boldly up and spake,[1]
"I see," quoth[2] he, "the Elephant
Is very like a snake!"

---

[1]**spake.** Spoke, said
[2]**quoth.** Said

The fourth reached out his eager hand,
And felt about the knee.
"What most this wondrous beast is like
Is mighty plain," quoth he.
"'Tis clear enough the Elephant
Is very like a tree!"

The fifth, who chanced to touch the ear,
Said, "E'en the blindest man
Can tell what this resembles most.
Deny the fact who can,
This marvel of an Elephant
Is very like a fan!"

The sixth no sooner had begun
About the beast to grope,
Than, seizing on the swinging tail
That fell within his scope,
"I see," quoth he, "the Elephant
Is very like a rope!"

And so these men of Indostan
Disputed loud and long,
Each in his own opinion
Exceeding stiff and strong,
Though each was partly in the right
And all were in the wrong.

The Hindus used this tale to teach that no one can fully understand the mysteries of life. We all are limited in what we know. So the next time you get into an argument with friends, remember the elephant. Are you seeing just the leg? What are you missing? What do your friends see? Could they be seeing part of the truth that you don't see? Should you be more tolerant of other people's opinions? ○

GO ON

30. Explain what this line of the poem means: "Though each was partly in the right, and all were in the wrong." Why was each man so convinced that he was right?

_____

_____

_____

_____

_____

_____

Leading the Way
by Victoria Fortune

"B anks!" Cody yelled. His voice echoed off the weather-worn walls of the old barn. "Banks, where are you?" he shouted again. A gooey, black mixture of mud and manure sucked at his boots as he walked around the barn, searching for his cousin.

He looked toward the horizon. A solid wall of heavy, dark clouds was moving in, and the sky was an eerie yellow-green. After three hot, muggy days, a thunderstorm was now approaching—the perfect recipe for a tornado. A chill ran up Cody's spine. The others were probably in the basement by now, where he should be.

"I oughta just leave her. Maybe that'd teach her," he grumbled as he trudged along the backside of the barn. "She ran off on her own; she can get back on her own." As the thought ran through his mind, he knew he couldn't leave his cousin out there alone—not in this weather.

When Banks's parents had died six months before, Mom had suggested that Banks come to live on the farm. "Banks is your responsibility," Mom had said to Cody. "You're going to have to look out for her, be her eyes." Cody felt awkward around Banks. He was always afraid he might say something to offend her. She was forever getting into things and asking if she could help out, but how could she help if she couldn't see? He felt sorry for her losing her parents and all, but deep down, having her around felt like one more chore. He was tired of looking for ways to keep her busy while he did his work.

Cody stomped angrily across the field. His boots sank into the freshly plowed rows of dirt. Raindrops began to splat against the rich brown soil, creating little circles of black mud. The air was thick with the musty smell of damp earth. Banks was nowhere in sight. He checked the sky again. The dark clouds were closer now. The wind whipped his shaggy blonde hair, and large drops of rain pelted his bony shoulders. He reached the edge of the pond and looked longingly toward home.

"Banks, where are you?" he screamed over the howling wind.

"Cody?" a voice yelled from nowhere. Cody glanced around to see Banks's head pop up out of the irrigation ditch that cut through the fields.

"What the heck are you doing down there?"

"There's gonna be a tornado," she screeched.

"No kidding," Cody snapped.

"It's gonna touch down any minute now," Banks panted. "Get down here."

"We're going home." Cody insisted. "C'mon." He grabbed her arm and yanked her out of the ditch.

"We'll never make it to the house," Banks yelled. "Let's get to the barn."

"I told Mom I'd bring you home," Cody snarled, dragging her behind him.

"Cody…" Banks struggled against his pull. Cody turned to yell at her to hurry up, but he froze before he could open his mouth. From the dense wall of clouds, a black funnel dipped down and hit the ground in a field south of the pond. It tore past the pond, devouring trees and fence and spitting out splinters. Cody's mind screamed "run," but his feet were rooted to the ground.

"Cody, the barn!" Banks yelled over the deafening roar.

Swirling debris stung Cody's eyes. He couldn't even see the barn, though he knew it was nearby. Then he felt himself being pulled. "This is it," he thought. "We're dead." But instead of flying upward, he was dragged forward. He could feel Banks's hand squeezing his. The next thing he knew, he was stumbling into the barn.

"C'mon, Cody," Banks screamed over the howling wind. "We've got to get to the grain bin."

Cody clutched the wall, terrified to move. The hay and straw that whipped around the room was blinding, and the walls were shaking violently. He could barely hear Banks yelling. She was right—the tornado was heading right for the barn. They had to move—but where…which way to go? He couldn't see. Again, he felt Banks grab his arm.

"This way!" she yelled, pulling him along the wall. They sidled toward the room where they kept the feed for the horses. Luckily, Cody had let the horses out in the far pasture that morning to graze. Banks kicked open the door to the feed room and leapt through the doorway, pulling Cody after her.

She struggled to lift the metal lid to the feed bin, but it was too heavy. Cody yanked it open, and they both dove in, pulling it down over their heads with a clang. Just as it slammed shut, there was a terrible sound of splintering wood and breaking glass. Debris smashed against the sides of the metal bin like a savage beast lunging repeatedly at its prey. The noise seemed to last forever. When it finally died down, Cody opened the lid slowly. He gasped. Wooden planks and shingles blanketed the fields all around them. The concrete floor, with the grain bin bolted to it, and a few jagged beams of wood were all that remained of the old barn. A pitchfork was stuck sideways in a beam near the bin.

"Cody? You OK?" Banks called.

"I'm fine," he whispered hoarsely. He struggled out of the bin and lifted Banks out.

As they walked home, Cody's legs felt wobbly. He hung his head low.

"That was close," Banks sighed. "We're pretty lucky."

"Yeah, lucky," Cody mumbled. "No thanks to me."

"What do you mean?" Banks asked.

"I froze up when I saw the tornado. If it weren't for you, we would've been killed."

Banks was quiet for a while. Then she said. "I'm glad I couldn't see it. The sound was scary enough."

Cody studied his cousin's deep brown eyes. He wondered what it was like to "see" in the dark.

"What made you think of the bin?" he asked.

"You know those big metal bolts that hold it to the floor? One day Uncle Jack caught me feeling 'em and he said, 'Those things are so solid, even a tornado couldn't budge 'em.'"

Cody smiled at Banks. He reached for her hand the way he usually did when he was leading her somewhere, but this time, he wasn't leading the way. ○

31. Explain why Banks is able to find a safe place to wait out the tornado when Cody cannot.

_____

_____

_____

_____

_____

_____

32. How does Cody's attitude toward Banks change during the story? Why does his attitude change?

_____

_____

_____

_____

_____

_____

Planning Page

You may PLAN your writing for question 33 here if you wish, but do NOT write your final answer on this page. Your writing on this Planning Page will NOT count toward your final score. Write your final answer on the next two pages.

Notes

33.

Often, a good way to figure out the theme of a story is to think about what lesson the main character has learned or how he or she has changed. In some cases, however, the opposite is true: The reader learns a lesson because the characters have not learned anything. The story and the poem have the same theme, but they teach it in different ways. Explain the theme that the story and the poem share. Compare and contrast the ways that the two selections get their theme across.

In your answer, be sure to

- explain the theme that the story and the poem share
- point out the similarities and differences in how the selections get across the theme
- use details and examples from both selections

Check your writing for correct spelling, grammar, and punctuation.

_____

_____

_____

_____

_____

_____

_____

_____

_____

_____

_____

_____

_____

_____

_____

_____

 Stop! End of Session 2, Part 1

Session 2
Part 2: Writing

Directions In this part of the test, you will be writing an original essay.
Follow the directions on the next two pages and begin your writing on page 310.

Planning Page

You may PLAN your writing for question 34 here if you wish, but do NOT write your final answer on this page. Your writing on this Planning Page will NOT count toward your final score. Write your final answer on the next three pages.

Notes

34.

Prejudice is an opinion or judgment made without knowledge of the facts. When people are prejudiced against another group of people, it is generally because they do not know any people in that group firsthand. Why is prejudice harmful? Describe some examples of prejudice and explain why they are harmful. What are some ways that people can overcome their prejudices?

In your answer, be sure to include

- one or more examples of prejudice
- an explanation of why prejudice is harmful
- some ways that people can overcome their prejudices

 Check your writing for correct spelling, grammar, and punctuation.

_____

_____

_____

_____

_____

_____

_____

_____

_____

_____

_____

_____

_____

_____

_____

_____

_____

_____

_____

_____

_____

_____

_____

_____

_____

_____

_____

_____

_____

Stop! End of Test

Appendix A: Punctuation and Capitalization Handbook

Meets
New York
Standards
1.B.6
2.B.4
3.B.4

1. End Marks

1.1 A declarative sentence ends with a period (.).

> Ravens look like crows but are bigger.

1.2 A question ends with a question mark (?).

> How long is forever?

1.3 An exclamation, or strong statement, ends with an exclamation mark (!). A strong imperative statement, or command, can also end with an exclamation mark.

> What a nice gift that was!
>
> Help!

2. Commas

2.1 Use a comma after an introductory exclamation, participial phrase, or adverbial clause.

AFTER INTERJECTION	Wow, that was one incredible play!
AFTER PARTICIPIAL PHRASE	Poking out from his shell, the box turtle saw that the fox had moved on.
ADVERBIAL CLAUSE	When she opens the door, I want you all to say "surprise."

2.2 Use a comma after two or more introductory prepositional phrases if these phrases are not immediately followed by a verb.

NOT FOLLOWED BY VERB	In April of 1912, the *Titanic* hit an iceberg.
FOLLOWED BY VERB	At the bottom of the canyon runs the Colorado River.

2.3 Use commas to set off an element that interrupts a sentence. Such an interrupter is known as a **parenthetical expression.**

> The teddy bear, by the way, was named after President Theodore ("Teddy") Roosevelt.

2.4 Use commas to separate items in a series, including words, phrases, and clauses.

TO SEPARATE WORDS	The park has a funhouse, a zoo, and a waterslide.
TO SEPARATE GROUPS OF WORDS	Good ways to get some exercise include riding a bike, walking a dog, and swimming.

Do not use commas to separate items when each is joined by a coordinating conjunction like *and, or,* or *nor.*

USE COMMAS	Which do you like most, soccer, lacrosse, or football?
DO NOT USE COMMAS	Which do you like most, soccer or lacrosse or football?

2.5 Use commas to separate two or more adjectives that describe a noun.

USE COMMAS	Look at those frosty, orange pumpkins!

2.6 Use commas to separate two sentences joined by *and, or, nor, for, but, so,* or *yet.*

> Winter came, but no snow fell.

2.7 Use commas to set off words of direct address.

> Joe, where have you been?

More ▶

3. Semicolons

Use a semicolon to separate a series of items if one or more of those items contains a comma.

> The teachers at the school included Mr. Snape, Potions; Mr. Lockhart, Defense against the Dark Arts; and Ms. Sprout, Herbology.

4. Colons

Use a colon to introduce a list either after "these" or "the following" or in a place where "and here it is" or "and here they are" could be inserted. Do not use a colon right after a verb.

CORRECT   These are the nine planets: Mercury, Venus, Earth, Mars, Jupiter, Saturn, Uranus, Neptune, and Pluto.

INCORRECT   The planets are: Mercury, Venus, Earth, Mars, Jupiter, Saturn, Uranus, Neptune, and Pluto.

5. Dashes

Use a dash to show an abrupt break in thought or speech.

> What a nice doggie you—ouch, you bit me!

6. Hyphens

6.1   Use a hyphen to link words in some compound words. If you have doubts about whether to use a hyphen in a compound, look the compound up in a dictionary.

HYPHENATED COMPOUNDS
- all-powerful queen
- twentieth-century history
- well-known musician
- middle-class person
- self-confident speaker
- living-room furniture
- blue-green color
- problem-solving ability
- five-year-old boy
- great-grandson

6.2   Use a hyphen to separate numbers.

> 2005-2006 school year
>
> pp. 21-43 and 183-85

7. Parentheses

Use parentheses to set off added information that is not the main idea of the sentence.

> My favorite artist is Maurice Sendak (author of *Where the Wild Things Are*).

8. Apostrophes

8.1 For most nouns and some, but not all, pronouns, use an apostrophe to show ownership or belonging.

For a singular noun, add an apostrophe and an *s*.

> the walrus's tusks
>
> the banker's keys

In some special cases, use an apostrophe by itself:

> for appearance' sake
>
> for goodness' sake

To show ownership or possession for a plural noun, add only an apostrophe if the plural noun ends in *s*. Add an apostrophe and an *s* if the plural noun ends in some letter other than *s*.

> the horses' stalls
>
> the geese's honking

To show ownership or belonging by all members of a group, use the apostrophe only for the last one in the group.

> Have you seen Maria, José, and George's skit?

8.2 To show belonging, use an apostrophe with a word that refers to a time or to an amount of currency or coin.

> a week's work
>
> a dollar's worth of peanuts

8.3 Use an apostrophe to form contractions.

> o'clock, rock 'n' roll, in the '60s and '70s, wouldn't

9. Italics and Underlining

9.1 Use italics (when word processing) or underlining (when writing longhand) for titles of

works of art: Leonardo da Vinci's *Mona Lisa*

books: E. B. White's *Charlotte's Web*

plays: *You're a Good Man, Charlie Brown*

films: *Star Wars: The Phantom Menace*

television series: *Sesame Street*

magazines: *Cricket*

long musical works such as ballet scores: the *Nutcracker Ballet, Peter and the Wolf*

Do not use italics or underlining for names of musical forms such as concertos or symphonies.

> Beethoven's Symphony no. 5

9.2 Use italics (when word processing) or underlining (when writing longhand) for words used as words, letters used as letters, and words from foreign languages.

> The vowels are *a, e, i, o,* and *u.*
>
> The word *radar,* spelled backward, is the word *radar.*
>
> The Sanskrit word *padme* means "lotus."
>
> "*Buenas dias,*" said Consuelo.

More ▶

Meets New York Standards
1.B.6
2.B.4
3.B.4

10. Quotation Marks

10.1 Use quotation marks to enclose direct quotations but not indirect quotations.

USE QUOTES   Shakespeare wrote, "All the world's a stage."

DO NOT USE QUOTES   Did Shakespeare write that the world was like a stage?

10.2 Commas or periods after a quotation should go inside the closing quotation marks.

"Living is learning," I always say.

10.3 Colons and semicolons should go outside the quotation marks.

I always say, "Good morning, Mr. Scrooge"; however, he sometimes acts as if he didn't hear me.

This is my favorite part of the story "The Boy Who Talked with Animals": the reports at the end of sightings of the turtle and the boy.

10.4 A question mark should go inside the quotation marks if the quoted material is a question. Otherwise, the question mark should go outside the quotation marks.

Did Mark say, "The woman is speaking Russian"?

Did Mark ask, "Does anyone here speak Russian?"

11. Ellipses

11.1 Use an **ellipsis** (...) to show that material has been left out.

"No sensible decision can be made ... without taking into account the world as it will be." —Isaac Asimov

11.2 Use an ellipsis to show a pause in dialogue or speech that is unfinished.

"Hey, ... wait for me," said Hector.

"This is really, really...." Ms. Nogales stopped, too choked up to finish her thank-you's.

12. Capitalization

12.1 Capitalize the first letter in each main word in the names of historical events, special events, periods of time, interjections used alone, brand names, letters used as grades or to refer to musical tones, names of organizations and institutions, personal names, place names, proper nouns and adjectives, the pronoun *I*, sacred names, course titles (as opposed to school subjects), vehicles, months, days, years, astronomical terms, and works of art, literature, and music.

the Battle of Shiloh

the Watermelon Seed-Spitting Contest

the Roaring Twenties

the Ice Age

Oh! Well! I never!

Converse, Gap

two As and 3 Bs on my report card

an E-flat scale

The Academy of Motion Picture Arts and Sciences

Ocala, Florida

me, myself, and I
Allah, Jehovah, Vishnu, Buddha, Mary, the Bible, the Koran
Fine Arts with Ms. Fleck
Air Force One
a Volkswagen Beetle
Tuesday, April 1, 1943
Neptune, Orion
The Wind in the Willows
"Happy Birthday"

12.2 Capitalize the first letter in each important word in the names of family relationships used as titles except when these names are preceded by a modifier such as a personal pronoun.

my dad

Thank you, Father.

Felicia's cousin

my brother-in-law

I say, Brother-in-Law dear, shall we depart?

12.3 Capitalize the first letter in each entry in an outline.

Things to do

    I. Get good grades

    II. Go to college

    III. Graduate with honors

    IV. Run for president

Meets
New York
Standards
1.B.6
2.B.4
3.B.4

Appendix B: Rubric for Writing Assessment

Factors Considered in the Writing Rubric

A **rubric** is a set of criteria used for evaluating something. The rubric on the next page can be used to assess the writing that you do for this book. That rubric takes into account such factors in good writing as Focus, Elaboration and Support, Organization, Voice and Style, and Conventions.

Focus. Writing is focused if it remains on topic and does not contain unnecessary or unrelated details.

Elaboration and Support. Writing is fully elaborated if its main idea is supported by sufficient details—ones that are appropriate and convincing.

Organization. Writing is well organized if details are presented in a logical order and if ideas are connected by means of transitions.

Voice and Style. Writing has voice and style if it is authentic, compelling, interesting, and unique. The voice, or sound, of a piece of writing is conveyed by elements of style, such as word choice and rhythm.

Conventions. When writing uses correct spelling, grammar, usage, capitalization, and punctuation, and when it follows the rules of proper manuscript form (such as use of margins and indented paragraphs), then it is said to follow the conventions of writing.

To use the rubric (on the next page), read over the piece of writing several times. Then, based upon your overall impression of the piece, assign a score from 0 to 6.

Six-Point Writing Rubric

6	The writing is exceptionally engaging, clear, and focused. Ideas are thoroughly developed using supporting details that are well chosen and convincing. The writer has organized the material and used transitions in such a way as to lead the reader smoothly through the text. The voice and tone are authentic and compelling. Precise use of language coupled with varied sentence structure make this piece interesting as well as understandable. The writing shows mastery of English usage and of conventions of grammar, mechanics, and spelling.
5	The writing is engaging, clear, and focused. Ideas are well developed and supported using interesting and appropriate details. The writer has organized the material and used transitions in such a way as to guide the reader through the text. Voice and tone are original, expressive, and authentic. The writing shows a command of English usage and of conventions of grammar, mechanics, and spelling but may contain minor lapses that do not interfere with meaning.
4	The writing is generally clear and focused. Ideas are developed and supported by relevant details. The organization is functional, and the writing is generally coherent. The voice and tone are appropriate. The writing may contain lapses in English usage and in conventions of grammar, mechanics, and spelling. However, these are not severe enough to impede meaning.
3	The writing has moments of clarity and focus. Ideas are developed using limited or partially complete details. The writing shows some evidence of structure, but the organization may seem artificial or ineffective. Voice and tone may be uneven or inappropriate. Problems in usage and in conventions of grammar, mechanics, and spelling may interfere with understanding some of the time.
2	The writing is only occasionally clear and focused. Ideas are underdeveloped and poorly connected. The writing shows slight evidence of organization or structure. Voice and tone may be uneven or inappropriate. Problems in usage and conventions may make the writing difficult to read.
1	The writing is generally unclear and unfocused. Ideas are not developed; descriptions or explanations are limited in length. The writing lacks noticeable structure. Problems in usage and in conventions make the writing difficult to read.
0	The writing is unreadable or was not done at all and so cannot be scored.

Glossary

Abstract. 1. Simplified or reduced to its barest elements. 2. General, not concrete.

Achievement test. A test that measures what a student has learned. Compare with *aptitude test.*

Active reading. The process of engaging critically and creatively with a text by asking questions, visualizing, predicting, drawing conclusions, summarizing, paraphrasing, evaluating, connecting, and extending.

Active vocabulary. All the words that a person uses when speaking and writing. Compare with *passive vocabulary.*

Active voice. Grammatical construction in which the subject (the doer of the action) comes before the verb (the action), in normal word order. *Dan washed the car* is a sentence in the active voice. Compare with *passive voice.*

Ad hominem. Latin, meaning "to the person." A type of argument in which a person casts doubts on an opposing opinion by attacking the person holding the opinion rather than the opinion itself.

Alliteration. The repetition of consonant sounds at the beginning of each word, as in "deep, dank, dark, dangerous, dewy, and dim."

Analogy. An extended comparison of one thing to another, usually to make a particular point.

Analysis. The process of breaking something down into its parts and studying the characteristics of the parts, how the parts function, and how they relate to one another and to the whole.

Anecdote. A very brief story, often a true one, told to make a point.

Antagonist. A character or force who struggles against the protagonist, or main character, in a story. Compare with *protagonist.*

Antonym. A word that is opposite or nearly opposite in meaning to another word. *Cold* and *hot* are antonyms. Compare with *synonym.*

Apposition. A word or phrase that follows another word or phrase, functions as the same part of speech, and provides an explanation, description, or definition of the word or phrase that it follows. In the following sentence, the italicized phrase is an apposition: J. K. Rowling, *author of the Harry Potter books,* is from Edinburgh, Scotland.

Aptitude test. A test that attempts to measure an individual's underlying ability or potential. Compare with *achievement test.*

Arrangement. See *organization.*

Audience. The people for whom one writes; the reader(s) of a piece.

Author. The writer of any written work.

Authoritative. Knowledgeable, expert. Said of a source of information, such as an encyclopedia or a human expert.

Autobiography. The true story of a person's life, or of some part thereof, as told by that person. See *biography.*

Base word. A complete word that is combined with one or more other word parts to form a new word. The base word *place* appears, for example, in the words *misplace* and *placemat.*

Benchmark. A point of reference for measuring or judging quality or value. In testing, the term is used to refer to a statement from a set of state standards that describes a concept or skill that students are expected to master at a particular level in their education.

Biography. The true story of a person's life, or of some part thereof, as told by someone else.

Body. In an essay, the main part of the piece of writing. It appears after the introduction and before the conclusion and supports, or elaborates upon, the thesis statement. See *elaboration.*

Brainstorming. A technique for generating ideas whereby two or more people list as many ideas on a topic as possible in as short a time as possible, without stopping to evaluate or critique the ideas.

Caption. Text that describes or explains an illustration. See *illustration.*

Cause. An event that brings about or helps to bring about one or more other events (the effects). Compare with *effect.*

Character. A person, animal, or other entity that takes part in or affects the action of a literary work.

Character analysis. The act of thinking about a character's features, including appearance, temperament, behavior, relationships, or motives and any changes in the character during the course of the story.

Chart. A graphic organizer that presents information in rows and columns. See *graphic organizer*.

Chronological order. Time order.

Class. A group or collection, or a subset of a larger whole.

Classification. The act of dividing things into groups, or classes, based on characteristics or features.

Classroom test. A test given to measure concepts and skills taught in class.

Clause. A group of words that has a subject and a verb.

Climax. The peak of interest or suspense in a story. The climax is sometimes, but not always, the same event as the crisis. See *crisis*.

Clincher sentence. A sentence that appears at or near the end of a paragraph and that summarizes or otherwise concludes the paragraph.

Cluster chart. See *word web*.

Coherent organization. The arrangement of ideas in a piece of writing in such a way that each idea follows reasonably from the one before it and leads reasonably to the one after it.

Comparison. 1. The act of showing the ways in which two or more things are similar. 2. The act of showing the similarities and differences between two or among more than two things. See *contrast*.

Complex sentence. A sentence that contains one independent clause and one or more dependent clauses.

Compound-complex sentence. A sentence that contains more than one independent clause and one or more dependent clauses.

Compound sentence. A sentence that contains more than one independent clause.

Compound word. A word made up of two or more base words, as in *eightfold* or *breakdown*. Compounds can be solid, meaning the word is unbroken, as in *spacecraft*; hyphenated, as in *space-time*; or open, as in *space shuttle*.

Conclusion. The final part of an essay, which sums up the piece and/or gives the reader the sense of an ending.

Concrete. Capable of being seen, touched, tasted, heard, or smelled.

Conflict. A struggle experienced by a character in a narrative. See *external conflict, internal conflict*.

Connecting. An active reading strategy that involves thinking about the ways in which information or ideas in the text relate to one's own life.

Context. The material that appears near a word in a reading passage. Often, the word(s) or phrase(s) around an unfamiliar word will provide clues to its meaning.

Context clue. In a reading passage, any word or phrase that provides information about the meaning of another word in that passage.

Contrast. The act of showing the ways in which two or more things differ.

Conventions. Rules of grammar, usage, punctuation, capitalization, and spelling.

Couplet. A two-line stanza in a poem.

Creative thinking. Any thinking that results in uncommon, original ideas or alternative solutions. Some techniques for creative thinking include creative combinations, doubting deeply, and asking "what if" questions.

Crisis. The point in a story where something happens to resolve the conflict faced by the central character or characters. Also called the *turning point*.

Criteria. The standards used to evaluate or make a judgment about something.

Criterion-referenced test. A test that assesses a student's ability to meet a set of *criteria*, or standards for achievement.

Critical thinking. Any thinking that involves reasoning to arrive at knowledge or truth. Types of critical thinking include careful observation, comparison, contrast, cause-and-effect reasoning, and analysis.

Dangling modifier. A word or phrase that is supposed to be a modifier but that appears in a sentence containing no word or phrase that the word or phrase can reasonably modify. The italicized phrase in this sentence is a dangling modifier: *After washing the car,* the real fun began.

Declarative sentence. A sentence that makes a statement.

Deduction. 1. A kind of argument in which, if the premises are true, the conclusion has to be true. 2. A conclusion reached by deduction. See *induction*.

Define. To explain the meaning of a term. A typical dictionary definition does this by first placing the item to be defined into a general class and then showing how it differs from other members of that class. For example, "A conifer is a tree (general class) that does not lose its leaves in the winter (difference from other members of the class)."

Definition, direct. See *restatement*.

Degree order. The organization of ideas or information from more to less or from less to more with regard to some characteristic or quality. Examples of organization by degree order include organization in order of familiarity, in order of importance, and in order of value.

Dénouement. Everything that happens after the central conflict in a story is ended, or resolved. The dénouement is the last part of a conventional plot. A writer may include a dénouement in a story in order to tie up loose ends.

Dependent clause, or subordinate clause. A group of words that has a subject and a verb but cannot stand alone as a sentence. Compare with *independent clause*.

Derived word. A word formed by adding one or more prefixes and/or suffixes to a base word or root. *Fashioned, fashionable,* and *unfashionable* are all derived words created from the base word *fashion*. Also called *derived forms*.

Descriptive writing. Writing that uses words to create a portrait of a subject.

Diary. See *journal*.

Direct definition. See *restatement*.

Distractor. Any one of the incorrect answers in a multiple-choice question.

Double-ledger chart. A T-chart in which one column includes quotations, and the other includes a reader's thoughts and responses. See *T-chart*.

Drafting. The stage of the writing process in which the writer gets his or her ideas down on paper in rough form.

Dynamic character. A character who changes during the course of a narrative. See *static character*.

Effect. One or more events that are caused by one or more other events. Compare with *cause*.

"Either/or" argument. See *false dichotomy*.

Elaboration. 1. The act of providing additional ideas or information in support of an idea, position, or description. Writers elaborate by including specific details, examples, facts, opinions, paraphrases, quotations, reasons, and summaries.

2. Any statement that supports a topic sentence or thesis statement. See *supporting details, thesis*.

Ellipsis. Three or four dots (...) used to show that material is missing from a quotation. An ellipsis can also indicate a pause in hesitant or faltering speech.

Essay. A short piece of nonfiction writing that explores a single part of a subject.

Etymology. 1. The study of the origins and history of the meaning of a word. 2. In a dictionary entry, the part of the entry that explains the origins or history of the entry word.

Evaluating. The act of making judgments about something, such as a piece of writing. Evaluating is an important active reading strategy and is essential for revising a piece of writing.

Events. The actions that take place in a story; what happens.

Evidence. Information provided to prove or support a general statement or opinion.

Example. Something selected to show the nature or character of the rest; a typical instance. Examples are a type of elaboration; they can also provide context clues for any unfamiliar words.

Exclamatory sentence. A sentence that expresses strong feeling and that ends with an exclamation point (!).

Exposition. The part of a plot, usually appearing at the beginning, which introduces the characters and setting and provides essential background information.

Expository writing. Writing that presents information. Also known as *informative writing*.

Expressive writing. Writing that is personal and subjective and that exists primarily to convey or embody the thoughts and feelings of the writer.

Extended-response question. A type of test question that asks the student to generate his or her own, often lengthy, response to a question.

Extending. Connecting ideas or information in a piece of writing to the world outside the piece of writing. Extending is an active reading strategy.

External conflict. A struggle between a character and an outside force, such as nature or another character. Compare with *internal conflict*.

Fact. A statement that can be proved to be true, either by definition or by observation.

Fallacy. An unreasonable mode of argument or an error in reasoning or logic.

Fallacy of omission. When important facts related to an argument have been left out.

Falling action. The plot events that occur after the crisis, or turning point.

False analogy. A comparison that falsely assumes that because two subjects are superficially similar, they share other, deeper similarities.

False dichotomy. A logical fallacy in which a speaker or writer falsely assumes that only two alternatives are possible. Also known as *"either/or" argument*.

Fiction. A story about imaginary characters and events. Compare with *nonfiction*.

Figurative language. See *figure of speech*.

Figure of speech. Descriptive statements that are not literal, including personifications, similes, and metaphors.

Final draft. A final version of a piece of writing—one that has been revised and, perhaps, proofread.

First-person point of view. The narrative standpoint from which the narrator tells the story using pronouns like *I* and *we*. Usually, in stories told from the first-person point of view, the narrator is a character in the story.

Five-paragraph theme. See *standard classroom theme*.

Flashback. A part of a narrative that presents an event or series of events that occurred earlier than the current time in the work.

Flow chart. A graphic organizer representing a sequence of steps or operations. See *graphic organizer*.

Focus. The quality that a piece of writing has when it does not wander off topic.

Folktale. A story that originated in the oral tradition and that has been passed down by word of mouth from generation to generation.

Foreshadowing. In a narrative, any hint about events to come.

Formal language. Language appropriate to ceremonial public occasions or audiences.

Free verse. Poetry that has no regular meter or rhyme. Compare with *traditional verse*.

Freewriting. A technique for generating ideas whereby one simply begins writing about a topic, putting down any and all ideas that come to mind, without stopping to edit and without worrying about grammar, usage, mechanics, spelling, or manuscript form.

Function. What something does; its purpose.

Generalization. A process of thinking by which a person arrives at a broad conclusion based upon specific facts. Same as *induction*.

Genre. A form or type of written work, such as the business letter, the persuasive essay, or the historical novel.

Graphic organizer. A chart, outline, table, or other visual representation of ideas or information. These tools can be used for any of a wide range of purposes, such as notetaking, planning pieces of writing, or presenting ideas to others.

Heading. A subtitle that appears within a reading passage.

History. A nonfiction narrative that tells about important events that happened in the past.

How-to writing. Writing that describes how to carry out some process, such as baking a cake or buying a house.

Illustration. Pictures or graphics that appear with text. See *caption*.

Image. A word or phrase that names something that can be seen, heard, touched, tasted, or smelled.

Imperative sentence. A sentence that gives a command or makes a request.

Implied topic sentence. A main idea that is suggested by a paragraph but not stated outright. See *topic sentence*.

Inciting incident. The part of the plot in which the central conflict is introduced.

Independent clause. A group of words that has a subject and a verb and that can stand alone as a sentence. Sometimes called a *main clause*. Compare with *dependent clause*.

Induction. 1. A kind of argument in which a general conclusion is drawn from specific facts. 2. A conclusion reached by induction. Compare with *deduction*.

Inference. 1. A conclusion drawn from a set of facts. 2. A reasoned argument from one or more premises to a conclusion. Types of inference include *induction* and *deduction*.

Inflected forms. Alternative forms of a word as listed in a dictionary. See *derived word*.

Informal language. Language appropriate to casual, nonpublic occasions or audiences.

Informative writing. Writing that primarily presents information and facts, not opinions.

Internal conflict. A struggle that takes place within a character. Compare with *external conflict*.

Interrogative sentence. A sentence that asks a question and that ends with a question mark (?).

Introduction. The beginning part of a piece of nonfiction writing that presents necessary background information and the main idea, or thesis. Introductions are usually meant to capture the reader's attention.

Inverted word order. The placement of words in a sentence in an order that is not usual or normal. *Works hard, he does* is a sentence that makes use of inverted word order.

Irony. A contradiction, such as a difference between what something appears to be and what it really is, or between what is said and what is meant.

Journal. A day-by-day account of thoughts, events, or any other happenings or impressions that a person wishes to record. Also called a *diary*.

Key terms. Especially important words that an author wants to emphasize. Key terms are often highlighted in special type, such as boldface or italics.

Leader line. The part of a multiple-choice question that comes before the answers. Sometimes the leader line is a question. Sometimes it is an incomplete statement that should be completed by the correct answer.

Learning log. A journal in which a person records what he or she has learned.

Line. In a poem, a group of words written out horizontally across a page.

Loaded word. A word that has strong emotional content, used to sway opinion.

Logical fallacy. See *fallacy*.

Logical organization. The arrangement of ideas in a piece of writing in an order that makes sense. See also *organization*.

Lyric poem. Verse, often short, that expresses the ideas and emotions of a speaker.

Main clause. See *independent clause*.

Main idea. The most important idea in a paragraph or piece of writing.

Manuscript form. The layout of a piece of writing, including its spacing, margin width, indention of paragraphs, and placement of titles, captions, headings, and page numbers.

Metaphor. A figure of speech in which one thing is described as if it were something quite different, as in *that undefeated wrestler, the sea*.

Meter. See *rhythm*.

Minor character. A character who does not play a major role in a story.

Misplaced modifier. A word or phrase placed in a sentence in such a way that it modifies the wrong word or phrase. The italicized phrase in this sentence is a misplaced modifier: *Taking pictures with their digital cameras,* the monkeys gave the tourists quite a treat.

Mode. A kind of writing, as determined by that writing's purpose. Common modes of writing include expressive, narrative, descriptive, expository, and persuasive.

Modifier. Grammatical term referring to a word, phrase, or clause that limits (by making more specific) the meaning of another word, phrase, or clause. Adjectives, adverbs, adjective phrases, adverb phrases, and other parts of speech that perform this function are examples of modifiers.

Mood. An emotional quality, such as gloom or joy, that is created by a passage in a literary work or by the work as a whole.

Moral. The lesson contained in or taught by a fable or story.

Motivation. 1. An internal or external reason that impels a character to think, feel, or act in a certain way; an incentive. 2. The state of being moved to think, feel, or act.

Motive. A reason that impels a character to think, feel, or act in a certain way; an incentive.

Multiple-choice question. A type of test question in which the student chooses the correct answer from among several possibilities.

Narrative. A story, either fiction or nonfiction.

Narrative nonfiction. A true story about real people, places, and events.

Narrative poem. A poem that tells a story.

Narrator. The person or voice that tells what happens in a story.

Negation. A statement that contradicts another statement.

Nonfiction. Writing about real people, places, things, or ideas. Compare with *fiction*.

Norm-referenced test. See *standardized test*.

Novel. A long piece of narrative fiction.

Objective. Presenting only verified facts and not personal opinions. News reports, for example, must be as objective as possible.

Observation. The process of taking in information using your senses—sight, hearing, touch, taste, and smell.

Onomatopoeia. The use of words or phrases, like *buzz* or *meow*, that sound like what they describe.

Opinion. A statement that cannot be proved, absolutely, to be true or false. Common types of opinion include predictions and statements of value, belief, policy, and obligation. See also *reasonable opinion*.

Order of impression. Arrangement of details in a piece of writing in order of the impact that they make on a viewer or in the order in which a person might typically encounter them.

Organization. The way a piece of writing is ordered, or the principle by which its parts are arranged. Common methods of organization include chronological order, spatial order, degree order, and part-by-part order. See also *coherent organization, dialectic organization, logical organization*.

Outline. See *rough outline*.

Overgeneralization. The act of making an inference based on too little evidence. See also *stereotyping*.

Paragraph. A unit of writing, usually containing more than one sentence, that communicates a main idea. A *paragraph in standard form* is a unit of writing containing a topic sentence, two or more supporting sentences, and, usually, a concluding or clincher sentence.

Parallelism. The use of similar grammatical forms to give items equal weight, as in Abraham Lincoln's "of the people, by the people, for the people."

Paraphrase. 1. (*v.*) To repeat in different words an idea taken from another speaker or writer. 2. (*n.*) A piece of speech or writing that repeats, in different words, an idea taken from another speaker or writer.

Part-by-part order. An arrangement in which ideas do not follow any overall organizational pattern, but each idea is logically connected to the one before it and to the one that follows it.

Part of speech label. The part of a dictionary entry that tells the part of speech of the entry word. Part of speech labels are usually abbreviated, as in *n.* for noun or *adj.* for adjective.

Participial phrase. A group of words that begins with a participle and that acts, as a group, as an adjective, modifying a noun or a pronoun, as in "the moon *peeking over the horizon*." See *participle*.

Participle. A verb form ending in –*ing*, –*ed*, –*d*, –*t*, or –*en* that functions as an adjective to modify a noun or pronoun, as in *singing* sailors, *broken* window, or *burnt* toast.

Passive vocabulary. All the words that a person understands but does not use in his or her writing or speech. Compare with *active vocabulary*.

Passive voice. Grammatical construction of a declarative sentence in which the doer of the action is either omitted from the sentence or follows the verb (the action) in a prepositional phrase. *The car was washed by Dan* is a sentence in the passive voice. Compare with *active voice*.

Personification. A figure of speech in which something that is not human is described as if it were.

Persuasion. The attempt, in writing or in speech, to convince an audience to take some action or to adopt some belief or point of view.

Persuasive writing. Writing that attempts to convince the reader to adopt a particular belief or viewpoint or to take a course of action.

Plot. The series of events in a story, often involving the introduction, intensification, and eventual resolution of a conflict. A plot may contain the following parts: introduction or exposition; rising action; climax; crisis, or turning point; falling action; resolution; and dénouement.

Plot analysis. The act of identifying and thinking about the parts of the plot of a story. See *plot*.

Poetry. Language used in special ways to communicate ideas or experiences more precisely or powerfully than they can be communicated in ordinary prose.

Point of view. The standpoint from which a story is told. See *first-person point of view, third-person point of view*.

Post hoc ergo propter hoc. Latin, meaning "after this; therefore, because of this." A logical fallacy in which two events are assumed, falsely, to have a cause-and-effect relationship simply because they occurred one after the other.

Predicate. Grammatical term referring to the part of a sentence or clause that is not the subject, including the verb and its attached modifiers or complements. Compare with *subject*.

Prediction. An opinion about what will happen in the future. Predicting is an excellent active reading strategy.

Prefix. A word part, such as *de-*, *in-*, or *mono-*, added to the beginning of a word or word part, as in *de- + value = devalue*.

Preposition. A word or group of words placed before a noun or nounlike word to indicate the relation of that word to a verb, adjective, or other noun or nounlike word. Examples of prepositions include *at, beyond, during, in spite of, except,* and *without*.

Prepositional phrase. A group of words that includes a preposition and its object, as in *across the bay* or *in regard to your letter*. See *preposition*.

Prereading. See *previewing*.

Previewing. Activities that a reader can carry out before reading a passage, including scanning, skimming, thinking about what you already know about the topic, and posing questions. Also called *prereading*.

Prewriting. The stage of the writing process in which the writer carries out such preliminary activities as choosing a topic, focusing the topic, gathering ideas, and organizing ideas.

Prior knowledge. What you already know about a subject.

Pro-and-con chart. A T-chart with reasons or arguments in favor of something (pros) listed on one side, and reasons or arguments against something (cons) on the other. See also *T-chart*.

Pronunciation. The way a word should be said.

Proofreading. The act of looking over a piece of writing and correcting errors in spelling, grammar, usage, punctuation, capitalization, and manuscript form. Also called *copyediting*.

Propaganda. The systematic spread or promotion of particular ideas, beliefs, practices, etc., especially by means of deception or distortion. Slander, loaded words, and fallacies are examples of propaganda techniques. See also *loaded words, rhetoric*.

Protagonist. The main character in a story; usually one who experiences some conflict, or struggle, and who goes through some important change. Compare with *antagonist*.

Publishing. The act of making a piece of writing available to others, as by distributing copies, posting it on the Internet or in an e-mail, or reading it aloud.

Purpose. What the writer wants to accomplish. See also *mode*.

Qualification. A limitation, restriction, or modification; a word or phrase that limits or modifies the meaning of another word or phrase.

Quatrain. A four-line stanza in a poem.

Quotation. The exact words of another speaker or writer, repeated verbatim (word for word).

Reading comprehension. The process of making meaning from a text; making sense of what you read.

Reading process. A systematic approach to reading that includes specific activities done before, during, and after reading. These activities include *previewing* and *posing questions* (before reading), *using active reading strategies* such as *predicting* and *connecting* (during reading), and *reflecting* and *responding* (after reading).

Reasonable opinion. An opinion that is supported by facts and consistent with accepted values.

Reference work. An authoritative source of information, such as a dictionary, almanac, encyclopedia, atlas, or database.

Reflecting. 1. The process of thinking seriously about something. 2. In the reading process, part of what one does after reading. Reflecting after reading might include summarizing the reading, answering one's prereading questions, and evaluating the reading.

Repetition. The use, again, of any element, such as a sound word, phrase, or image, in order to create an effect.

Resolution. The part of a plot in which the central conflict is ended (resolved).

Responding. Thinking about and otherwise reacting to what you are hearing, seeing, or reading.

Restatement. A context clue in which the meaning of a word is stated again in other words. Also known as *direct definition*.

Revising. Making changes to improve aspects of a piece of writing, including its focus, content, accuracy, interest, organization, degree of formality, appropriateness to the audience, voice, mood, and tone.

Rhetoric. 1. The art of using speech or writing to move or persuade others. 2. The art of oral or written composition.

Rhyme. The repetition of sounds at the ends of words. See also *rhyme scheme*.

Rhyme scheme. The pattern of rhymes within each stanza of a poem. See *stanza*.

Rhythm. A regular pattern of stressed and unstressed syllables in a poem; also called *meter*.

Rising action. The part of the plot in which the central conflict is developed.

Root. A basic word part that carries primary meaning in a word even though it cannot stand alone as a word. Examples of roots include *capt* in *captive* and *capture* and *dem* in *democracy* and *endemic*.

Rough draft. A preliminary, unfinished version of a piece of writing. See *final draft*.

Rough outline. An brief outline containing main ideas above supporting ideas that are introduced by dashes (—).

Rubric. A listing or explanation of the standards by which a piece of writing will be evaluated.

Run-on sentence. An error in which two separate sentences are written as though they were one.

Scanning. Looking through a piece of writing quickly to find specific parts or specific information.

Sensory details. Details that tell how something looks, tastes, smells, sounds, or feels.

Sentence. A group of words that is grammatically complete and that expresses a complete idea. (Exception: A single word can be a sentence if that word is an imperative verb with an implied subject, as in "Wait!")

Sentence combining. The act of putting separate sentences together into a single sentence.

Sentence expanding. Revision of a sentence by adding material, such as words, phrases, or clauses, to it.

Sentence fragment. A group of words that does not form a complete sentence.

Sequence. The order of events in a piece of writing.

Setting. The time and place in which the action of a work of literature occurs.

Short story. A brief work of fiction.

Significance. Importance, meaning.

Simile. A figure of speech in which unlike things are compared using *like, as,* or *than,* as in "Spring came like a freight train, fast and furious." See *metaphor*.

Simple sentence. A sentence that does not contain any dependent, or subordinate, clauses.

Skimming. Looking over a piece of writing quickly to get a general idea about its content.

Spatial order. Arrangement of details in a piece of writing by their distance from the observer (near to far, or vice versa) or in order of their position in space: top to bottom (or vice versa), left to right, and so on. See also *order of importance*.

Speaker. In a lyric poem, the voice that expresses ideas and emotions.

Standard classroom theme. An essay that contains an introductory paragraph, two or three body paragraphs that support the thesis given in the introductory paragraph, and a concluding paragraph.

Standards. A set of statements telling what students should know or be able to do in a particular subject at a given grade level.

Standardized test. A test or group of tests, like the Iowa Tests of Basic Skills, used to compare the skills of individuals and groups. Also called a *norm-referenced test*.

Stanza. A group of lines within a poem, a unit somewhat similar to a paragraph.

Statement of belief. An opinion that a person thinks is true but that he or she cannot prove beyond doubt.

Statement of obligation. An opinion about what individuals or groups of people should or should not do.

Statement of policy. An opinion about what should or should not be done by a group as a matter of course.

Statement of value. An opinion about the worth (value) of something.

Static character. A character who does not change or develop in the course of a story. See *dynamic character*.

Statistic. Information presented in numerical form.

Stereotyping. The act of unfairly attributing a quality to a whole group of people or to an individual based upon an unfair characterization of the group to which he or she belongs. Stereotyping is often a kind of *overgeneralization*.

Stringy sentence. A sentence that contains many clauses loosely combined with conjunctions such as *and* or *but*.

Structure. How something is organized or put together.

Style. The features that characterize a piece of writing, especially those features that are chosen by the writer as a matter of technique, such as alliteration, rhythm, inverted word order, word choice, and sentence complexity. Style creates voice. See *voice*.

Subject. 1. What a piece of writing is about. 2. In grammar, the doer of the action of the verb. The subject and the predicate, together, make up a clause or sentence. Compare with *predicate*.

Subordinate clause. See *dependent clause*.

Suffix. A word part, such as *-al*, *-ment*, or *-tion*, added to the end of a word or word part, as in *merry + -ment = merriment*.

Summarize. To repeat, in fewer and different words, an idea or ideas taken from another speaker or writer. Summarizing is an excellent active reading strategy.

Summary. A piece of speech or writing that repeats, in different and fewer words, an idea or ideas taken from another speaker or writer.

Support. See *elaboration, supporting detail*.

Supporting detail. A fact, opinion, example, or other kind of detail related to a main idea.

Suspense. A feeling of curiosity or expectation, often accompanied by anxiety, created by raising questions in the reader's mind about the outcome of events in a literary work.

Syllable. A unit of spoken language consisting of one uninterrupted sound.

Symbol. An image that stands for something else. A rose is a traditional symbol of love and beauty. An ampersand (&) is one symbol for *and*.

Synonym. A word that is the same or similar in meaning to another word. *Gigantic* and *enormous* are synonyms. Compare with *antonym*.

Synthesis. A type of thinking in which separate or conflicting ideas are combined to create or support a new idea. See *thesis*.

T-chart. A graphic organizer divided into two columns that fall under one heading or title. See *graphic organizer*.

Tercet. A three-line stanza in a poem.

Theme. A main idea or message conveyed by a literary work. In a story, the theme is often something that the main character learns as a result of the central conflict in the story.

Thesis. In an essay, a one- or two-sentence statement of the main idea. The thesis usually appears in the introduction and often appears again, in other words, in the conclusion. Also called the *thesis statement*.

Thesis statement. One or more sentences that express the main idea, or thesis, of an extended piece of nonfiction writing such as an essay.

Third-person point of view. The narrative standpoint from which the narrator tells the story using pronouns like *he, she, it*, and *they*. In stories told from the third-person point of view, the narrator reports but does not directly participate in the action.

Timeline. A graphic organizer used to show the chronological order of events. Events are usually displayed as marks along a single line that represent a certain time period. See *graphic organizer*.

Tone. The attitude conveyed by the voice of a narrator.

Topic sentence. In a paragraph, a sentence that expresses the main idea.

Traditional verse. Poetry that has regular meter and rhyme scheme. Compare with *free verse*.

Transfer. The attempt to get a person to shift or move his or her strong feelings about something to something else that is unrelated.

Transition. See *transitional words and phrases*.

Transitional words and phrases. Words and phrases, such as *after, then, next, as a result, in summary*, and *therefore*, used to show connections between or among ideas.

Turning point. The point in a story where something happens to determine the ultimate fate of the central character or characters. Also called the *crisis*.

Values. Opinions about what human actions are worthwhile or desirable.

Venn diagram. A graphic organizer that uses circles to compare and contrast subjects. See *graphic organizer*.

Verify. To confirm or prove the truth of a statement of fact by making one or more observations or by checking one or more authoritative sources of information, such as reference works or experts.

Verse. Language organized into lines and often containing a regular rhythmical pattern or meter. See *line* and *meter*, or *rhythm*.

Visualizing. An active reading strategy in which you picture something in your mind.

Vocabulary. A list of words, particularly of new or unfamiliar words from a reading passage.